FINDING PURPOSE IN LOSING A HAND

DL BOOTHE

Printed in the United States of America

ISBN 10: 06920-62351

ISBN 13: 978-0-6920-6235-7

Cover design by Zach Lezniewicz of ZJL Designs
www.zjldesigns.com.

Print Edition 10 9 8 7 6 5 4 3 2 1

ISBN: 06920-62351
ISBN-13: 978-0-6920-6253-7

DEDICATION

This book is dedicated to my savior Jesus, for without Him, none of this would be possible. Your grace is sufficient for me.

ACKNOWLEDGMENTS

To my bride Shelly, thank you for the countless days, weeks, and months of time sacrificed to allow me to write this book. Your loving support and gentle nudges helped me overcome some of the greatest obstacles in working through it all. All my love!

To my legacy; my kids Gerrod, Marlee, Asher, and Amelia, you are the jewels in my crown and I am so grateful for the honor and privilege of being your dad. I love each of you immensely!

To the countless people who have prayed for, and supported me in a myriad of ways over the years, Thank you just doesn't do enough but it's what I have. There are far too many to list here but much love to you all!

Mom and Dad, you believed in me even when I didn't. Your love and support have never wavered for which I am eternally grateful. Mom, you are the strongest woman I have ever known. I love you both deeply!

Kim and Shawn, thank you for always being my biggest fans. The most protective younger siblings ever, you have always been my greatest defenders. I love you both more than you know.

To all my extended family and friends, each of you holds a near and dear place in my heart. Thank you for all your love and support over the years, it means the world to me. Love you guys!

Last, but not least. To my precious grandson Alastor, may the Lord pour out multitudes of blessing upon you. I am so happy that you have come and I can't wait to take you camping. I love you to the moon and back, grampa!

1

A PISTOL IN MY HAND, A SINGLE BULLET IN THE GUN. I WAS about to play the game of Russian Roulette. With the bullet in the cylinder, I gave it a spin, and locked it in place. Never having handled a gun, I had no intention of handling one again after my intended use for it.

Crouched down on the living room floor, I was the sole occupant in the house. This was the home I had spent the longest span of time in my twenty-two years. It was the first home my parents owned, but they were overseas. The gun rested on the floor beside me as I mentally rehearsed the instructions on its use. As I picked up the gun, I noticed how aged it looked. I lifted the barrel to my right temple in slow motion.

The pain which tormented me since the age of five was about to resolve. The pending act would also relieve the world from tolerating my existence. My finger shook as I placed it on the trigger.

The floor was cold; the surrounding air was cold, everything was cold. Even my heart had grown cold. No longer were the resources of running water and natural gas connected to the home. The electricity disconnection was next as that bill was also unpaid.

The silence in the room was deafening. You could have heard a pin drop on the gold shag carpet stretching across the floor. As I sat alone, reflecting on the misery of my life to that point, my resolve grew stronger to carry out my plan. The ongoing pain was unbearable. I closed my eyes and pulled the trigger.

Silence... What went wrong?

If at first you don't succeed, try again. A phrase I remembered hearing from my mom. I opened the cylinder of the pistol again to ensure everything was in place. The shiny brass casing was still in place, waiting to fulfill its destiny. I gave the cylinder another spin, locking it in place. Ready, aim... fire!

Continued silence.

Something wasn't working right. I opened the cylinder once more, removed the bullet, replaced the cylinder and test fired the weapon unloaded. I pulled the trigger nine or ten times to confirm the gun functioned the way it should. Everything seemed operational.

Frustration building, I loaded the round into the chamber, figuring the odds had to be in my favor. Locked and loaded, with a fresh roulette spin, the end of the cold barrel found its way back into position at the right side of my head.

In pulling the trigger, time stood still. The deafening silence gave way to the distinct sounds made by a handgun as mechanical parts perform their function.

When the hammer came down, my body collapsed into a heap there on the living room floor. Still alive, the pain intensified, though it was emotional rather than physical. For most of my years I thought I was a complete failure, unworthy of living. Three failed attempts at Russian roulette confirmed my belief. I failed at being a failure!

What was I to do? I wasn't getting life right, and now it was obvious I couldn't get death right either. In my tears, I repeated one word - failure. Where would I go from here? When will this pain ever end? Would it end?

When had it begun, and what purpose could it serve?

2

M Y PARENTS WERE BOTH BORN AND RAISED IN THE SOUTH, Alabama to be exact. My father might well have been an unwanted child. His parents owned a small farm and were in the barn one day preparing feed for the cows. My grandmother, a petite woman, was eight months along in her pregnancy. My grandfather was a bovine inspector for the state and they had just lived through the Great Depression of 1929 before they married. Both came from large families and times had been difficult for them.

Because he faced many financial challenges growing up, after marriage my grandfather rode the pendulum the opposite direction, determined to go from extreme poverty to becoming wealthy. To him, having a child hindered that goal. Making the selfish decision to take care of the perceived problem, he picked up a piece of wood and swung it at my grandmother, attempting to abort the child. Though his efforts were unsuccessful, it could explain future behaviors of my father.

My grandmother delivered her only baby though the relationship between parents and child was less than a loving one. Grandfather never fostered a loving bond with his son, and grandmother was overprotective, to a fault. She risked abuse to give my father things her husband would never approve of. My father grew up with no understanding of healthy boundaries nor would he experience genuine from his parents. These conditions created a breeding ground for many deviant behaviors.

My mom was the middle child of three, flanked by two brothers. Her father had abandoned the family marriage when she was around eight years old. Her mother, my granny, never remarried. I don't know many details surrounding the divorce but granny took out her frustration on her daughter. Her sons were her pride and joy but her daughter could do nothing right.

Beaten so often, and for trivial things, mom longed for freedom from her mother's tyrannical grip. In Alabama, in the late 1950's and early 1960's, it was unacceptable for a white girl to have any relationships with people of color. Mom could not understand why she was not allowed to play with any black children in the neighborhood. Whenever Granny discovered her playing with the kids, mom received a beating.

Once mom graduated from high school she and my father married right away. My father sought refuge from his abusive father and controlling mother while my mom was escaping her own personal nightmare, the result of which set the stage for a perfect storm. My parents moved to southern Alabama to start their new life together. Soon after their nuptials, they became pregnant with their first child. The little girl was stillborn, with no explanation why or how it happened. In those days, the doctors considered it best the mother not see the baby, to reduce the amount of grieving for the parent of the dead child. Mom has never spoken much about this event but I know she carries wounds which only compounded an already complicated life.

A year later I entered the world. A healthy baby, with all fingers and toes accounted for. My sister came along seventeen months after me, and thirteen months later, my little brother debuted as the last child.

Now a dysfunctional family of five, my father enlisted in the US Army and served in the Payroll/Finance division. He was soon deployed overseas. When he enlisted, the Vietnam War was still going on. He received orders for a solo TDY (Temporary Duty) assignment to a unit in Camp Samae San, Thailand. He was to leave his family behind while he served a one year tour.

My father had developed bad habits which included being sneaky and hiding things from his father while his mother "covered" for him. He also tended to be melodramatic.

After a few years of marriage, mom found it difficult to trust her husband. His stories sometimes didn't match up when he claimed to work late or when he missed appointments. He was flirtatious with other women, even in the presence of his wife.

The original plan was for the four of us to stay with an aunt and uncle on my father's side of the family while he served in Thailand. With their marriage on shaky ground, mom's distrust intensified, as she was certain her husband would be unfaithful while overseas.

With good intentions, my great aunt convinced my mom to have our family join my father in Thailand so they could work on their struggling marriage.

Mom had much trepidation about going. My father had been in Thailand three months and she could imagine how many prostitutes he may have solicited in the red light districts.

Her uneasiness was compounded by frequent occurrences of dark premonitions. The sex trade in Thailand was prolific, and many people warned to keep her kids close at all times. In those premonitions, mom envisioned many awful things involving me in particular.

Her greatest fear was me getting kidnapped and sold into the sex trafficking trade in Thailand. The premonitions and fears increased to the point she considered aborting the trip. Aunt E. encouraged mom face her fears and we boarded a plane bound for our new home, halfway around the world.

We arrived in Thailand, on my fifth birthday, in October 1972. My father met us at the Bangkok International Airport and drove us to Samae San, a three hour car ride southeast.

Since we had not been "command sponsored", we had to live off-post in civilian housing. A Private in the US Army; my father's take home pay only afforded us a small hut like structure several miles from his office. Elevated on pillars of bamboo, to avoid flooding during the monsoon season, our hut was across the road from a field where the US Army stored its "dead ordinance".

My siblings and I found many enticing things to play with in the field, items such as bullets, mortars, bombs, and tear gas canisters. You might say that was miracle number one in my story; that we never blew ourselves up playing in the ammo dump.

On November fourth, one month after I turned five, mom thought it would be fun to go have lunch at my father's office, and then catch a USO show at U-tapao Air Force Base, a short drive to the east.

A baht bus was a small Toyota pickup truck outfitted with padded seats which ran along both sides of the bed from the back of the cab to the tailgate. The passenger seating area had a canvas canopy to deflect the rain and sun. Seatbelts were not even optional equipment back then.

The hut we rented was in a compound of several, overseen by a landlord known as "Papasan". He had warned us to never take a baht bus when it was raining. The rain came down in heavy spurts and caused flash flooding. Add an erratic driver to the mix and it could get dangerous.

On that day it had been raining all morning, and following the advice of Papasan, mom waited out the rain before asking him to hail a bus for us.

After a while, the rain tapered off and sunshine broke through the clouds. Mom walked over to Papasan's hut and asked him to call for a bus.

Almost a grown man, since turning the ripe old age of five the month before, I asserted some independence by telling mom I was going to sit on the opposite side of the bus by myself. My little demonstration of autonomy angered her as mom insisted I return to her side. As fate would have it, the vehicle pulled away, so I sat down and held on. Ah, sweet victory, my negotiation skills had reigned supreme as I heard mom tell me to stay put and off we went.

I have little recollection of the details after the crash. The following is the narrative my father gave.

After delivering lunch to my father, we continued on our journey. From nowhere, a US Army jeep came up behind us. Two US soldiers, draftees, one seventeen and the other eighteen, intoxicated, high on some narcotic, and now AWOL (Absent With Out Leave), had stolen the vehicle from the base motor pool. They were out on a joy ride, looking to inflict "collateral damage" severe enough to get them sent back to the United States, even if it meant the military prison at Fort Leavenworth. In their minds, prison was a better option than going back into a war zone.

As I reflect on what happened next, it always amazes me no one saw the jeep as it came up fast behind us. I sat close to the rear area of the bus with my arms extended behind me, holding on to the metal rails when the collision happened. In a flash, the jeep struck the back of the truck, pinning my left hand between the two vehicles. The collision crushed my hand and almost severed it at the wrist. Moments later, as the vehicles separated, our vehicle left the road and rolled down an embankment, flipping several times, before coming to rest on its side. Everyone was ejected from the vehicle, including the driver.

Our driver, a Thai national, took off running, not to get help, but to save his own life. There was an agreement in place between the US and Thai governments which meant he could have been charged with criminal negligence if involved in an accident involving American citizens. His only perceived option was to flee the scene. The soldiers in the jeep fled the scene as well.

We found ourselves some fifteen feet below the road surface, in a jungle somewhere in Thailand. A young mother and her three children, the oldest of which was bleeding out, had no way of calling for help. My brother and sister sustained only minor bumps and bruises and maybe a small laceration or two, nothing serious. Mom had a mild concussion along with a few cuts and bruises.

As a parent myself, I can only imagine how horrifying it must have been for my mom as she faced this unwanted challenge. The strength and courage it took for her to endure that event has always impressed me.

It's difficult to ascertain just how much time we spent near the wreckage before help came. It was only because smoke rose from the crashed baht bus that another bus stopped to investigate. On board were an Army Captain and two of his soldiers.

With a great deal of blood loss, my body went into shock and I passed in and out of consciousness. Without recollection of being loaded into the other bus, I regained consciousness long enough to realize someone had picked me up out of the jungle. As I looked at the mangled and bloody mess of my hand I lost consciousness again.

The men got us to the Air Force hospital at U-tapao where doctors wheeled me straight into surgery. There were many challenges to overcome. U-tapao was an installation for active duty soldiers only, no spouses or dependent children.

<u>**3**</u>

GREEN JELLO, GREEN JELLO, ALL I WANTED WAS GREEN Jello. There was no green Jello in the hospital cafeteria, so my father returned with a chocolate milkshake. The shake was acceptable, but I wanted Jello. After surgery, although confined to a bed in a US field hospital, I was ready to resume life a feisty five-year-old.

Upon our arrival to the hospital, the doctor informed my mom that had we been five minutes later in getting there, I would have bled to death.

Once stabilized, the doctors worked to re-attach my hand. As a field hospital, doctors were accustomed to seeing injuries involving limb loss, but without a pediatrics unit, it was a daunting task to serve a child with such severe trauma. Surgeons did the best they could to save the hand. Every tiny bone crushed, every vein, muscle, and tendon mutilated.

After a short stint in recovery, they wheeled me back to the operating room to remove the hand. When gangrene developed at the fingertips, my father requested only the affected areas be removed. The surgeon was reluctant to do so. If the gangrene spread, death was imminent. Gangrene is necrosis of flesh; the flesh dies, turns black, and rots, opening the door to more infection. A quick Google search for the word "gangrene" could help you understand why amputation was the best course to take. The Chief surgeon said it was critical to get me back to the United States where I would have a better chance of survival.

Stabilized and ready for flight, mom and I boarded a B-52 bomber to take "hops" across the world on a med-evac mission. The final destination was Ft. Gordon, Georgia. Two weeks after the amputation, another doctor performed a skin graft, removing flesh from my left thigh to cap the stump. Again, in retrospect, I stand in complete awe of my mom for the way she handled the stress of the whole situation. Mom has always been my rock. She has taken a great number of hits in her lifetime; she is the strongest woman I have ever known.

4

PHYSICAL THERAPY COMMENCED IMMEDIATELY AFTER I was fitted with my first prosthesis. In two days I learned to reach, open, and grasp things with the hook. Resiliency is the name of the game when you are five.

In the interim, my father worked through the process of transferring back to the US early. His time in Thailand equated to about half of his one year deployment. His next duty station was Fort Benning, GA.

It was two or three months after mom and I returned before our family reunited at Fort Benning. I wonder what it was like for my siblings during the tragedy. Were they concerned if they would ever see their big brother again? When they saw me again for the first time, with a hook, what thoughts passed through their young minds?

At Fort Benning we lived in government quarters on post. We settled into our "new normal" back in the United States. Living on post had it perks. My father's commute to work was easy, and we were near the hospital, shopping, and other community services.

Mom was a housewife (or domestic engineer as I prefer to call her) who took care of her family at home. My father worked 8 to 5, Monday through Friday, in the Payroll Office on post. Life was safer back in the US, with medical facilities able to provide the necessary care.

We had been in our house two weeks when one day a knock on the door surprised us all. As mom worked to prepare lunch in the kitchen, my siblings and I played together in the living room.

Mom was not expecting to receive any visitors that day. She opened the door to a man dressed in an Army combat uniform. Without a word, the soldier let himself in, dropped to the living room floor, and did push-ups. His was a "shock and awe" entrance, which might get him killed today.

He completed twenty and as he rose from the floor, he asked my mom to go get a pair of shoes; "for the young man with the hook."

Mom left us with this man and returned a few moments later with a pair of shoes. My siblings and I remained frozen in bewilderment at the sight of this stranger. Just moments later mom returned with a pair of shoes, and as she passed them over to the man, she noticed he had a hook. She failed to notice during his unconventional entry.

The soldier took the shoes with his right hook and turned toward me. As he approached, before kneeling to meet me on the floor, he removed his prosthetic leg. Now at my level, he passed to the shoes me. It was then we discovered the man had two hooks, he was a triple amputee!

His mission was to teach me how to tie my shoes. "If I can do this with two hooks, you can get it done with one," the soldier said as he asked me to put the shoes on by myself. I had used the hook for less than a month and had not dressed myself since the crash. That was about to change.

He showed me how to tie the laces. After he tied both shoes, he asked me to untie them. I reached with my right hand to pull the string. He tapped my hook with his and said, "No, use the hook."

Using my prosthesis to tie shoes was a foreign concept for me; one, because I was right-handed, and two, because I had not yet learned to use my hook in that way.

I untied the second shoe with the hook. "Now pay close attention young man because I will only do this once more", he declared, as you would expect a drill sergeant to. With two hooks, he tied both shoes a second time. I untied them with my hook.

Once I untied both shoes, he insisted it was my turn to tie them. Mom said the first try was slow-going, and somewhat sloppy, but the soldier remained steadfast in his mission as he untied them and told me to try again. We went through the procedure three or four more times until he was satisfied I grasped the concept.

With his mission complete; the soldier rose, re-attached his leg, and saluted me as he would one of his military superiors. He turned to my mother and saluted her before he walked back into oblivion.

The soldier never gave his name, nor did he say much during his visit. In the days following, Mom asked around the hospital if anyone knew who the mystery man was. She wanted to thank him for what had done for me. No one knew anything about him.

Frazzled by his visit, it never occurred to mom to read the nametag on his uniform.

Our best guess was he must have been a war vet from either the Korean War or World War II and heard about a kid coming back from Thailand who lost a hand. His mission was to "pay-it-forward", if you will. He sought no recognition, he only wanted to help.

That event holds a huge place in my heart after all these years. It is my motivation for helping others dealing with limb loss. The man was a guardian angel, an incredible mentor. He gave me something that day I didn't realize I needed.

I had received teddy bears and things of that nature, but that recalibrated warrior gave me a gift far greater. He renewed my sense of independence. Had he not selflessly offered what only he had to give, I might wear slip-ons or Velcro shoes to this day. Although mom did her best to teach me, she could not teach me something she didn't know how to do herself.

As I reflect on this experience, it is my belief we should all look for ways to give back, just like that soldier did for me. Each of us has a duty to reach out, lifting others up by whatever means we have. You need not be an amputee in order to help someone either. If you've experienced a chronic illness; there are people to whom you could offer encouragement who may not be as far along in their journey.

Perhaps you could even reach out without having survived trauma or illness and simply serve others with the gifts and talents you have. Schools are always in need of people to serve as reading mentors or lunch buddies. Senior care facilities are full of people longing for visits and people to spend time with.

If you find yourself on the opposite side of the coin, it could be good to seek assistance from someone else who has traveled father down the path. Sometimes, even just a listening ear can help someone get unstuck. We are creatures built for community and it is not a sign of weakness to ask for help when you need it.

Everyone can benefit from mentorship. Through mentorship, you might discover the purpose for your pain.

5

FORT BENNING WAS OUR HOME FOR THE NEXT YEAR OR SO and life just carried on in our family. I adjusted quickly to using my prosthetic and soon discovered many uses for it.

One new thing I discovered about the hook, it was superb for dragging my siblings around. If I wanted them to do something, I would grab the back of their shirt collar, or maybe a belt loop, and take them where I wanted them to go.

There were also more sinister things I used the hook for. A mischievous kid, I situated myself on the couch and summoned my brother. The little guy rushed in to see what I wanted. To their credit, my brother and sister always cared about me and wanted to help in any way they could. As my brother approached the couch, I waited for him to plop down beside me. I would position my hook on the couch cushion next to me, with the pointy side up, just in time for him to sit down on it. That little act of brotherly love made him jump!

That trick never got old for me and he fell for it many times. I'm certain I tried that trick on my sister too but after one or two times, she never fell for it again.

In the summer of 1973 we received new plastic skates as gifts. They were the kind you slipped over a pair of tennis shoes. Competing to determine who was fastest, the winner was the first person to reach the grass at the end of the sidewalk. One day, my brother kept going. Instead of a soft grassy landing, he lost control and barreled over the curb into the street. He crashed hard on his left arm and broke it.

Mom scooped him up and took him to the hospital. The break required having the bones reset and his arm cast. When he came out of the cast room, he wore the biggest smile on his face because he looked like me. I thought it was cool too until the next time I pulled the sit-on-the-hook trick on him.

One day, I waited for my brother to sit next to me, so I could try a new enhancement. I opened the hook, pointy side up, and just as he sat on it, I closed the hook, catching a sizeable chunk of his backside. That little trick did not sit well with him, and he swung his cast as hard as he could, clobbering me on the head. Mom ran into the living room to find both of us in tears. After discovering what happened, she couldn't help laughing. As often as I did that to him, it's amazing my brother still loves me.

I met a kid who became my best friend, Desmond. He may have been my only friend, to be honest.

I noticed a difference between myself and other kids, at least in the way others saw me. It was rare to see a kid wearing a prosthetic back then. Most parents did not educate their kids about a topic such as limb loss. That lack of education is an ongoing issue.

Without guidance, kids can be brutal in the way they treat one another. They have few filters. Kids would point and jeer, snicker and laugh, and there was always at least one in a pack who had to start the name calling. I wish I had a dime for every time someone called me Captain Hook.

To make matters worse, there were parents who would add insult to injury by telling their kids to run up and touch the hook. I suspect most had good intentions. Perhaps it was the way for some to show their children I was a real person who was "different", but their lack of social sensitivity contributed to the wounds caused by their words and actions.

I withdrew into my shell as that behavior occurred again and again. Everywhere we went, people stared, pointed, and worst of all, whispered things to each other with disgusted looks on their faces. It wasn't long before I didn't want to go anywhere. I wanted to stay home with my brother and sister. They had always accepted me and never made fun of me, ever.

Because of the issues with other kids, I did not start school when I should have. I skipped kindergarten altogether; the age kids learn about friendships and how to get along with others. It was a critical loss in my development which had lasting effects on my social development.

By this time, I had refused to play with other kids because they said I was different and treated me like a reject. Desmond caught me on the street one day as we were roaring down the sidewalks on our *Big Wheel* tricycles.

Desmond and his family moved into our housing area not long before we did. The chains of racism in our branch of the family tree broke when I met Des.

Desmond was different. In my six-year-old mind I could process that his skin color was different, but I didn't understand why. What also intrigued me about Des was he didn't seem to care about anything but having fun.

He asked if I wanted to race, and I said, "Sure, but don't you see I'm different?" "Yeah," he said, "but I don't care. Do you care if I look different from you?" "But I have a hook, and you still want to play with me?" I queried. "Can you still race?" he asked. "Yeah!" I shouted.

Then he said something which resonates with me to this day. "As long as you can race, who cares what makes either of us different? Let's go!" So off we went.

We must have burned the wheels off of at least two trikes each. Together as often as possible, we raced and spun around the neighborhood without a care in the world.

I credit Desmond as another life saver in my journey. His friendship reached in and grabbed hold of me when I needed it most. At the time of this writing, it has been forty-four years since our first race and I still consider him my friend. Not long after making such a good friend, my father received orders for a transfer to Fort Clayton, Panama.

In December 1995, twenty-two years after we parted ways, our paths crossed again as adults. Des came to visit me at Fort Benning, when I went through a mini basic training. I had been deployed by AAFES to the Former Republic of Yugoslavia. I will touch on the deployment in a later chapter.

Friendships should be considered in terms of quality rather than numbers. One good friend can be worth their weight in pure gold and everybody needs at least one. If you don't have a friend relationship that is golden, let me encourage you *to be* that kind of friend to someone else.

6

ONTO OUR NEXT ADVENTURE. ONCE AGAIN, THANKS TO THE US Army, we were world travelers. My father's next assignment was at Fort Clayton, Panama. Of all the many places I have had the privilege of traveling to, Panama ranks at number one, despite some painful memories.

It was summer when we got there but in a tropical location like Panama, it's like summer all year round. Fort Clayton was close to the bustling city of Balboa. It was also near the infamous Panama Canal Zone. I always enjoyed going to the locks to see the big ships.

We often picked up Kentucky Fried Chicken on the way to the beach for a picnic lunch. It was a tradition to use the empty KFC bucket to collect shells in after we ate. There was quite an array of stunning seashells to be found there. It was 1974, before Noriega came to power, so it was a very pleasant place.

That fall I started my school career at Curundu Elementary. The school was an American run school on post at Fort Clayton. It was a good-sized school and a bus picked me up near my house.

On the first day of school I wore the finest in seventies clothing, which included a navy blue shirt and the loudest navy, yellow, and white plaid bell bottomed pants you have ever seen. You could have seen me coming from a mile away in that outfit.

School life was not as horrible as I feared. There was the occasional name calling and teasing but those instances were fewer in frequency than in Georgia. I was exposed to kids who had experience with various forms of diversity.

Our quarters were apartment buildings which housed eight families each if memory serves me. We lived on the bottom floor and our unit was the closest to the street. We had assigned carports which paralleled the street.

Across the street was an open jungle. It was like living next to a zoo as creatures would wander out from the trees to investigate us.

There were many kids in the area. Sometimes the animals behaved more like zoo patrons as they watched crazy kids run around in our natural habitat instead of the other way around.

Some of the creatures who visited us included iguana, kudamundi (monkeys), and wolf rats. The iguanas were often over six feet long and fearless of humans. They would just stroll across the street like they owned the place.

The kudamundi would visit in teams of three or four. They would plop down on the curb to watch the activities of the human monkeys as if studying us.

We soon learned these cute, furry little creatures were not our friends. If we ventured too close to their side of the road, they would defecate in their hands and throw it at us. One of the older kids antagonized the monkeys by charging toward them. He got hit with rapid fire excrement bombs. The monkeys had superior aim and almost never missed a target.

One time the monkeys antagonized us. To our great surprise, they ran across the street and every kid scattered, each to his own home, screaming for help. Even in pursuit, they could still defecate and throw their bombs at us.

I recall another scary interaction we had with the local wildlife. We were going into town; and after we piled into the lovely dodge station wagon, my father backed the car out from under the carport. The car rolled over what felt like a speed bump. Horrified, because there were no speed bumps, and thinking he had run over a child, my father jumped out of the car to see what he had run over. To his relief, it was just a rat. It was no ordinary rat, it was a wolf rat. Angry the rat had given him a scare, my father gave the rat a swift kick in the head and rolled over it again as we pulled away.

I turned to look at the rat monster, hoping he was squashed to bits. To my shock and horror, the rat stood up and walked back into the jungle. It was like a scene from a Stephen King movie as the four foot long tail slowly disappeared from sight.

While the outside environment was exciting in Panama, inside our home was a different story. My parents' marriage, already stressed since their wedding, soon reached its boiling point.

Mom suspected infidelity two years prior, when my father received orders to go to Thailand. In Panama, her suspicions were confirmed.

The sexual revolution was in full swing in the mid nineteen seventies and free love was the name of the game. It started with the magazines. My father always kept stacks of pornographic magazines around our home. In the beginning they were hidden; but the more he fed his demon of lust, the more conspicuous they became. There was a large pile in the bathroom, in the open for anyone to see.

I remember looking at them, as a seven-year-old boy, trying to understand what they were for. Sometimes my siblings and I would go into the bathroom to view the mags together.

We got caught viewing his stash, but he never scolded us for looking. He would say, "Put those back and go play before your mother catches you." He tried to make our mom look like the bad guy because *she* didn't want those magazines in her home.

My father would go to the bathroom, and then call for one of us. We were his servants who fetched things for him all the time.

Whenever summoned, he enjoyed showing me the girls in the magazines, pointing out certain characteristics of their anatomy. I am sure if someone had questioned, he would say he was just schooling his son in the *birds and the bees*.

If one's lusts go unchecked, there is a progression which takes place as the individual seeks greater thrill experiences. It's like the effect of narcotics. My father acted as though his behavior was normal, every dad did these things.

In no time, he transitioned from showing us elicit materials to photographing us in the shower. Mom would go run errands and my father would gather us up to take "showers". Sometimes he would photograph us in the shower individually, posing in ways similar to the women in the magazines. Other times he would have all three of us pose together. We thought we would be famous like the girls in the pictures, but for now he told us to keep it a secret.

Meanwhile, my father was engaged in an extramarital affair. He would sneak away for a secret rendezvous with a woman he met on post. The other woman knew my father was married, with children.

Mom's intuition alerted her to something which caused her to investigate. She questioned our father about dates and times and people. She wanted to know the name of the woman who called our house asking for him.

With his secrets exposed, my father became defensive and combative with words. Arguments occurred with increased frequency, and then he got physical.

Their "discussions" often took place after the kids were in bed but we still heard them. My father's frustrations affected the way he interacted with his children. The photo shoots in the shower reached a point where we felt unsafe. He demanded we do things which didn't seem right; he got angry if we resisted and whipped us when we didn't do as he instructed.

The perfect storm continued to brew.

One day, mom answered the phone and discovered it was the "other" woman. Something she said confirmed my father was guilty of infidelity. Mom told the woman if she wanted him, she could have him and handed the phone to my father. He pleaded with the woman on the phone as he tried to keep from losing his side-pocket relationship. She offered him an ultimatum; she would stay in the relationship if he could convince my mom to take part in a three-way affair.

Craziness elevated to insanity.

After hanging up the phone, caught up in a self-absorbed state of mind, my father shared the ultimatum he had been given and mom responded with an emphatic NO! He pleaded with mom to participate, he even cried as he begged, saying the other woman would dump him. Mom still refused.

Faced with rejection from his wife, and the possibility of losing his lover, my father transitioned from crying like a spoiled brat to a raging lunatic. He got physical with my mom, which he had done during earlier arguments. She took those hits in the past, out of fear, but her tolerance for abuse ended with that altercation.

On that day, my siblings and I came into the living room where they were fighting and tried to stop them. As we piled in on my father, he hit us and knocked us down. That was the proverbial straw that broke the camel's back. She tolerated his violence toward her, but she would not allow him to abuse their children. I don't remember if we left the apartment or if she told him to go, but that was the day my family exploded and fell apart. A short time later we boarded on a plane bound for the United States.

7

WE LEFT OUR FATHER IN PANAMA AND RETURNED TO THE home of Uncle N.B. and Aunt E., the same family we stayed with before leaving for Thailand.

They were great people. As wonderful as they were, it was difficult for my mom to ask for their help but we had no other place to go. Mom couldn't return to her mother; as she had burned that bridge when she married my father. Housing options were limited for a single mom with no job, car, furniture, and three children to feed.

We stayed for two or three months as pressure increased for my mom to determine her next move. Mom received a call from a man who was a member of a motorcycle club she and my father belonged to in Panama. Robert harbored an attraction to my mom, but since he was married, and had a daughter, he could not act on his attraction. Like my parents, Robert and his wife divorced in Panama, and he transferred to Fort Leavenworth to work in the military prison as a guard. As time passed a relationship formed but distance was an issue, he was in Kansas and we were in Georgia.

Mom grew uncomfortable living with her ex-husband's family and wanted to move out.

Rebound relationships are often doomed from the start. Those who fail to resolve problems in their former relationship and forego the difficult soul-searching work before getting into another, find themselves on a familiar path to "Splitsville".

On short notice, we traveled across the country to join Robert in Kansas. I mentioned in an earlier chapter, the chains of racism were broken in our family line, but that came at a high price. The relationship between mom and Robert was interracial. It was unheard of, in that part of the country, for a white woman to marry a black man, and none of our extended family approved.

I have many scars but one of the deepest comes from abandonment by family. Regardless of anyone's family of origin, there exists dysfunction, that's just part of life. While no one is perfect, everyone needs family. As a child grows up, they get their sense of well-being from their family. From the joy visiting grandparents, to growing up with cousins, to family gatherings at holidays and special events, a child learns to fit into this great big world through his extended family. That stability was stripped away from us. At the time of this writing, forty-three years have passed since my parents' divorce and I have yet to meet any of my cousins.

We had access to our extended family until I was four, which reduced to just our nuclear family after we moved overseas. When my parents divorced, all I had left were my mom, sister, and brother. To grow up without an extended family structure had lasting ramifications which took years to overcome.

I also missed out on critical school time because of losing a hand and moving. It was difficult to foster genuine friendships. The lack of social skills took me to a dark place of isolationism and set the stage for years of intense inner pain.

Robert became our only family, and because the marriage was interracial, his family of origin didn't accept us either.

The five of us moved into a single-wide mobile home near Kansas City. It was the middle of the school year when mom enrolled us. A civilian school, this one did not understand diversity. I was the outsider and the local kids had plenty of things they could pick on, and bully me over.

"Captain Hook", "one-armed bandit", and "nigger-lover" were just a few terms of endearment the kids had for me. It was never fun walking to and from school. Every day the bullies were there, pouring out hatred fueled by their ignorance and fear.

Summer in Kansas can be exciting for a meteorologist. Storms can develop ominous clouds which sometimes give birth to tornados. I am still baffled by the number of mobile homes in tornado prone states such as Kansas.

Not long after we arrived in Kansas, we moved from one single-wide trailer to another a short distance away. The new trailer had a corrugated metal exterior with a lovely wood-grained panel interior and shag carpeting. Whatever the reason for the move, divine providence had something to do with it. A week after we moved, a tornado ripped through our old trailer park and destroyed our former home. I remember feeling lucky we moved but fearful a tornado might find us in the new place.

21

As a way of helping her children cope with the aftermath of the tornado, mom purchased a little fish tank and three fish, one for each of the kids. She thought a pet would help us move past the fear. I remember mine was just a long and skinny, silvery scaled fish, maybe a minnow. I didn't care what type of fish it was, it was mine and I loved it. My sister and brother each had colorful ones, most likely both male Beta fish. Anyone who knows fish would understand you don't put two male betas in the same tank. It didn't take long for the two fish to become territorial.

The Beta fish fought and died after a few days. None of us understood why those two beautiful fish floated on top of the water. Mom removed them from the water as my grieving siblings wept. My brother, who was about five, thought I had killed the fish, so he plotted revenge. Every day when I fed my fish and watched it swim around the tank.

About a week after the two fish died, I wanted to feed my little fish but could not find him. Fearing he must have died too, I expected to find him floating at the top of the water. I searched the house in tears to see if mom had removed the fish. I found Fishie behind the couch, in a sandwich baggie, dead; his shiny, silvery corpse pressed against the plastic bag in a Z-formation.

Later that day, upon mom's interrogation, my brother confessed to his crime. In a fit of jealousy, he removed the fish from the tank, and placed it in the bag. Mom asked my brother to show her what he did to the fish. He demonstrated how he put the fish in the baggie, placed it on the carpet, and then stepped on it. The new "Z" shape of the fish matched the heel of the shoes my brother had on.

I hold no animosity towards my brother; he was just a jealous kid who reacted like a normal five-year-old. I share that story because it was the event which pushed me passed the point of no return. Kids at school, and the trailer park where we lived, picked on me and called me names. The death of my fish and the name calling, combined with the abuse which occurred in Panama and Thailand, crushed my spirit. What that fish represented was an unconditional love, and that love was dead.

Summer came to a close, and I started third grade. It was not uncommon for a seven-year-old to walk his siblings to school, without parents. The older kids were excited to start a new school year of bullying and name calling. My kindergarten sister, always at my defense, yelled back at them. While my siblings and I had our squabbles, they were always protective of me. The bullies never let up, and though they never got physical with us, they inflicted a lot of psychological damage.

8

JUST AFTER I STARTED THIRD GRADE, ROBERT RECEIVED orders transferring him from Fort Leavenworth to Fort Sill, OK. In his time as a prison guard, Robert put on some additional weight. While the extra weight may have been helpful in subduing an inmate, a battle-ready soldier it did not make.

He needed to get back in shape. Robert's former commander thought he would benefit from a post change, a new location which would facilitate weight loss. Fort Sill is a large installation which exposed him to daily physical training, and down range practice exercises. In reality, the transfer was an ultimatum. The Army directed him to lose weight or face dishonorable discharge.

Accustomed to frequent moves, this one was easy. We moved from northeast Kansas to southwest Oklahoma, just one state south.

The movers packed our household belongings, and we hit the road. In reflection, I picked up the nomadic lifestyle and acceptance of change so easily because, in moving, I hoped to find acceptance in a new place. We celebrated my eighth birthday after settling into our new residence in Oklahoma.

Once we arrived at Fort Sill, the transfers between posts came to an end, but that didn't keep us from moving around town. In Lawton, our family had six addresses from the time I was eight to seventeen. Those were my formative years, and I did not develop many friendships. It takes time to build trust with someone, more so for a wounded child like me.

I read research which states that by the time a child reaches the age of eight or nine; he solidifies his identity in the world, and how he fits into it. Since the crash, my mom always encouraged me to believe I could do anything. She never wanted me to think of myself as handicapped, but the world treated me otherwise.

If moving to a different city was an opportunity for change, hopeful change, then Lawton was not the right move. By the age of eight, I'd already been through more trauma than children should have to endure. In Lawton, I went from the proverbial pan to the fire.

Predators groom their victims through subtle means. It's like the frog in the pot analogy. You toss a live frog into a pot of boiling water and it will struggle to get out. On the other hand, if you place a frog in a pot of room temperature water and slowly add heat, the frog will not try to escape, even as the temperature rises.

When Robert was working, home life was okay. When our homework assignments and household chores were complete, there was little drama in the house, at least for the kids. After we took care of our responsibilities, we could go outside to play or ride bikes around the neighborhood.

Several kids lived in the neighborhood, but none of them invited us into their circles. It was rare for other kids to invite us to their homes to play, and no one came over to our house. Perhaps the neighborhood parents were fearful of us due to the interracial aspect of our family. Who knows, but the fact remains, we were loners.

I don't remember a single encouraging word from Robert. He discouraged us making friends with neighboring kids. He wanted us to stay in the house and make dinner. Mom worked later than Robert and he didn't want us out playing anyway, especially when he was hungry.

"GO MAKE ME A SANDWICH!" he often barked. We knew better than to dilly dally or fight about whose turn it was to make the sandwich. We worked together to get it done. White bread, two slices of the mystery meat known as liver cheese, two slices of American cheese with mustard spread across one piece of bread and mayonnaise across the other.

The sandwich required perfect assembly or Robert would throw it back at us. One kid presented the food and waited until Robert completed his inspection. If the sandwich met with his approval, another kid brought the Kool-Aid, while the last kid brought the fried pork rinds. Afterward, we sat on the floor between Robert and the television while he watched his favorite shows, programs such as Wheel of Fortune, Jeopardy, and soap operas. Since watching television was a "privilege" for us, we knew not to ask for cartoons.

We were the frogs in the pot of slow boiling water, unaware of the increase in water temperature.

Our lease expired, so we had to move. The new house was in an older neighborhood across town. I remember it being dark inside with little natural light reflecting off the dark wood paneling.

The neighbors next door, Rick and Sue, were also a military family. They had no kids of their own. Rick was a mechanic and Sue did not work outside the home, as I recall. When working on cars he would call me over to assist as tool boy. One day, when I came home from school, I found a gift Rick had left for me in the front yard. It was an inline six cylinder engine he pulled out of one of his cars. He handed me a little tool box and told me to tinker away. That engine became my anchor to reality, my means of escape from what took place in our house.

I disassembled the engine and put it all back together with only a few bolts leftover. Not bad for a third grader.

During that time, Robert received a discharge from the Army. At three hundred fifty pounds, there was no way he could keep his job as a soldier. In his recliner all day, he never got up except to use the bathroom; never even got dressed. He sat there, nude, with a towel draped across his lap as he watched TV, all day long.

His prized possession was a Harley Davidson 1300 Electra Glide motorcycle. It had a lot of chrome on it, which he kept polished. The bike was his only reason to turn off the television. He would have had us kids detail it except no one else could touch it.

Since he no longer contributed to the household finances, mom had to work double shifts. She worked in the mess hall on post, serving three meals a day to hungry troops. It was backbreaking work. She didn't earn much money, even working twelve to sixteen hours per day, six, and sometimes seven days a week. To supplement our food budget, she brought home leftovers. Mom left around 6 am and got home around 9 pm most days. Home from work, with whatever leftovers were available, she ate dinner, said goodnight, and went to bed before repeating the next day.

Mom carried a great burden, at high risk for her own health and the safety of her kids. The need to provide for the family trumped everything else, so she worked.

Conditions were now ripe for Robert to act on temptations which had been building. I don't believe Robert intended to become a molester, but there were exit ramps he could have taken to avoid the collision course he was on.

Robert grew less and less patient with us kids and spanked us for trivial things. Spankings started out with him using that rather large leather belt of his. He required us to lie down across his lap as he inflicted his version of discipline. If you moved, you got more whacks.

It proceeded to having us strip naked before he whipped us. Most days, at least one of us endured the flogging. Some days we had to cut a switch, a small limb from the tree, for our spankings. We didn't dare return with a switch he considered too small. Other times he would use an extension cord.

We remained house bound at that point. Robert avoided hitting us where bruises were visible to others and warned if ever we told anyone, the punishment would get even worse.

Robert's teenage daughter came to live with us. She was not exempt from the beatings; he was very violent with her too. One time she had an accident with a feminine hygiene product and the school sent her home to get cleaned up.

I had the misfortune of witnessing Robert beat her before making her strip down so he could "teach" her the proper way of applying pads. It was a horrible thing to watch as I shivered in a corner hoping he would not turn his rage against me too. He told her to get dressed while he continued hitting her. I don't recall how long she stayed with us but, she returned to live with her mom before the school year ended.

Robert's anger ebbed and flowed. His temper flared when we got home from school as he waited for us to get him something to eat. Forever in his recliner, always naked, with only that towel draped over his lap. The brown towel was a close match to his skin color, as was the chair.

It was always dark in that living room, save for the light of the TV. Robert sometimes fell asleep in the chair after we got home from school. While he napped, we could play in our rooms. The walk from our bedrooms to the kitchen for a snack was scary. We tiptoed past Robert, hoping not to wake him. He was never in a good mood when we interrupted his sleep.

One evening, while sitting on the living room floor eating dinner, the recorded video tape of TV game shows changed to something we were familiar with. It was a pornographic video which somehow got recorded over with game shows. Though familiar, it was still jolting to see. He was surprised by the switch up, but Robert didn't stop the tape.

Before I started this project, I asked a friend, Paul Young, for some writing advice. He has written a few books and I thought he could provide insight. Paul is the author of the bestselling book "The Shack" and had given the message at my church one Sunday. After service, I shared my dilemma about this writing project God was calling me to.

As we talked, I mentioned that our pasts were similar as we are both survivors of childhood molestation. In The Shack, he told his story through the use of allegory, giving fictional names to characters that represent various aspects of his life experiences.

I wasn't sure how or where to begin, whether I should use allegory or write in more of a testimony style. Paul answered by asking a series of questions. First, he asked if I believed God told me to write. Yes. Next, did I believe God inspired the writers of the Bible. Yes. Third, did I believe God placed every star in the sky and painted every fish in the sea. Of course. His final question drove it home, "Then do you not also believe God can speak through you and give you the right words?"

He suggested I pray and ask God to guide my keystrokes. "In the beginning don't worry about punctuation, chronology, or spelling, just start writing. In time it will come together to form a cohesive story." That conversation stuck with me over the course of this project. Thank you for the insight Paul!

Even after Paul's great advice, I still resisted the call to write. Two more years passed before I started the process. Finally, at a place of surrender in my heart, I was ready. My bride suggested we go away for a weekend, without the kids, so I could have uninterrupted time to write. We spent a weekend at a family cabin close to the central Oregon coast. The hurdle of where to begin was difficult to overcome, but once I got started, I wrote for eight hours straight.

I feel I must warn you before going any further. The following scenes are graphic, and I will only share a few details to paint the picture. Some things are just better left unsaid.

As I typed, tears flowed onto the keyboard of my laptop. The memories of molestation I had repressed for so many years came flooding back, in vivid detail. I relived nightmares long since buried. Over 17,000 words poured out, covering in great detail the abuse I suffered. Writing those words was one of the most difficult things I have done. It was painful, so dreadfully painful, I wanted to quit. I argued with God, telling Him how done I was, adamant I would go no farther with the project.

A few months later, after feeling convicted over my refusal, I tried to write more. I often opened the file to re-read what I had written, but added no more words. Every time I looked at those words, I felt as though a piece of me got cut away, like a cancerous tumor removed by surgery.

The day I sat down to continue writing, to my shock and horror, all 17,000 words had disappeared. The file was there but no words. I searched my hard drive, flash drives, and laptop–nothing found. I was devastated. After all the effort of working through painful events, I had nothing to show for it. That's how it appeared.

I told my brother what happened with the words, and after hearing the story, he uttered some of the most profound words. He thought I had a divine appointment with the Author of Life himself and the writing session was a journey of deep healing for me. The purpose of the exercise was to face the demons in my past, reconcile the pain, and redeem the loss of my innocence.

My brother said it was necessary that I tap into that horrible place, but inappropriate for a reader to consume all the darkness and evil described in those words. He suggested I share enough for the reader to imagine what took place without having to experience one of the ugliest facets of humanity in such gory detail.

Therefore, I will share only what is necessary for you to understand how it affected my life.

Back to the living room scene.

Addictions begin with a person believing they can handle the fire they are playing with. These things always go somewhere, places one never dreams of.

A daily occurrence for us, to watch videos with images of adults doing things to one another which didn't seem right to us kids. With the faces the actors made, it didn't look like they enjoyed themselves. At the ages of eight and nine, I remember feeling filthy after watching those movies.

As this activity progressed, Robert lost more inhibition. With his signature towel in place across his lap, he masturbated while viewing the tapes. That progressed to ditching the towel, exposing his entire anatomy. If we turned around, he yelled at us to turn back toward the TV.

When he finished, he would send one of us for a warm wash cloth to clean himself with. He took it to the next level when he made one of us kids do the cleanup. If a person allows himself to go this far, exercising no self-control, then the sky is the limit for what he is capable of doing.

Robert must have viewed me as the perfect little victim. He had been destroying my sense of self-worth, telling me nobody would want me since I was a cripple. His behavior worsened until he passed the point of no return, sodomy. The physical pain was intense! The abuse made bowel movements so painful I tried to hold them back. Days, sometimes weeks, passed without having a bowel movement for fear of the pain.

My bowels were impacted after several days. My underwear soiled as I attempted to hold the feces in. Embarrassed, and not knowing what to do about the soiled underwear, I wore them for several days before hiding them in a bag. I knew how Robert felt about soiled underwear having witnessed him beating his daughter over hers.

Mom couldn't figure out where all my underwear disappeared to. She struggled to make ends meet, and buying more cut into an already tight budget. I lived in such fear at that point. Robert made it crystal clear, through regular intimidation and warning, if I ever told anyone about what he did to any of us, he would kill me. He even threatened to kill our mother.

As a child, I didn't know how to escape the situation, so I complied. I kept Robert's secret, and I kept my underwear issue a secret. I feared mom would get angry about the cost of replacing the underwear. Since I couldn't reveal the truth of why they got soiled, I presumed she would spank me if she found the stash. If only she had known...

9

WE NEVER WENT OUT TO RESTAURANTS. THERE WAS never any extra money so it was a real treat when mom took us out for dinner one evening. Just the four of us, Robert did not come along.

The restaurant was almost empty when we sat down to order. Mom started the conversation with small talk, asking how our day was at school. I remember thinking how great it was to eat out but even happier to spend quality time with my mom. With her working all those double shifts, it was rare to spend much time together. As the evening progressed, I tried to find the courage to tell her about what we had been experiencing at home. Robert's threats to keep us silent were convincing and I couldn't muster the guts to do it.

As she toyed with the food on her plate, mom said she needed to get something out in the open. "No sense in beating around the bush," she uttered. "I have decided to divorce Robert."

Our faces looked like three baby deer caught in the headlights of an oncoming vehicle. Mom may have assumed I would be sad, but her announcement was music to my ears. She said we could continue loving Robert but their marriage was over. I didn't love Robert; I wanted to get away from him. The pressure to tell mom about Robert's "little secrets" subsided, for the time being.

Moving day! Into the house of horrors walked our rescuer. Charles came to remove the four of us, and our belongings, from the house. Mom met Charles at the mess hall where she worked. His office was in the adjacent building.

Robert was present when Charles walked in the door. We rushed into the living room in time to witness Robert threaten Charles. Robert was over six feet tall and almost four hundred pounds. Charles was approximately five foot nine and one hundred sixty five. I'll never forget how Charles stood in defiance as he told Robert to sit down and shut up.

Robert retreated to his recliner where he remained seated until we left. The valiant confrontation overshadows anything else which happened that day. Liberated and free from my abuser, the stress and emotional release swept over me.

Lawton was a small town of around one hundred thousand. We moved across town, into a house Charles shared with a military buddy. That fall we attended yet another new school. Latch key kids again, I walked my brother and sister to and from school every day, several blocks away.

I was in the fifth grade at Lee Elementary school. Home life improved since mom did not have to work double shifts anymore. She and Charles were both home by 6 pm. Life with Charles was like night versus day compared to Robert. Charles was also black which perpetuated the separation from our extended family. Harassment from the local people also continued.

My fifth grade year was relatively uneventful. While it never seemed to get old for other kids to call me Captain Hook, I tried to ignore it. Sticks and stones will break my bones, but words.... Whoever came up with that phrase never walked a mile in my shoes.

During the summer after fifth grade, we moved again when Charles and mom bought their first house. We moved back into the Swinney school boundary, close to where we once lived with Robert. While the house was very modest, it would be *our* home.

In July 1979, on mom's birthday, we all piled into the car for a trip to Wichita Falls, Texas. Once we got to the highway, I asked mom where we were going. "To get married!" she replied. I guess I had never considered they were unmarried. What would a twelve-year-old boy know about the subject, anyway? After hearing mom's answer, I replied, "Oh cool, I've never been to one of your weddings before!"

"Thanks David, now you've made me feel like Elizabeth Taylor!" exclaimed mom in an offended tone. I didn't catch the reference but continued on, "I couldn't be at the first one because I wasn't born yet. I wasn't there for the second one when you married Robert, so this is my first time going to one of your weddings." While she seemed less than amused by my comments, she detected my approval of their decision.

The journey was about forty five miles to the courthouse, just across the state line. We had to go to Texas because Oklahoma

31

would not grant a marriage license because of the difference in race. The State of Oklahoma required blood testing to get a marriage license. None of that made any sense.

Charles is seven years younger than mom, making him only thirteen years older than me. He was just days past his twenty-fifth birthday when they got married and had assumed the role of a father to three very blonde, white children. As complicated as the responsibility was, a great deal of baggage and brokenness came along with it. He did not realize what he had signed up for.

To his credit, Charles treated me with love and respect. Ever encouraging, almost to a fault, he treated me more like a contemporary. That fall, after my thirteenth birthday, he taught me how to drive.

It started with practice on the living room floor. We sat down with legs spread and feet touching as he simulated the foot pedals of the car. I held onto a pretend steering wheel as he created scenarios to make sure I understood which the gas pedal was and which the brake was. We also practiced a scenario for a manual transmission because he thought I should know how to drive a car with either transmission.

After he felt I had mastered the "simulator", he took me for a real driving lesson. We drove to a large paved area on Fort Sill where there was no traffic and I practiced driving for the first time, in a real car.

On another occasion, with the whole family in the car, he let me drive down a city street that straddled the border between Lawton and Fort Sill. The road was just two lanes and in horrible disrepair. Good thing the traffic was light. I did well though it was difficult to see the road well through the steering wheel.

I followed the speed limit with Charles in the middle and mom in the passenger seat. Mom wasn't happy with the idea. She was unaware Charles had been teaching me to drive. I was three years away from getting my driver's license. Less concerned with my driving ability, she worried about what might happen if we got caught.

Not thirty seconds after those words left her mouth, she saw a police officer in the passenger side mirror. Imagine the view from behind the car. Since my head didn't rise above the headrest, to the officer it looked like there was no driver and two passengers. Mom got really frazzled at that point. She kept thinking someone would go to jail that day.

Charles reached picked me up to trade places. We coasted down a slight hill, so we never lost speed and the officer never noticed the switch. Charles made the next right turn, and the officer continued straight. Narrowly avoiding a heart attack, mom put an end to driving until it was legal for me to do so.

What a great adventure that was. I could not wait to drive again, and I got other opportunities, unbeknownst to mom. My affinity for cars established in that land yacht.

<u>1 0</u>

LIFE WAS SO MUCH DIFFERENT LIVING WITH CHARLES. IT started with adding friends to our lives. People came by our house to visit, have BBQ's, and play games. No longer did we experience isolation as we had with Robert. Charles has an outgoing personality and would give the literal shirt off his back to anyone who needed it.

Sometimes he allowed people to stay with us until they could find housing. He often loaned our cars to others. If someone had a need, whether he knew them or not, he helped any way he could. Mom might say his willingness to help went overboard a few times as people took advantage on more than one occasion.

Life was never boring after Charles. We associated with other military families, which meant there was a lot of turnover. That part was tough for me. It was difficult to trust others and just when I opened up; they left. A couple of times families we knew transferred to other posts, and within a few years, the Army transferred them back to Fort Sill. Military life has a way of making the big world feel smaller.

Meanwhile, interaction with hospital staff on post was frustrating. We got the run around a couple times when I needed my prosthetic replaced. As I grew, I had to get a new arm every year. Not only because I outgrew them, I also beat them up pretty bad. I never let the hook stop me from at least attempting to do things.

As large an installation as Fort Sill is, they lacked an orthopedic clinic. For several years they referred me to a civilian provider for a new hook. It was a long drawn out process which involved seeing a doctor to get a prescription for a new prosthesis. I never understood having to get a prescription every time; my hand will never grow back.

At some point, the Army decided the cost was prohibitive to do business that way and changed their protocol. For the next couple of years we had to drive seven hours south, to Fort Sam Houston Army hospital near San Antonio, Texas to get new hooks.

One of those trips stands out. Sam Houston was a teaching hospital. Prior to going there, I never showed my arm to more than one doctor. I was self-conscious of the way it looked. On that trip, I had to remove my clothing and put on one of those hospital gowns, the type that ties in the back. Taken from one exam room to another, away from my family, I met a dozen new doctors. Each one, amazed by its appearance, pressed in for a turn to examine my stump.

Behind me was a large curtain which parted, revealing more than three hundred medical students in the audience. My exposed backside was in plain view and I felt violated. The doctors never informed me I would be on stage. It was hard enough to endure the dozen doctors, who pointed, poked, and prodded, but even more so to be a lab rat in front of such a large group. We never traveled to Sam Houston again for a hook which was fine by me.

After we left the hospital, it started raining. Infrequent in Texas; when it rained, it came down with fierceness. As we traveled down the interstate, the wiper blades could not keep up with the quarter sized raindrops pelting the car. The three kids, now teens / pre-teen were in the back seat doing what kids do well at that age, argue and complain. Crammed in the back seat, our long legs competed for space. Ongoing comments included, "Mom, he's touching me!" "Mom, she kicked me!" After hearing enough, mom told us to knock it off. We passed a tractor trailer, and a gust of wind hit the car so hard we hydroplaned.

We spun three hundred sixty degrees, four or five times before we landed wheels down, in the gulley of the center median. Not one other driver stopped to check on us. Charles asked if everyone was okay, and then got back on the highway as if nothing happened. I remember how relaxed he was during, and after that event; the literal "calm in the storm". For the rest of the journey, no one spoke. It no longer mattered if our knees or feet touched.

Summer 1980, my father arranged for us to stay with him for three months. Though he always knew where we were, he never visited prior. He called once per year, on his birthday.

He remarried by that time and became a step-parent to three younger children.

He drove from Alabama to Oklahoma to pick us up and then drove straight back. That was quite a long drive with a man we hadn't seen in six years. For most of the trip he took every opportunity to ridicule and discredit our mom. Barely a teenager, even I knew the tactic he used would not bring the results he hoped for.

As we got close to the home of his parents, he had to teach us the ways of proper etiquette. We were never to discuss, in front of his parents, certain activities such as going to the movies. My grandfather was vehement in his opposition of "picture shows" as he believed they came straight from the pit of hell. Certain language was also off limits. We were never to utter the word fart, for any reason.

Once we arrived at our grandparents' home, I made an incriminating remark which resulted in a verbal altercation between my father and his parents. I shared an observation I made while on our cross country drive. Several times my father had taken his hands off the steering wheel, and waved them in the air, pretending he was not in control of the car. I later learned, after he received a scolding from my grandparents for endangering our lives, he used his knees to guide the steering wheel. It is ironic how this little scene embodies his performance as a father. He had taken his hands off the proverbial *steering wheel* with us by abandoning us after the divorce.

We stayed with our paternal grandparents for a few days before my father took us to visit our maternal grandmother, about an hour's drive east. Granny, as we called her, lived alone in a retirement center. I only know of seeing my maternal grandfather one time, when we returned from Thailand, but I don't remember him. I'll share more about Grampa Jasper in a future chapter.

Granny took us to the space center in Huntsville, Alabama. Happy to spoil us, she bought sugary soda which we could drink anytime at her house. She also took us to the five and dime where we chose our own toys; it was like Christmas in July! We had not received many gifts since the Christmas in Panama when we got more toys than any three kids should own.

As a teenager, I enjoyed building plastic models. I picked out a jeep-like vehicle which came with a trailer and two motorcycles. All my cares vanished whenever assembling models. Once I started one, I would not stop until I finished. I developed a high skill level as a builder and aimed for perfection with each one. In hindsight, my struggle with perfectionism started out with those plastic models. I was in control of the finished project. If there was one flaw, even if no one else noticed, I felt like I had failed and beat myself up over it.

At both grandparents' homes, we endured the twenty-question routine. None of the adults seemed concerned about how my siblings and I were doing at home. They were more interested in how "that black man" behaved; an idea unfathomable to my ancestors. They asked if Charles drank orange Kool-Aid and ate watermelon and fried chicken.

None of them had any qualms about using the word nigger. It rolled across their lips as smoothly as *bless your little heart*. Mom taught us we were never to use that word, ever. I have never spoken the word; it disgusts me to type it, to be honest. Our grandparents used us to gather information, perhaps for the purpose of helping my father regain custody of us.

After several days at Granny's house, my father drove us to his home in Georgia where we met his new wife and step-children. We stayed at their home for a few days before we loaded everybody into the station wagon to head north, to visit my father's in-laws in Massachusetts.

It was clear from the start where my siblings and I stood in the ranks. My father's car had a jump seat in the back that flipped up to provide additional seating. While the step-children enjoyed the sprawling expanse of the second row seating, we sat in the jump seat, which offered no leg room. We tried to make the best of it by requesting truckers honk their horns or making silly faces at other cars. Each time we stopped at a restaurant, my father, his wife, and her three kids sat at one table and we sat at another. We felt tainted, unworthy to sit with them.

11

WE ARRIVED AT OUR DESTINATION, NEW BEDFORD, Massachusetts, and spent the better part of a month there. I remember how beautiful the scenery was; and how the beach reminded me of Panama. It was fun to collect seashells and play in the sand.

On one occasion, my father took us to into the gift shops and allowed us to choose two special treasures each. I chose a ship inside a bottle and a bag full of colorful polished rocks. You could have as many as you could stuff into a little blue velvet bag. We could also choose one postcard each to send home to mom.

New England differed from other places we had lived. My father's new wife had a large and boisterous family of Polish heritage. They served traditional cuisine at most meals. Two dishes stand out, one was *Gwumpkies* (a mixture of ground beef, rice, onion, and seasonings wrapped in a cabbage leaf and baked in a sauce made from gravy mix and ketchup). The other was *Pierogi* (a mixture of potato, cheese, and spices wrapped in a dough shell, which they boiled and topped with sautéed onions).

Since leaving Thailand I had become a rather picky eater. At home with my mom, I developed a method for getting through meal times with food I found offensive. Mom often served green beans, a food I despise. I would place a spoonful in my mouth and take a swig of water or milk to wash the food down without chewing. There were many foods which I could not stand the smell, taste, or texture of. Eating that way required a lot of drink so I went through two or three glasses per meal.

At the gatherings in Massachusetts, food was a celebration. It was tortuous for me. We each got one small glass of whatever drink they offered. If I didn't have liquid to wash the food down with, I couldn't eat it. That didn't sit well with the cooks, or my father. My refusal to eat resulted in a spanking and being sent to the bedroom. I received many spankings while we were there.

My father took us for a drive to the state of Maine, for one simple reason, so we could say we'd been there. I asked if the older kids could sit in the middle row for that trip but got shot down by my father's wife. That seat was for her kids only. Any resistance on our part resulted in a spanking. She may have had a valid reason but I thought it was because she didn't like us.

It was lunch time when we arrived in the town of Kittery, and my father stopped at a cafeteria style restaurant. Pleased with the chosen restaurant, I thought I would find something on the buffet I liked to eat and then eat a lot of it.

I don't recall the name of the restaurant but not much of the food met my peculiar eating concerns. As we moved through the line, the others found several options. Nearing the end of the line, I had nothing on my plate. My father insisted I choose something because he did not want to spend any of his good money for me to eat nothing.

After a second trip down the line I chose dinner rolls and half a cantaloupe. The outer skin wasn't removed but figured I would take care of it on my own. After my father paid the bill, the cashier reached over my tray and grabbed the cantaloupe, explaining the fruit was only a garnishment to the salad bar. It was not for consumption. Embarrassed, I wanted to run and hide because he made me feel like I had stolen the fruit. After we sat down, my father marched me off to the restroom for a spanking. Back at the table, I sat and stared off in the distance as everyone else ate.

Instead of pushing two tables together to accommodate the eight of us, my father and his second family sat together in a booth while we sat by ourselves at another table. Impressed with how well-behaved the children were, an older couple stopped at the booth to commend my father. My father's wife beamed with pride as she looked at her kids, who had been acting like wild monkeys. The woman clarified it was us, the older kids, about whom she was speaking.

Our return to New Bedford felt twice as long, and we still had to endure the drive back to Georgia. My siblings and I couldn't wait to go back to Oklahoma, the sooner the better. While grateful for the opportunity to see places I had never been, I knew I never wanted to visit my father again.

When our visit in New Bedford was over, we returned to my father's house in Georgia to finish out the summer there. The Brady

Bunch we were not. We tried to get along with the younger kids; but if there were disagreements between us, we knew who would end up in trouble.

During our stay, we had to use my father's bathroom. I still remember the piles of porn magazines he kept in there. Knowing what we experienced with him in Panama, I couldn't help but wonder if he subjected his step-kids, two girls and a boy, to the same torment. Did he take nude photos of them? Did he allow them to view his porn magazines too? I sure hope not.

It felt like an eternity passed before we finally went back to Oklahoma. We said our goodbyes, took instruction again on what we could discuss with our mom, and walked out to the car. The younger kids were sad to see us go. We wore the biggest smiles as we waved goodbye because were going home.

Without the younger kids in the car, we sat in the middle row. Leg room was a joy to experience. We drove straight through, from Georgia to Oklahoma. We got irritable and argued after long stretches. When our behavior upset my father, he would extend his arm over the front seat and hit whoever was closest. It didn't matter if he hit the guilty party or not. Looking back, I realize he was under a lot of pressure and perhaps reacted out of frustration. Blending families is challenging, but I didn't understand that then. We felt inferior, like we weren't good enough for him and his new family. That summer experience should have brought us closer together, but it pushed us farther apart.

My sister and I never had to endure another visit with him again. My brother went back and spent his sophomore year in high school living with our father. He had to know where he stood.

<u>12</u>

PROBABLY THE BEST THING MY FATHER EVER DID WAS TO buy a lawnmower for me. After the summer visit, I used the mower to earn money cutting grass around the neighborhood.

The mower gave me the opportunity to experience new things. It fostered a strong work ethic, and gave me the drive to finish what I started. With proceeds from the lawn mowing, I bought a bicycle to get around town. I then expanded my business endeavors farther into the neighborhood.

I didn't mow lawns for long before a new business opportunity presented itself; newspaper delivery. My bicycle enabled me to have a large route. I woke up extra early to deliver the morning paper, with more time spent after school delivering the evening edition. Sunday deliveries were demanding because the papers were an inch thick and took several trips to get them all delivered. I was in seventh grade, the first year of junior high school.

While most kids were hanging out at friends' houses, or playing video games at the local arcade, I was busy earning a living. If memory serves me, I averaged $60 per month from the paper delivery business.

I could buy candy whenever I wanted. Another perk of becoming an entrepreneur was having my first girlfriend. Cathy lived one street over and was a year younger. Cathy was problematic for my social status because in junior high my contemporaries frowned upon dating a girl in elementary school. I didn't care; I never fit in with the social circles, anyway. I was elated to have a girl even show interest in me.

Thinking things were innocent enough, mom allowed her to sleep over at our house one Saturday night. We camped out on the living room floor with my brother and sister.

We ate popcorn and candy and stayed up to watch Saturday Night Live. When the show ended, it was lights out and my siblings fell asleep. Lying there, unable to sleep due to the evening's sugar intake, Cathy startled me when she grabbed my hand and placed it between her legs. I was even more surprised to find her undressed. She then pulled my pants down and rolled me on top of her, thrusting her pelvis as a sign she was ready to have sex.

I watched people having sex in videos, but I wasn't prepared to engage in intercourse with Cathy. I remember thinking, how do I get out of this situation? With no experience to reference, I pretended to fall asleep. To continue the ruse, I faked snoring as she continued to thrust. She felt rejected and pushed me back onto the floor. I lay there, continuing the charade of snoring, until she fell asleep. Only then did I pull up my pants.

Our relationship didn't survive long after that incident. We remained friends for until she took an interest Raymond. He was happy to oblige when she presented him with the same opportunity.

I met Raymond when he moved in with his grandfather who lived across the street from us. He and his mom had moved to Lawton from Bakersfield, California. Like Desmond, Raymond was never bothered by my hook. We hit it off right away and soon became best friends. His mom found a house behind ours which made it easy to be at one another's house anytime. Raymond was like an adopted brother though he looked like he would have been a son of Charles rather than my mom.

We built a fort in his back yard out of pallets we had found in a local lot. Technically I guess we had stolen the pallets since we asked no one for permission to use them. We worked on the fort every day after school. Scraps of plywood, two by fours, pallets, and bricks comprised the fort. We built a fire pit inside to keep us warm in the winter months. We even lined it with wallpaper. That "wallpaper" was pages torn from porn magazines. There was no escaping the imagery.

In my mind, grown-ups obsessed over sex. Images and connotations were everywhere and sex was a part of almost every conversation. I felt trapped in a spider's weavings, long before the days of the world-wide-web.

Raymond waited for me at my house one afternoon. He shared his conquest of my former girlfriend with Charles and his friend Don. They thought it would be fun to tease me when I got home from school. All three guys waited to ambush me in my bedroom.

When I walked in, all three of them had grins on their faces like the Cheshire cat. Their behavior raised my suspicion. Charles and Don started with the questioning and teasing, asking me if I was too afraid of Cindy. They offered go with me next time, to hold my hand and walk me through it. Raymond laughed through the entire experience.

Charles and Don continued to press as I tried to change clothes for work. "Grandkids, grandkids, when you gonna make me some grandkids?" Charles taunted. They continued advancing until I tripped and fell backwards into the closet and hit something with the end of my stump, which caused intense pain to shoot up my arm. That was it, I had had enough! I chased Charles out of my room, tackling him in the living room where I began a full on assault. Pinning him to the floor, I sat on his stomach and pounded his chest repeatedly.

I unleashed anger which had developed over many years; most of which he was not responsible for. He took my pounding without hitting me back. Like a pressure relief valve in a piping system, he enabled me to bleed off a little pressure. Not to condone their behavior, but they did not know any of what I had experienced. Those guys weren't aware of the abuse, the molestation, or the threats. They were unaware Robert often came by after midnight to reinforce those threats by sitting on his Harley in front of our house, revving the engine to let me know he was still there.

If they had known those details, they would not have teased me the way they did, but I remained silent out of fear. Fear that if I told anyone, Robert would carry out his threat to kill us. Fear of an altercation between Charles and Robert, something I wanted to avoid. It was a great weight upon my shoulders that aged me far beyond my years. Not only was my innocence lost, and my childhood robbed from me, my teen years grew more miserable by the day. I felt I had nowhere to turn, so I turned inward. I retreated into my mind, to create a safe place where I could survive. My trust destroyed, I didn't believe most of what anyone said or did.

I lost my self-worth. Human beings crave relationship. Feelings of unworthiness amplified my perfectionism which began with the model car building. Perfectionism was my cry for acceptance. It motivated me to do my best at anything I attempted, to garner validation and acceptance.

For instance, when I built a model car, I did things over and above what the kit offered. I once built a 1/4th scale model Camaro Z28. The car was about twenty inches long and had cool features, but I took it to another level by adding working headlights and taillights. I even set it up so you could reach inside with a pencil and touch the brake pedal to light up the brake lights. The local

Radio Shack store knew me as a regular customer since most of the electronic parts I bought there.

I drifted away from "so-called" masculine pursuits and related more to the feminine persuasion. I wasn't interested in becoming a girl. The feminine world I found less aggressive. In my woundedness, I sought healing and comfort, something the world of bravado and machismo could not offer.

In social settings I conversed with the girls rather than the guys. I was the guy friend the girls hung out with who represented no threat. Never one to hit on them, or try to have sex with them, established me squarely, pun intended, in the *friend zone*. The friend zone would haunt me in the high school years.

13

SINCE AROUND SIXTH GRADE, I NOTICED I HAD A WAY WITH children, specifically babies. We often had visitors who brought their little ones along. I had many opportunities to hold a baby for a mom looking for a few minutes of peace without having to tend to her little one while engaged in adult conversation.

Always willing to help, I became known as a baby whisperer. When a visiting baby was fussy, my mom called me to care for the child. Most times, the baby would calm down for me. Many of them found the shiny stainless steel hook to be of great interest.

With each child I held, I saw something in them which had been destroyed within me. There is a beautiful innocence in a child's eyes and their wonderment with the world was something I envied. I often wished I could go back to redo my childhood where I would never have been a victim of grown men's insatiable lusts. Babies are very perceptive and compassionate; I think they sensed the melancholy within my soul.

If ever I had a child, I would shower that child with unconditional love and vigilantly protect their innocence. I would defend them from the evil that abounds in this world. It also seemed like the best way to receive love in reciprocity. A child naturally loves its parents and looks to them for all their needs, regardless of the parent's social status, career, or bank account balance.

My mother's love for me I have never doubted and I also knew my siblings loved me, but we lacked a fundamental component in our family dynamics. Though we knew we loved each other, we didn't express it in tangible ways. Seldom were those three little words, "I love you", uttered. Hugs were infrequent.

The lack of positive physical contact contributed to the downward trajectory I was on. With every baby I had the chance to hold, however, the desire to have a child of my own grew stronger. I purposed in my heart to love my child so fiercely that he/she would never doubt my love for them. My child would never endure the things I experienced if I had any say in the matter.

Every child was a life line, a little beacon of hope. I've heard it said when you look into the face of a baby; it's akin to seeing the face of God. To this day, babies still hold that power for me, the power of hope.

It breaks my heart to hear all the tragic stories of abuse and neglect inflicted upon our most vulnerable citizens. When I see a news article describing a horrible situation for a child, I feel their pain. I weep for them. Children should never have to endure abuse. When the perpetrator is a family member, the abuse is more heinous. I realize the altruistic nature of these words, but as a society, we must break the chains of abuse.

<u>14</u>

MOM ALWAYS ENCOURAGED ME TO BELIEVE I COULD DO anything. In seventh grade she supported me playing team sports. I expressed an interest in baseball so she petitioned the military to provide an adaptive device which made it possible to catch a ball with my prosthesis. The wrist unit of the arm was a screw type. I could use a device which fit into a baseball mitt when I played outfield and then switch back to the hook when up to bat.

It took less than a minute to make the switch. I may have been the most surprised the first time I caught the ball. Catching the ball every time took practice, but I determined I would succeed at it. While I could try out for the team, I was the first one cut. The coach may have feared I would hurt other players by accident when sliding to a base or something. He appreciated the heart and effort I put forth. He offered me the trainer position which allowed me to be part of the team.

Basketball tryouts were a different story. Since there was no special device required, maybe I would make the team. Once again, fearful thinking by the coach resulted in my being offered the trainer position. The main part of my job was to collect towels and uniforms once the team hit the showers. There wasn't much fun to do. During practice, I often made my way to the upper level in the gym to work out on the weightlifting equipment. When I set my mind to do something, I adapted. Lifting weights was no different, and since it was not a team sport, the coach no problems with it.

After seventh grade, it was clear I would not play on any team so I moved away from sports. I didn't attend another sporting event until my senior year, the town rivalry football game.

In eighth and ninth grades I took part in the visual aids department. Before school I set up film projectors in various classrooms, and after school I retrieved the equipment. It was easier for me to serve from the background. I felt connected with no one knowing I was there, the anonymity I enjoyed.

At home, no one considered me handicapped, but the world outside had a different opinion. I was repeatedly denied participation in various activities because of the hook. Every time I faced rejection, two things conjured up within me. First, rejection increased my determination to do the thing someone said I couldn't, and to do it better than any so-called "able bodied" person. Second, it made me withdraw further from any sense of community. Isolationism took root in my life in junior high school.

Most of the cliques did not accept me, even the nerd squad rejected me. A few people knew my step-father was black, so I found a little acceptance in the black community. There was some joking and teasing, but they did it in jest.

I already listened to rap and R&B music and my friend Raymond kept me supplied with cassette tapes of the latest jams. We were on a school field trip one time and I had a tape playing in my Walkman. I stared through the bus window, listening to a mix tape, when a girl popped into the seat next to mine. She pulled my headphones off so she could hear the music. She danced in her seat a little and then told everybody on the bus I had the cool jams.

Within seconds, I found myself surrounded by several curious black girls. They were curious to know why a dorky little white kid had the latest and greatest music, and mix tapes at that. It was not normal in their eyes.

Half the bus crowded around me as we traveled. Some people thought it was amazing, for others it was disgusting. My face red from embarrassment, I didn't know how to handle that kind of attention. Someone in the group coined a new nickname for me that day; OREO. The idea being, I was the white cream in the middle, flanked by two black cookies. One represented my black stepfather; the other represented my new black friends.

Charles always wore baseball hats which he personalized with his initials, CSW. He had them in every color available and hung them on all four walls of his bedroom. I emulated him and bought hats personalized with OREO. I'm not sure it was a good idea, but I had fifteen or twenty hats made up. Maybe it was me telling people I found my tribe.

15

THE NEWSPAPER DELIVERY BUSINESS HAD HELPED ME grow in terms of responsibility and work ethic. The papers got delivered whether or not I was in good health. During the winter one year it had gotten too cold to deliver my route via my bicycle so mom helped out. We loaded the papers in her van and with the passenger sliding door held open; I tossed them from the relative comfort of the vehicle.

The car option didn't last long. It became a burden on the family, from a financial perspective and time-wise. A customer of mine owned a restaurant near my home and one day he offered me a job. He had witnessed my dedication in delivering newspapers so he offered me a position as a dishwasher in his pizza franchise.

At age fourteen I got a part-time job washing dishes in a very busy restaurant. It was difficult but it sure beat delivering papers. I also made more money! My starting wage was $1.65 per hour.

In ninth grade I was at the top level on campus. That was also the year for prom. With a source of income, it was incumbent upon me to find a date for the prom. Mom stepped in to help with that. She knew someone who had a daughter at my school and our parents arranged for us to go to the dance together.

Dating was a new concept for me. With my first dance less than a month away, I asked for as many hours as I could get at work. I needed to earn enough money for a suit and pay for flowers and dinner.

With funds in hand, I walked the five or six miles to the nearest clothing store and purchased my suit. It was a camel color blazer with matching slacks, a white shirt, and a chocolate brown knit tie.

It was the nicest outfit I had ever owned and the best part was I earned the money to pay for it myself. The empowering feeling squelched my anxiety about going to the dance.

The day of the dance finally came. Saturday night, and after my shift at the pizza parlor; I went home to get showered up. My suit fit well and Charles helped me get my tie situated. He enjoyed teasing me, as he worked the knot, with his favorite question, "So when are you going to give me a grandchild?"

Mom grabbed the corsage from the refrigerator and pinned the boutonniere on my lapel. She instructed me on the proper way to pin the corsage on my date, and then the phone rang. Mom excused herself to go take the call. My date's mom called to say her daughter did not want to go to the dance.

Moments later mom walked back into the living room to give me the news. She tried to soften the blow by offering encouragement but it was evident her words did not help much. Mom and Charles both encouraged me to go have fun anyway. They drove me to the school and dropped me off. I wandered through the venue assuming all eyes were upon me and after ten or fifteen minutes I left and walked home.

Embarrassed to go with me, the girl feigned illness. Her friends teased her about having to go to the dance with the one-armed bandit and feeling pressured; she couldn't go through with it. We never spoke again.

Like every other junior high school boy, I wanted to experience dating and to have a special girl in my life. That was not to be. I had many "friend girls" but no girlfriends. One of those friend-girls was Margaret, who I would walk home from school with. I thought she was attractive, and we always talked as we walked but she saw nothing in me other than a friend.

As my junior high school career came to a close, I decided there was no use in trying to find someone to date. All prior attempts were exercises in futility and I began to resent females too. No longer could I trust them. Many times I heard them say how "sweet" I was. I also heard the gossip about how gross it would be for any girl to date an amputee.

It was that shunning which caused me to retreat to what my father had shown me; pornographic magazines. In viewing the images in those magazines, I could imagine myself having the prettiest girl. It was sweet revenge in some twisted sense. What I didn't realize was just how damaging the viewing of that material was to my mental state, and my understanding of true intimacy and love. Unbeknownst to me, I compounded the devastation levied upon me by my father and first step-father, continuing the destructive pattern.

16

SOPHOMORE YEAR IN HIGH SCHOOL AND ONCE AGAIN I found myself at the bottom of the pecking order. A new school means new people, but being the only amputee student amongst 1,500 makes one stand out. My best friend was left behind as I moved up to the high school campus. He was a year younger and a grade level behind me.

After the school year started, a fellow student asked a question of me, and the response I gave haunts me to this day. I don't remember her name or much about her features except that she was rather small and had short, curly hair.

I stood in the hallway, near the lobby area of the school, when she approached me. We had not met before, but she was well aware of me. She introduced herself in a very soft-spoken, but cordial way. After a few pleasantries she popped the question, "Would you be willing to speak at our meeting for the handicapped?"

How I wish I could travel back in time to right the wrong I created that day. My response to her came out of anger, perhaps even fear and I regret it to this day. I responded by saying, "Absolutely not! Do I look like I am handicapped?" As the tears welled in her eyes, she walked away. I could do anything anybody else could, and I would prove it if given the chance. I didn't view myself as handicapped, and I did not want others to see me that way either. Many souls wander this planet with a handicap; they just may not identify it. My real handicap was the inability to see the characteristics within me which she found so inspirational.

That young lady saw something, and believed others would too, which prompted her invitation. I had become a very cynical and jaded person. While she and I could have become friends, I am certain I hurt her with my negative words and attitude. I hope she has found it in her heart to forgive me.

During my sophomore year I picked up more hours at the pizza parlor. Money was scarce in our home so I took on extra hours to contribute to our family finances. At school from 7:15 am to 2:30 pm, I got home by 3:00 pm, completed homework assignments, and then prepared to start work at 5 pm. Most weeks I worked thirty hours, on top of going to school.

I worked the closing shift every Friday night and the opening shift on Saturdays. Sundays rotated between day shift and night shift and then I had two or three closing shifts during the week. As much as my family appreciated the financial help, it always upset my mom to accept money from me to cover expenses. I recognized it was painful for her and I did things in secret so she wouldn't have to accept money directly.

Since I worked late on many nights, I would take their cars after work and fill them with gas while my parents slept. We lived three blocks from a gas station so it didn't take much time to do.

Both parents thought their cars had defective gas gauges and feared running out of gas. They caught on that it was me filling the tanks. I also paid for anything I needed for school to lessen that burden for them. Mom received child support from my father which totaled of $250.00 per month. The court ordered him to pay $83.00 per month, per child. In an act of generosity, he had rounded the payment to $250.00 to make accounting easier. That extra dollar didn't go very far.

One of Charles' army buddies got orders for temporary duty in Korea and asked him to take care of a motorcycle while he served overseas. The guy preferred the bike got used rather than sit in storage for a year. Charles thought I would like to ride it to and from school.

It was a small bike, with a 60cc engine, but it was better than riding the bus. Charles took me to the elementary school playground and taught me how to ride. I used the hook to pull the clutch lever when changing gears and work the turn signal switch.

In Oklahoma, you could get a motorcycle license at fourteen so I got the driver's handbook and studied for the test. We set a date for a week later and went down to the office of the Oklahoma Highway Patrol.

Charles was always very proud to refer to us kids as his own, calling us his sons and daughter no matter whose company we

52

kept. We walked into the OHP station and stepped up to the counter. The lady behind the counter asked how she could help and Charles replied, "My son is here to test for his motorcycle license". The lady scanned the waiting room, looking for the son.

I stood right beside my step-father and because he is black, and I am white, the lady didn't realize I was the son to whom he referred. Her face blushed, and she stumbled on her words when I said it was me who wanted to take the test. She gave me the paperwork, told me where to go to begin, and then consulted a trooper in private as I walked away from her counter.

When I finished the written part of the test, I handed it back to the lady. She notified the trooper I passed and was ready for the road test. The trooper had no qualms sharing his opinion about interracial marriage. He confronted Charles as though he had committed a crime by bringing me in and claiming to be my father.

The trooper looked for ways to deny me taking the road test. He requested identification for both Charles and me. We produced valid military ID cards which showed me as the dependent son but they didn't suffice. The trooper called the military police at Fort Sill to verify the authenticity of the identification.

Since that didn't work, the trooper turned his sights to the motorcycle. He checked the tread depth on the tires, the tension on the chain, and all the lights to insure proper function. With everything checking out okay, he had no other legal reason to deny me the road test.

The trooper explained the route before we left. He followed in his patrol car, which was very unnerving. Just before the turns he gave direction over the loudspeaker on the car, all while the red light on top of the car flashed. People in the area may have thought the officer was chasing me.

I paid extreme attention to every speed limit and made full and complete stops. I rode with caution hoping he would not take away any points. To pass, I had to achieve a score of 80% or better. As we returned to the station, I felt confident I passed. The trooper told me to stand near the building while he remained in his car for several minutes.

The trooper tried to fail me but came up short. My grade was 80%, based on four mistakes which took away five points each. I made an improper lane change four times. In his directions over the loudspeaker, he instructed me to make a left turn and then make a right turn at the next corner. There were two lane streets in each direction and the mistake I made, all four times, was turning into my destination lane rather than the closest lane. It felt like he tried to trick me with the lane changes, but rather than argue with the man, we took the passing grade and got the license. The trooper told Charles not to bring me back expecting to take the driver's test for the automobile license. He promised he would not grant one if we did.

Even though I lived about a thousand yards from work, I still loved to ride the motorcycle there. One Monday night, after working the closing shift, I locked the restaurant and walked to where I had parked the motorcycle. It wasn't there, someone stole it. I called the police who recovered it the following day in a trailer park just south of the pizza parlor.

My book bag, still attached, had all my school books inside, but no homework. The motorcycle was not in good condition. When I parked it I locked the forks, they were still in the locked position when recovered. The thief broke just about everything else there was to break on the bike. The clutch and break handles snapped off, the turn signals smashed, and all the wiring stripped and cut.

Without insurance coverage on the bike, there was no way my parents could pay for the damage. My boss loaned me $700.00 to get the bike repaired. That was a tough lesson learned.

We never found out who stole the bike. I have always suspected it was someone who did not approve of our family and the damage done to the motorcycle was a subliminal message. After that incident, I stopped riding it to work for fear of it happening again.

After a few errands around town on the motorcycle, I rear-ended a car. The street had two lanes running each direction, plus a center turning lane. In the left lane, cruising at forty miles per hour, the car in front of me slammed on the brakes, stopping at the intersection under a green light.

With a high curbed median to my left, and several cars in the lane to my right, I had nowhere to go. I hit the brakes as hard as I could and wound up laying the bike down on its left side. I slid under the stopped car, wedging my right leg up against the gas tank. The rate of speed at impact was 30 mph.

I laid there for a few moments, stunned by what happened, as the driver pulled away. The driver proceeded through the intersection on a red light and left me there on the ground. I was wearing a helmet and because I laid the bike down on the left side, my hook protected my arm from road rash. It was a miracle I did not get injured. I stood the bike up, got back on it, and waited for the green light. No one got out of their car to check on me. They stared at me in disbelief.

I rode the bike for a short while longer before parking it for good. The time soon came to drive a car, and the motorcycle faded into history. When the owner returned, he pretty much got a brand new motorcycle back after all the repairs it had.

I took Driver's Education as an elective in tenth grade where I received my permit to drive with a licensed adult. After my sixteenth birthday we went back to the Highway Patrol station to visit with the same trooper who had promised to fail me.

As with the previous test, I passed the vision screening, and the written part with no problems. The grumpy trooper began his "checklist" by verifying the registration and insurance paperwork. The first thing he noticed was our vehicle inspection, which was due to expire within a week so he declined to test.

Charles was not happy about it but we drove to the closest inspection station, got the certificate, and returned to the Highway Patrol office in less than thirty minutes. With disdain, the trooper performed a basic safety check and found everything operational. Checking the tread depth on the tires, he once again refused to test.

Determined he would not let the trooper beat us, Charles raced to a tire store and had four new tires installed on the car. He left rubber on the street when he raced back to the station. The trooper got angry when Charles threatened to sue the department if they refused to give me the test. After checking the clock, the trooper said we had run out of time for testing. Charles demanded someone test me at that moment or he would contact an attorney.

The trooper relented and tested me moments later. He tried everything he could to rattle me into making mistakes. He rode in the passenger seat as he ordered me to do various maneuvers. The car was a stick shift, and he had me parallel park in uphill and downhill conditions, with and without curbs. He tried to get me for improper lane changes but I already knew about that little trick. Almost closing time, the trooper directed me back to the station.

On the way back, we crossed a set of railroad tracks which caused the trooper to hit his head against the roof of the car. I could tell it angered him and thought he would fail me on the spot. We got back to the station where he exited the vehicle and sprinted into his office. A few minutes later I had my license, and one last threat to go with it. The trooper warned me to do nothing wrong because he would have no leniency on me if I did.

Having the legal ability to drive myself was a great feeling. Driving brought with it the responsibility of maintenance. My first car was a 1978 Chevrolet Chevette four door hatchback. Though the loan was in my parent's name, I made all the payments. I even made double payments to reduce my balance quicker. I came home from school one day and as I parked front of our house, the transmission dropped to the street under the car. That was a surprise!

17

AFTER PAYING FOR THE TRANSMISSION REPAIR, I TRADED the car for a 1979 Olds Cutlass Supreme Brougham. My parents owned a similar car, so I had achieved a huge milestone catching up to them. At sixteen I secured the financing in my name, without need of a co-signer.

Many of the abuse survivors I've met develop addictions as they turn to drugs or alcohol to numb their pain. My addiction was less damaging to the body but still had a high cost. Cars were my addiction, which led to another, becoming a workaholic.

A full-time student in high school with a car payment of $225.00 per month, I had to work full time to cover my bills. Fortunate to still live with my parents, I could not afford to live on my own with so many expenses.

I suppose I snubbed my nose at the world with my actions. I had no value in the eyes of others, so I set out to prove my worth. Gaining material possessions "to keep up with the Jones" was how I went about it.

Even on a tight budget, I bought accessories to customize my car. Chrome wheels, tinted windows, sun visor, and a simulated spare tire on the trunk lid were a few of the customizations I did to the car. I also spent many hours every weekend waxing and detailing that car. The tires were always super glossy with the brightest whitewalls.

I befriended Gino, a guy two years older who had already graduated from high school. We used to cruise the strip together.

His car was a 1980 Pontiac Grand Prix, customized like mine. Our goal was to make the cars resemble limousines.

Gino had a baby boy he sometimes brought to the car wash. Gino Jr would lie sleeping on the front seat as we cruised, not the most responsible thing to do.

I envied Gino for having a son. While I kept up well in the car competition with my friend, it would be a few years before I had a child of my own.

The summer before my junior year I worked a lot of hard hours at the pizza parlor. The owner also had a sub sandwich restaurant a few blocks up the road. One guy who worked at the sub shop was a schoolmate, in the same grade as me. He had an older brother who dated one of the boss's daughters, and I often saw them around both restaurants.

One Saturday morning, as I prepared for the lunch buffet, my classmate stopped into the pizza parlor on business, accompanied by a young lady. She sat at a video game console within my field of vision. I found her attractive but didn't pay much attention to her. She was out of my league.

She chatted with another daughter of the owner and they kept looking my way and giggling. I felt self-conscious, wondering why they were laughing at me. The smirking and giggling continued for several minutes which frustrated me. It was bad enough girls saw me as friend material but to make matters worse, this girl laughed and giggled at my expense. The owner's daughter walked behind the beverage counter to continue her work, leaving the mystery girl alone at the video game.

Not yet open for business, she was the only non-employee in the building. She put a quarter in the jukebox and resumed watching me work. As the song ended, she said something to me but I couldn't hear it. Not accustomed to having many girls speak to me, I thought she was making fun of me. I tried to ignore her.

I looked up as she mouthed the comment again, but with the cacophony of noise surrounding me, it was impossible to hear her. The boss's daughter walked by and yelled, "She said she likes you! What are you deaf or something?"

I must have appeared aloof, but it took a few seconds to process what she said as it was not what I expected. Not knowing how to respond to a beautiful girl expressing an interest in me, I nodded and continued working. She later told me she thought I was rude and arrogant. In later years, I discovered many people had that perception of me.

Misunderstood is what I was. No one knew about the emotional scars I wore, or the baggage I carried. I was desperate for relationships but did not understand how to cultivate them.

Wounded, and naïve, I lived in fear that Robert would still come after me as he threatened on so many past occasions. My classmate/co-worker came out of the office once his business dealings were complete and then I learned the mystery girl was his sister. He motioned for her to join him as he left. On her way out, she gave me her telephone number and asked me to call her.

Dumfounded, I didn't know what the next step was. After she left, I asked the boss's daughter what that interaction was all about and she told me the girl had a crush on me. I didn't believe her. I thought they were teasing me with all the laughing and giggling. "If you don't call and ask her out, I will make fun of you!" scoffed the boss's daughter.

I waited a few days before I got the nerve to call. She agreed to come to the pizza parlor the next day, and we enjoyed conversation over a pizza. Our relationship jumped onto the fast track. I don't recall taking her out on any dates. Somehow, we became a couple. Denise often came home with me after school and we watched TV in my room. I shared a bedroom with my younger brother, who often joined us.

We became sexually active within days of becoming a couple. Denise enjoyed our after school rendezvous, and as our relationship progressed, she became increasingly amorous. Risky behavior motivated her.

We had intercourse almost every day after school, but it got boring for her. The anticipation of getting caught in the act excited Denise. I was sixteen, she was fifteen; and we had no business engaging in sexual activity. With my brother in the room, as we watched TV, Denise discreetly pulled the covers up over us and slid my pants down to my ankles. My brother was oblivious to what we were doing. Moments later my mom opened the door to ask something. All movement ceased. We were in the direct line of sight of my mother as she stood in the doorway. Caught in the act, I waited for mom to pull back the covers. Instead, she questioned us about dinner and left the room. I couldn't handle the craziness.

Twice, during sex, Denise disclosed earlier sexual encounters she had with others. I don't know what purpose she thought it served, but telling the stories, while graphic and disturbing to hear, increased her level of pleasure. At sixteen, I wasn't thinking about disease but it disgusted me to learn how many guys she had been with before me.

I confided with my buddies what I learned about Denise and they encouraged me to keep going. The male mantra was "Look out for number one". Everyone I knew, kids and grownups alike, encouraged selfishness in sexual pursuits. Since Charles and Don continued to press me with the grandchild talk, it appeared I was on the right track.

Within a month or two, as word got out that Denise and I were a couple, I received warnings from others. There were four or five guys, more acquaintances than friends, who warned me no to get involved with her. They never gave details as to why so I dismissed their warnings as jealousy. Denise was the first girl I was intimate with and since she was so pretty, those other guys had to be jealous.

When other girls approached me with similar messages, it gave me pause for concern. The girls were from various factions, including the popular, nerdy, and cheerleaders. Why would they insist I stay away from Denise? I thought they were mean, toying with me for fun. Small town antics in high school settings I suspected – drama llamas.

In my junior and senior years I enrolled in the vocational/technical school across town to study Design Drafting & Architecture. I attended the high school campus for morning classes, and then after lunch drove across town to the Vo-Tech campus for afternoon classes. Denise fooled around with other guys when I was not on campus. Her liaisons she did not keep discreet and people noticed.

I received threats from two dudes at school. Both were former boyfriends of Denise. To break off the relationship with one, she dated the other. The guys restored their friendship after she dumped them.

When leaving for the other campus, on more than one occasion, their pickup trucks flanked both sides of my car such that I could not back out without hitting them. I was more concerned about scratching my car than theirs.

The guys hid inside their trucks and when I got in my car, they would just sit there, revving the engines in a show of intimidation. Other times they would stand on the sidewalk yelling obscenities, threats, and racial slurs as I pulled out of the parking lot. Their bullying never got addressed by any of the teachers or staff.

One morning, as I walked Denise to her class, an ambush awaited me. My face turned toward her, we walked and talked. The classroom doors sat back a foot behind the walls of lockers. I don't know if she was aware of the plan, I hope not, but one guy landed an unseen punch to my right jaw, catching me by surprise.

The coward launched his attack that way because he would have received a mean left hook (pun intended) in response had I seen it coming. The punch dropped me to the concrete floor, knocking me out cold.

I regained consciousness in the passenger seat of my car as my guidance counselor drove me home to my mother. I couldn't understand why Mr. Blackburn drove my car home. Standard protocol was to seek medical attention and notify the parents after calling an ambulance, but that did not happen.

Mom took me to the emergency room where a doctor diagnosed a concussion. He rang my bell hard. On the way to the hospital I faded in and out of consciousness, causing mom great anxiety. I'm sure she exceeded the posted speed limits along the way.

Back to school the next day, I was surprised when called into the disciplinarian's office. Why? I had done nothing wrong. Mr. Barker, a rather large man, gave me five swats with the paddle as a punishment for fighting on campus. He used a wooden paddle, about two feet long, which had holes drilled in it to reduce wind drag. To my knowledge, the other guys received no disciplinary action for their part.

I got paddled plenty of times at home, but just that one time at school.

<u>18</u>

AFTER THE INCIDENT OF BEING KNOCKED OUT COLD AT school, things escalated with the two former boyfriends. They would stalk me in my car as I drove around town. Sometimes they would pull up so close to the back of my car that our bumpers touched. When the light turned green I wouldn't move and they would lie on the horn until they passed, staring, yelling, and making obscene gestures as they drove by.

I can't prove it was those guys, but I frequently found items missing from my car while at work. Little things like chrome valve stem covers. While they didn't cost much, it got old having to replace them all the time.

I was in quite a conundrum. Stalked by my former stepfather while being stalked by my girlfriend's former beaus, I lost the ability to trust people. It felt like the world hated me, for reasons I couldn't understand. I did nothing to warrant such treatment from others.

The two former beaus never pulled any stunts at my family home. Perhaps they feared what they would encounter if Charles caught them.

The boys continued their verbal harassment for quite some time. I thought I must have scored because I had the girl and they didn't. Their intimidation tactics went on for the better part of my junior year before fading away.

Senior year rolled around. I was still sixteen when my last year in high school began. While I hadn't done well on the social scene, I was doing well in other areas. I purchased a car on my own, I was the assistant manager at the pizza parlor, and I had a serious girlfriend who was quite the catch.

While my time at the main campus was not fun, I enjoyed my drafting class at the other campus. Most of the students at the Vo-tech campus were high school students but the atmosphere was very different. It was less about pettiness and more about business.

On Fridays we attended Vo-tech all day rather than the split between campuses. Almost every Friday, for two school years, we only drew letters. More than penmanship, this was about learning to write in the distinctive architectural font. As soon as class started, we grabbed sheets of 8-1/2 x 11 paper and lined out 1/8" spacing to fill the pages using capital letters. You could copy text from any source. Eight hours of nothing but lettering. It was mundane work but it developed perseverance and a nice lettering style.

During my senior year, the school had gained the latest and greatest technology which changed the way drafting and architectural design was done. CAD, or computer aided drafting, was new to the market and there was no pointing and clicking done with a mouse. If you wanted to draw a line, you had to type in the X/Y/Z coordinates. Compared with what is available today it was like carving words in stone, very cumbersome.

To gain proficiency, a student had to type a minimum number of words per minute. With no prior exposure to a computer, I fretted over other students typing ability. I wasn't sure how I would ever get up to their speed typing one-handed.

I never reached the sixty words per minute goal but I became better than a hen-pecker using my one hand. One afternoon we had a test and the instructor was walking around the room peering over student's shoulders checking their work. She saw me typing one-handed and slammed her scale (non-drafters call them rulers) against the back of my chair before stating, "Use both hands Boothe!"

Startled by the sound, I adjusted the point on the hook and covered the keyboard in a two-handed manner. I then told the instructor this double hen-pecking was slowing me down. It dawned on her I didn't have two hands and she turned red in the face. The class enjoyed a big laugh at her expense.

Back to the tried and true tools of the trade, using a T-square, vellum, and mechanical pencil, we took on a project for statewide competition. The mechanical T-square was like an extension of my hook and the two worked well together. One advantage I had over the other students was the hook never sweats, leaving my drawings cleaner with less smudging.

The project involved a three dimensional, exploded view drawing of an overhead pulley which had two rollers and a hook. I worked hard on that project and was very proud of the final product. Mine tied for first place. When the judges critiqued further to break the tie, a detail I had done to showcase two through bolts with their thread patterns cost me the prize.

The bolts looked great, however, an exploded view gets drawn in such a way that when the explosion reversed, the parts migrated back into place. Showing the bolts on the outside of the two steel plates that should have sandwiched them meant the parts would not go back together as designed.

With points deducted, I lost first place but secured third. Since I didn't think I stood a chance at winning, it was awesome to have placed in the top three in the state. The educators didn't think I would succeed in the class, so my third place victory feel like first place.

During my tenure at Vo-tech, I also drafted plans for an office expansion at the school and a greenhouse for one of the other instructors. Both were constructed from my blueprints. I had accomplished something and it motivated me to continue my pursuit of becoming an architect, despite all the opposition in the field.

<u>19</u>

AS MY HIGH SCHOOL CAREER CAME TO A CLOSE, I couldn't wait to get out. There was pressure coming from all corners for me; pressure to measure up to unrealistic standards, pressure to outperform everyone else at work, pressure at home regarding family finances. In grades 6-12, the peer pressure to have sex with as many girls possible never let up. Pressured to do drugs and alcohol, to smoke cigarettes, to skip school and just act like a juvenile delinquent, all in the name of fun. I wanted release from the pressure.

There were the different social factions at school; the brainy crowd, the nerds, the jocks and cheerleaders, the popular crew, all jockeying to be the greatest people on earth. I didn't click with any of the cliques. High school could not be over with fast enough.

Aside from the graduation ceremony, the biggest social event of my senior year was the prom. There was still a bad taste in my mouth from the train wreck that was my junior high prom. The thought of attending this one was a dreadful.

Denise wanted to go, and she wouldn't accept no as my answer. She ordered a pink dress, and I rented a burgundy tux. We kept with prom night tradition and went to a fancy restaurant before the dance. While several groups rented limos and sat together at large tables, we sat at a table for two. Denise was a popular girl, or at the very least, well known so it was weird to sit alone, like outsiders looking in.

For a picky eater like me, the meal was a bust. I would rather have grabbed a pizza or burger instead, and saved a bunch of money, but I digress. After dinner, we made our way to the gymnasium at school, the venue for the dance. My stomach in knots, I wanted out of there.

She led me around the gym, stopping to visit with her friends along the way. Music played as we meandered around the second floor mezzanine, songs I had never heard. When her favorite song played, "Cuts Like A Knife" by Bryan Adams, she wanted to dance. I felt my dinner reappear in my throat as she dragged me onto the dance floor. Not only the first couple on the floor, we remained the only couple for the entire song.

I didn't have an ounce of rhythm, and I could not figure out how anyone danced to such a song. Since we were the only ones on the floor, the DJ hit us with the spotlights. My only time on the dance floor, the next three and a half minutes were sheer torture for this wallflower. The song ended and I dragged her off the floor as the rest of the school walked on. I don't recall anyone laugh at me but in my mind they all did; a horrible experience for an introvert.

Not content to hold up the walls with me, Denise danced the night away with anyone willing. She checked in when a rest was in order. That night couldn't end fast enough as far as I was concerned.

We left a little early though. After leaving the dance, we made our way to one of the cheap motels on the main drag through town. Denise wanted a fling before going home. Nervously, I stood at the counter in my tuxedo, filling out paperwork to rent a room for an hour.

I was sixteen years old pretending to be older. I wrote a fake name and address hoping the guy wouldn't ask for my driver's license. If he did, I pictured myself getting arrested or something. Sweating bullets, I was way outside my comfort zone.

The motel clerk knew exactly what I was up to. It was prom night, and many more couples would check in before the night ended. What did he care as long as we paid the money?

Even for a hormone ravaged teenaged boy, I couldn't wait to escape the situation. The thrill of it all was exciting for her but I thought I would drop dead out of fear. In retrospect, our relationship started to dissolve that very night. My girlfriend's sexual desires were on the extreme side while I was more like a prude, for lack of a better term. With greater risk, there was more pleasure for Denise. For me, even though intercourse was an enjoyable, I couldn't handle all the extra excitement. Her sexual appetite was approaching addiction while I regressed further into my shell.

After surviving my senior prom, I counted the days to graduation. I would liken the anticipation to someone anticipating release from prison, how I longed to be free.

May 1985 arrived and we were back in the gymnasium, this time dressed in a red cap and gown. It was the last time I subjected myself to standing in front of an audience. Ready to begin life on my own terms as an adult, it was worth the discomfort. One by one, we walked across the stage to receive our diplomas. They called our names in alphabetical order which put me toward the front.

For many, high school is the greatest time in the life, but I hated it. I suffered many embarrassing moments; from falling asleep in Business Law class as the other students laughed me awake, to sending flowers to the wrong girl. Knocked out in front of everyone, senior prom, the name calling; those events made high school less than fun.

Once school ended, I poured myself into work at the pizza parlor, taking on as many hours as the boss would give. I continued to customize my car, my only outlet for self-expression. It was an obsession for me really.

A month after graduation I was ready to launch out on my own. Life at home was not bad, but I wanted to lessen the burden on my family by not having to support me anymore. I found a property management company willing to let me sign a lease on a rental home at seventeen and prepared to fly the nest.

<u>20</u>

SIGNED THE LEASE AGREEMENT BEFORE TELLING ANYONE in the family, even my girlfriend. If bound by contract to a lease, I figured my parents could do nothing to prevent me from moving out. I just considered myself a burden to the family. I also wanted a private space so I could begin the search for who I was.

The lease was signed and I picked up keys to my first humble abode. It was a 400 square foot, one bedroom duplex, about five miles from home. Far enough away to change zip codes. It was moving day when I surprised my mom with my plans. She was the only one home when I approached her with the news.

Without beating around the bush, I told her why I had to leave. Tears formed in her eyes as I spoke. Her reaction I did not expect; on the contrary, I thought she would get angry and send me to my room to forget about it.

After she gathered her composure; she asked me to sit beside her. As she wiped her tears, she said it was no surprise. Feeling it was her own fault, she could not be angry with me. Mom knew I would fly the nest someday, and blamed herself for encouraging my independent spirit. With a warm embrace, she said she was excited to see where I would go in life.

In retrospect, I realize why my leaving saddened her; I was her first born, and she was not ready to let me go. Mom saw me face adversity many times, and despite her own fears, tried her best to protect me. She was forced to prepare me to fly from a much earlier age than she ever dreamed of. She thought she had seen me endure adversity, but she didn't know the half of it. Mindful only of the impact of the crash in Thailand, mom was unaware of the abuse, neglect, or molestation. A decade passed before I found the courage to reveal the darkness to her.

I left that day with my mom's blessing and moved what little earthly possessions I had into my new place. With the money I had been saving, I stocked my home with the necessities. To buy a toilet brush was an exciting milestone.

I found a sofa and loveseat for $50 so I had a place to sleep. I put up curtains and got a big TV. With my stereo and its big speakers, I was ready to take on adult life. I remembered what mom had always told me at meal times. "When you move out, you can eat whatever you want, until then you will eat what I serve." Never again would a green bean cross my lips. No more pepper steak, no more rice, meat loaf, or mashed potatoes. No more ice tea or Kool-Aid, only Coca-Cola from then on.

Most of my meals I ate at work. Meals at home included things like macaroni and cheese, hamburgers, and hot dogs. Gone were the corn flakes, replaced with all the yummy sugary cereals. Some nights, dinner was a sleeve of Pillsbury biscuits with grape jelly and a Coke. That was my little taste of Heaven on earth, at least I thought so.

To have my own home was great. I could stay up all night watching TV if I so desired. I came and left as I pleased. Because my car was so identifiable, it didn't take long for trouble to find me though. At three o'clock one morning, someone knocked on my front door. Not expecting anyone, I wondered if Denise had snuck out of her parent's home to come over for a conjugal visit so I answered the door.

I saw a strange light flickering through the half round window in the front door. When I opened to door to investigate, in the middle of my little porch sat a flaming paper sack. With no shoes on my feet, I couldn't kick the bag away from the door. I ran to the kitchen for water to douse the flames. When I returned, the bag was consumed by the fire, revealing its contents. The bottom third of the bag held a bunch of fecal matter which emitted a horrendous odor.

At once, I suspected who had done this, but I also understood calling the police would be an exercise in futility. Someone was sending a message. Any police officer responding to a call like that would recognize the modus operandi, and would offer no help. There were two prime suspects who caused many problems in the past, it had to be them! I cleaned up the mess, hoping they would get bored and go away.

A couple weeks later, another early morning knock at the door came. I jumped out of bed fast, hoping to catch someone. No fire that time, no flaming bag of poop, just a bunch of large, bloody catfish heads. One of them affixed to the front door, with the rest strewn across the porch. Blood was everywhere. The porch looked like a murder scene.

The two troublemakers came to mind again. There were messages being sent. The first action represented their opinion of me, the second was about intimidation. This time I told Denise to make these guys stop. I would not tolerate their behavior anymore. Whatever she said to them worked. Maybe she had one of her older brothers pay the guys a visit, I can only guess, but I never had to deal with that crap again, pun intended.

Soon after, I got another late night knock at my door. This time it was who I had hoped it was, my girlfriend. She was all fired up after having a fight with her father. She was sent to her bedroom after the altercation. After packing a few things, she climbed out her bedroom window and made the trek over to my place, claiming she was never going back. Our relationship advanced to the next level, living together, which was fine with me.

Her father found out she ran away and put her out of his mind. Her brothers and mother knew where she was safe with me. For about a week we played house. Her mother insisted she come home as her father had cooled down. I was seventeen; she was sixteen, so her parents trumped our wishes.

Fall classes started at the local university and I was late deciding whether to go to college. I submitted paperwork for scholarships and financial aid but they took time to process. After a week together with my girlfriend, I realized I would have to work toward a better career if I wanted to start a family.

Since I was late turning in my paperwork, it surprised me when the school processed it so quick. The semester was already two weeks in; making my first day was tough. Missing two weeks in a university setting was far worse than missing time in high school. One of my courses was "Introduction to Fluid Power", a class on hydraulics. It was a required course for my major in architecture.

Except for an Algebra class in high school, my educational experience was a breeze. College, in contrast, was like taking a drink from a fire hose. There was a lot of information to process and I playing catch-up.

My eighteenth birthday was approaching, and I received another one of those surprise late night visits from my girlfriend. She wanted to be together for my birthday. After another fight with her father she ran away from home again. Denise resolved she would never go back to living with her parents.

As before, her mother came to my house after about a week. The two ladies stood in the doorway, engaged in discussion, while I waited in another room. I heard parts of the discussion, which got heated once or twice. Summoned to the door, her mother told me she would not allow her daughter to shack up with me.

I never knew the family to be religious but her mother's Catholic faith suddenly brought conviction on the situation. While certain sins were okay, living together out of wedlock was not. Her mother then hit us with the ultimatum; either Denise went home with her mother, or we were to get married.

I was all for marrying this girl. I just didn't think it would be so soon. Denise responded by telling her mother she and I would rather get married. There was no way she would go back to live under her father's rules.

Just days before my birthday, rather than focus on a birthday party, we planned a clandestine wedding. No one else was to know, for various reasons. I didn't want my family to know for two reasons. First, they considered this girl too much trouble. Second, if I was attending college, and unwed, my father's child support would continue. I didn't want that money to stop going to my family because they needed it.

Denise hoped her father would accept her getting married without his permission if enough time passed before he found out. I wasn't so sure he would. Excited about being married and thinking I was prepared to handle it, the voice of doubt still whispered in my ears. I ignored it.

My future mother-in-law was a registered nurse and worked varying shifts at the hospital. On the weekend of my birthday she stopped by my house after work to tell us we would drive to Wichita Falls, Texas to get married the following Wednesday. We met early that morning and drove together.

My bride-to-be was still in high school and her mother had to call in to report the absence. The big day came, and we found ourselves on the road, southbound about forty-five miles to a town just over the border in Texas.

Oklahoma did not issue marriage licenses to anyone under the age of eighteen. In Texas, we could get married if the parent of the minor signed an emancipation document, which her mother did. After we took care of that paperwork, and got a marriage license, we then chose a Justice of the Peace to perform the ceremony.

We had two options, and it boiled down to which one's name sounded more upstanding. We settled on one whose first name was Henry. That sounded official enough. We entered the chambers of the Justice and waited for him to join us. A rather tall black woman strolled in to take a seat at the bench. Not what we expected.

Justice Henry performed a rather solemn ceremony and then told me to kiss my bride. As I positioned myself for the kiss, Denise turned and I ended up just giving her a quick peck on the cheek. It seemed odd she was uncomfortable kissing in front of her mother.

With no real plans following the ceremony, I thought it would be nice to go out to dinner in celebration our nuptials. My wife was not interested. We made our way back home and parted in three separate ways. There was no celebratory dinner, no honeymoon, and no consummation of marriage. I found myself in my little home, all alone on my wedding night, without a clue of my new bride's location.

The next day it was back to our routine; school in the morning, and work in the evening. After two weeks, I dropped out of college because having only one car made the logistics too difficult. Those first weeks we only saw one another in passing. I pictured married life looking better.

21

THE CHASM BETWEEN PERCEPTION AND REALITY OF married was greater than I expected. Even after dropping out of college, our schedule was still crazy. School began at 7:15 am so when she left, I was still asleep. School let out around 2:30 but she wouldn't come home until 4:30. She picked me up and we went to work by 5 pm. My shift was 5 pm–1 am. I asked others at work to take me home so my wife wouldn't have to wake up to come get me.

Denise worked part time at a restaurant down the street from mine which closed at 9 pm. On one of those first nights of our new schedule, I walked out to the parking lot just as my wife passed by. My car had two layers of limo tint on the windows and she couldn't see out at night time so she drove with the windows rolled down.

If my wife saw me waving to her as she drove by, she pretended she hadn't. I noticed another guy in the passenger seat. The next morning, as she was getting ready, I asked Denise why she didn't wave, and who the guy was in the car with her. Her immediate response was that she didn't see me and the guy was a co-worker who had asked for a ride home. She claimed to have taken him home, and then went to our house. Something about the story did not sit well with me.

Both of our restaurants served beer. I never touched the stuff but Denise used to drink it, along with her coworkers, as they cleaned up after closing. It worried me for her to drive after drinking. Whenever I broached the subject she got defensive and told me I was acting just like her father. She would remind me how she had left her father's house over similar issues and suggested I not act like him.

Seeing her in the car that night with this other guy, invoked feelings of suspicion and jealousy I had never experienced. I didn't know what to do, but it kept gnawing at my soul to find out.

Monday night, less than a week after getting married, suspicion was getting the best of me. I was the shift manager and since business had been slow, all but one delivery driver went home. We did not have a home telephone line so I could not call her and this was long before cell phones.

Something wasn't right and I could not wait until we closed the restaurant to investigate. I took a delivery myself and chose one with an address near mine, expecting to drop off the pizza then drive by my house to check on my wife. My anxiety level rose as I approached my house.

Happy to see my car parked out front, I noticed all the exterior and interior lights were off. I walked the perimeter searching for anything out of the ordinary. At each window, I listened, but everything was quiet. Since I was there, I thought I would say goodnight before heading back to work.

I slid the key in the lock and opened the door, trying to avoid being noisy in case she was asleep. The house was dark but the street light outside illuminated a small path toward the bedroom through the glass in the front door.

I opened the bedroom door to find people having sex in my bed. Startled by my presence, the guy fled to the little closet to hide. My wife, of five days, got out of bed and redirected me to the living room to talk. Stunned, I listened as she explained what I had just seen was not what it looked like. "Good, because it looked like you were having sex with another guy!" was my reply.

Denise explained the guy asked for a ride home. She didn't work that evening and had no reason to leave home to pick up another guy from work. His girlfriend, who worked at the same place, left early after an argument, leaving him stranded at work. The argument was over the flirtatious bantering between her boyfriend and my wife.

The guy got tipsy after drinking too much company beer. Denise further explained she brought him to our house to let him sober up before taking him home. She claimed she didn't want him getting into any more trouble with his girlfriend, or his family.

My father-in-law was a prejudiced man. He hated anyone with skin darker than his. Of German descent, he married a woman born and raised in Mexico, who had skin much darker than his. I never understood how he reconciled his hatred for others based on their skin color.

Denise had a curiosity of black people, and since my step-father was black, she was more interested. I believe another reason for the attraction was in rebellion to her father's strict control. At one point he even installed bars on her bedroom window to keep her from sneaking out.

"How did you two happen to crawl into bed to have sex?" I asked my wife. She had shared our secret with him; that we had gotten married and showed him the red see-through lingerie I had purchased for our wedding night. When she showed it to him, he insisted she model it for him, which she was happy to do. "One thing led to another and well... wait, what are you doing home so early?" To redirect her guilt, she got angry because I caught them in the act.

Her tone changed again, back to a comforting one, saying I was the one she loved. What just happened with this guy meant nothing to her. She tried her best to convince me, but I was not buying it.

I walked back to the bedroom and opened the closet door. The guy stood there naked, still in performance mode if you will. He assumed I would leave and allow him to continue what he was doing before I interrupted. It was the same guy she had given a ride home a few nights prior. The same one I saw in the car with her that night.

I pointed toward the door and told him to leave. He grabbed his clothes and asked if he could get dressed first. "GET OUT!" I yelled. "OK man, but do you mind if she gives me a ride home?" he asked. "GET OUT OF MY HOUSE, NOW!!!!" He scurried off into the darkness naked, carrying his clothes in his hands.

My wife, still naked on the couch, tried to entice me into having sex. I asked her where the lingerie was. She retrieved it from the bedroom and handed it over. I said I would be right back and when I returned, I wanted her to gone.

In the kitchen I grabbed a lighter on my way to the back yard. I set the lingerie on a cinder block and tried to light it on fire. I had tried so hard to keep my cool in the house because what I wanted to do was kill them both. Instead, I tried to kill the lingerie. The irony was I had purchased the lingerie hoping my bride would wear it on our wedding night. Not only had I not seen her in the lingerie myself, I had not yet tasted the fruit of marriage. This guy beat me to it.

As hard as I tried, that lacey fabric would not catch fire. Angered by this, I stomped back in the house for scissors and cut it to shreds. Once inside, I saw she left. She walked into the night just like her lover, bound for where I did not know, nor did I care. I locked the doors and drove back to the pizza parlor.

After returning to work, I fretted over the house and my car, wondering if either of them would come back to cause damage. Thankfully, no one did.

22

A FEW DAYS PASSED, GIVING ME THE CHANCE TO REFLECT on all that had taken place during my first week of marriage. I recalled the devastation caused by the divorces my mom had been through. Divorce is painful, regardless how amicable the split and an option best avoided in my opinion. Divorce equated to failure and as I had only just begun, I couldn't throw in the towel after less than a week. Naively, I also believed I could change my wife so she would no longer need to be promiscuous. Besides, I would never find another woman willing to marry me. I decided to show her we could make it as a married couple.

She ended up staying with one of her brothers after I asked her to leave. We spoke on the phone and I told her to come back home. We both agreed we would try to make our marriage work. Three days after the betrayal we reunited. We slipped right back into the routine of hectic schedules, seeing little of one another.

Nine days had passed since the betrayal. As usual, my wife dropped me off at work at 5 pm and then headed off to her job. It was a Wednesday night and business was slow, a little slower than usual. I called Denise to see how her night was going. It was about 8:30 pm, close to her quitting time, so I figured she would be ahead in her cleaning duties with few customers to serve.

A co-worker said Denise went home around 7:30 pm. Their manager sent a few people home early due to slow business. That guttural feeling of suspicion hit me again. I wondered why she had not called to let me know she was going home early. I soon found out why.

HOOKED BY GRACE

Once again, I delivered a pizza near my home and with knots in my stomach, drove to my house afterward. My car was backed into the driveway. She never parked that way; it was too difficult for her to see through the tinted windows. The porch light was off.

I checked the perimeter of the house. Nothing seemed out of the ordinary so I slowly slipped my key into the lock. Quietly, I opened the door until the security chain stopped me. As I peered inside, through the gap in the door, I saw my best friend's girlfriend with a book up to her face as if she were reading. The troubling part was there were no lights on in the house, and the book she held was upside down.

"Susan, what are you doing here?" I asked. "Reading," she replied. "In the dark? Open this door right now!" I ordered. I was no longer being quiet. She removed the chain from the door, and without turning on any lights, returned to her place on the couch. I hoped I was not going catch my wife with that guy again.

I flung the door open to find my wife having sex. "Not again," I shouted. The guy tried to hide under the bed. "GET OUT!" I demanded. "Everybody, get out of my house right now!" The guy gathered his clothes. Although black, he was not the same guy I caught her with last time.

Was this what everyone tried to warn me about?

The two non-residents left while my wife, as before, tried to convince me what I had just seen was not as it seemed. She must have thought I was stupid. I asked if she planned to model the red lingerie for him too.

It had been two weeks since we committed ourselves to each other in a marriage ceremony. It was obvious one of us was having a very difficult time understanding the concept of monogamy. An issue of great importance; we had not had sex in five or six weeks. "We've been married two weeks, and we have not consummated our marriage because there has been no time, yet you have made time for two other people."

Before I went back to work, I grabbed her keys. As I walked through the front door, I said nothing. I didn't know what to tell her, or what I would do about the situation. I didn't know who to talk to about it either.

<u>23</u>

DREADED GOING HOME AFTER WORK, FEARFUL OF WHAT I
might find. I had taken her keys, figuring my car would still be
there, and I assumed Denise would be too.

I asked no one for a ride home that night; as I figured it would
be better to walk. It was three o'clock in the morning when I arrived
at my doorstep. With a heavy sigh I unlocked the door to an empty
house. I did not know my wife's whereabouts. Did she go home
with the other guy, or the watch guard friend? Exhausted by it all, I
fell asleep, but not before stripping the sheets from the bed.

She had gone back to the same brother's house to stay the
night. Several days later, after wearing out her welcome there,
Denise came back with tears in her eyes, asking my forgiveness. I
hoped her remorse was genuine, but I knew she had burned bridges
with her brother and had nowhere else to go but home.

I don't want to pretend I was in my right mind, taking her back
after two brutal betrayals. The situation far exceeded my level of
maturity to handle. I allowed her to come back. From the outside
looking in, I would agree it was crazy; crazy to think I could ever
change her, crazy to tolerate the behavior, crazy to think I had no
other choice.

The following week held new surprises. As usual, I slept as
Denise went off to school. I was still asleep when she burst in the
front door around lunch time. She slammed the door and tried to
hide in the bedroom.

Minutes later, there was a knock at the front door. "Don't
answer it," she whispered. Another knock; followed by a voice

identifying the knocker as a police officer. He knew someone was in the house and made it clear he was not leaving until he spoke with us.

I answered the door. The officer asked for my wife by name, and when I asked what this was about, he stated he needed to speak with her at once.

Denise came out of the bedroom, shaken and in tears. Still confused about what happened, I repeated my question. The officer said my wife understood why he was there and she needed to explain her side of the story.

My wife told the officer she left school to go home for lunch when she noticed a car following close behind. She sped away after recognizing the driver, expecting her pursuer her would get caught at the red light. There were other students in crosswalks nearly hit by the ensuing car chase.

Denise realized she did not want the girl following to discover where she lived so she pulled the car over behind a shoe store. She exited the car to confront the driver who chased her. It was Melissa, the disgruntled girlfriend of the guy with whom I had caught Denise in bed with the first time she betrayed me.

Melissa learned of the affair and showed up to confront my wife. With threats of violence, Melissa insisted Denise quit sleeping with *her* boyfriend. Both girls shouted at each other while other students and passersby watched. Melissa screamed, "Denise, you should be ashamed of yourself, a married woman carrying on multiple affairs." The embarrassment caused my wife to snap. She produced a switchblade and lunged at the girl, stabbing her in the cheek.

Upon hearing this, I was at a loss for words. First, I had her affairs to contend with, and now it appeared my wife might go to jail for assault. Crazy just got crazier!

The officer questioned Denise about Melissa's accusations. The response given stunned me even further. She explained that we were newlyweds, and the guy was a co-worker of hers who made several unwanted sexual advances toward her at their workplace. She declined his advances, not only because we were newlyweds, but the guy in question was black.

She continued, maintaining his unwanted advances had gotten to the point of harassment and she considered calling the police herself. Hearing this, the officer questioned her about Melissa. Sensing her plan was working, my wife laid it on with the victim mode. Denise played the race card saying Melissa, who was white, was angry because her boyfriend kept coming on to her.

With a straight face, my wife then claimed she feared for her life. Never would she let a black man touch her. The "white trash girlfriend" had become enraged with jealousy, and she only pulled the knife in self-defense. The officer bought every bit of the story and left, pressing no charges against my wife.

I stood there in disbelief as I tried to process everything. I don't know what possessed me, but I got dressed and we went for a drive. Nervous there would be retaliation coming our way, I thought it best to get out of town.

24

WE SPENT THE NEXT COUPLE OF WEEKS JUST TRYING TO survive. Most shifts I worked were at night, and I got home after 1 or 2 am. The euphoria of living away from our parents' homes was waning fast. I was on constant alert, just waiting for the next surprise to happen.

Halloween passed without incident. I expected another flaming bag of poop, or something of the sort, but things had quieted down on that front.

It was the middle of November and people prepared for Thanksgiving. With the shops decorated, the festiveness of the season was in full swing.

I had dropped out of college due to the logistics of having one car. I thought it was important for Denise to get her diploma, but it became more difficult to make sure she showed up to classes. She couldn't wait to finish school. My persistence in making her go was met with resistance. She viewed me as an oppressive father figure rather than a husband.

A problem arose when we planned where to spend Thanksgiving. Most of our family members were still unaware of our marriage. It had been a while since I had been to her parent's house. I had only been there a few times during my junior and senior years. The last time was when I picked her up for my senior prom.

Denise hated being around my family. She never established a relationship with anyone in my family, except my younger brother. She had a somewhat sinister motive behind her friendliness with him. Fortunately, her attempts to seduce my brother failed.

In fact, our respective families never met. Since my stepfather is black, we could not introduce him to her dad. My wife always feared the potential repercussions if her dad found out. Her mother knew, and so did her brothers, but no one wanted to break the news to my father-in-law.

We settled on going to our homes of origin to celebrate Thanksgiving and meet up later. It was no problem for me; I went home to be with my family. For Denise, she had to lie to her father about where she was living. It was easy enough for her fabricate a story.

Later that evening, when we reconvened at our humble abode, it was obvious she had been drinking. I hated drugs and alcohol because their use contributed to the two soldiers crashing into us in Thailand. Denise did not share the same values on controlled substances. She often smoked marijuana before going to school. Beer consumption at work after closing happened regularly too.

I hated to smell the stuff on her, and when I made comments about it she ignored them. When I asked how much she had to drink, she claimed it was only two beers. My disappointment was hard to mask. Rather than get into a fight over it, she decided it was time to consummate our marriage. I suppose she figured it was the easiest way to avoid an argument, and illicit substances apparently put her "in the mood".

A couple days later she came with news that rocked my world. Without mincing words, she got straight to the point, "I'm PREGNANT!"

While those words I longed to hear, I calculated time lines. "When did you find out? How far along are you?" I asked. She had gone to a clinic that day, and they had estimated four to six weeks gestation.

I had wanted a child of my own since the age of twelve. I wanted to get excited, but my analytical mind was busy determining whether to be excited or angry. Denise was not excited about it. I was all of eighteen years old, she was seventeen. She was in no hurry to have a baby and made that point abundantly clear.

Not interested in being pregnant while still in high school, the greater concern was what pregnancy would do to her female form. Her body was of great importance to her and stretch marks would not be acceptable.

As she gave me the reasons this was bad news, I was still running the numbers. My posture seemed uncaring to her in this dilemma which angered her. She stormed off to the bedroom and closed the door.

As I scrolled through recent memory, I figured out we had not been sexually active for at least four weeks before we got married. On that day, we were seven and a half weeks into our marriage and our first intimate moment occurred only a few days prior. My math skills told me it had been about eleven weeks between our moments of intimacy. It was impossible; the baby could not be mine.

It's one thing to catch your wife in bed with another man, let alone two, but to receive that news was like getting hit by a wrecking ball. I questioned who the father of the child was. She scolded me for my insensitivity, and said I should be ashamed for asking such a question. "You are the father!"

"How could I be? It's been at least eleven weeks and you are four to six weeks pregnant. The father has to be one of the two guys I caught you in bed with." To point out her indiscretions showed further coldness on my part.

She demanded I leave the room. No further discussion took place that night. What a quagmire. When she delivered a multiracial baby, it would be obvious it was not mine. How would that affect me? What would be the outcome? Would we stay married, or would we separate so the baby could be with its father?

These questions needed answers, and fast. Answers came the next day. She consulted a few friends and decided to terminate the pregnancy. The decision process didn't involve me. Being the husband, I had no input. Denise knew I could not be the father though she kept trying to convince me otherwise. She needed to do that to protect her reputation and make me responsible for the pending outcome. Perhaps the greatest fear she had was the reaction her father would have.

Denise found a clinic in the same city in Texas where we got married. Abortion was not legal in Oklahoma when this occurred. The cost of the procedure was $250.

Denise continued to play the mind game; insisting the problem was my responsibility to clean up. I knew in my heart the child couldn't be mine. Over the next few days, so desperate for unconditional love, I reasoned in my mind I could still love the child and raise it as my own. Today, I realize codependency drove that logic. The life of an innocent child hung in the balance, and I was uncomfortable taking that life.

Not open to any further discussion or debate, she took an appointment for a few days later. We needed to come up with the $250 post haste. That was a big chunk of change and we did not have that money in our budget. After rearranging our bills, I only came up with $125. Denise said she would try to borrow the rest from friends. By the date of the appointment we had the full amount. We drove to the clinic with few words spoken between us.

In the interim, I had talked to the sister of affair number two. After sharing the events which led up to this predicament, I told her I would be in the room with Denise and watch as they removed the fetus. Because her brother was the father, the color of the baby would confirm it wasn't mine.

It was a cold and cloudy winter day when we arrived at the clinic. I imagined what people in the waiting room thought of two teenagers showing up at an abortion clinic. Even more pressing were my thoughts about this innocent baby my wife carried. The tiny baby, torn apart as they sucked it from the womb by some crazy vacuum, haunted my thoughts.

Together, we sat in the waiting room until they called her name. If nervous, she did a fantastic job of hiding it. I was a mess and felt a huge burden of guilt for my part in what was taking place. I was contributing money to cause the death of an innocent person whose only crime was being "inconvenient". It tore my heart to shreds. My convictions were not based on religious reasons as I was an agnostic.

Her name was called and we stood to make our way to the procedure room. At the doorway, a staff person told me I could not go with my wife and suggested I sit and wait for her. That was the longest thirty minutes of my life. Denise came out with a smile on her face and motioned for us to leave. I wept all the way home.

Back at the house, neither of us spoke. I broke the silence when I queried Denise about the other half of the money. I wanted to know who I owed the other $125. She told me the money had come from Susan, my best friend's girlfriend who had been the watch guard for affair number two. She claimed the money came as a gift, but I later learned the truth. The actual father, affair number one, provided the funds.

The pressure relieved, her mission accomplished, Denise was free to go on with life while I became a prisoner of guilt.

I needed a change, to begin a new chapter, so to speak. My beloved car had to go. A new car would be exciting and fun, and I thought it would be a good way to redirect my focus. I rolled into the Oldsmobile dealership and traded my "pimpmobile", as the salesman called it, for a 1984 Olds Cutlass Supreme. The car was in pristine shape and only a year old. It gave me something new to concentrate on, but it also added more responsibility, with a higher payment and higher cost to insure.

25

AS IS TYPICALLY THE CASE WITH MATERIAL POSSESSIONS, the novelty of the new car faded and no longer pacified the situation. With trust for Denise damaged, it was no surprise that our problems were common knowledge in the community, having spread by way of gossip. Many people called me a fool for sticking with the marriage. The chatter around town; I wasn't man enough to handle my wife. By some twist of fate, I wore the scarlet letter and carried the brunt of scrutiny and ridicule by others.

Lawton was a small town full of folks who knew each other's personal business. Denise had been promiscuous with so many guys, before and after we married, and folks talked about it. For our marriage to succeed, I would need to get her out of Lawton. Relocation seemed like a rational way to solve the problem, so we moved to Tulsa.

We had to to let our families know we planned to move, which meant we had to tell everyone about the marriage. To my surprise, my father-in-law took the news well. He even told his daughter he was proud of her. My parents tried to support me as best they could, but they were disappointed. More than the fact I had kept the marriage from them, they feared what Denise might do when she got bored with me. My parents had trepidations, which is why I couldn't share everything that happened since our wedding day. If they knew even half of it, I am certain they would have intervened in the name of rescuing me from the situation.

Our target move in date in Tulsa was January 1, 1986. Unlike the Thanksgiving holiday, with our marriage no longer a secret, we celebrated Christmas with both sides of the family before moving.

On New Year's Eve, with help from another brother-in-law, we set out on the new adventure. Once we arrived in Tulsa, we slept in the vehicles until morning when the leasing office opened. We signed the lease papers, got the keys, and moved in. We didn't have much to move in, and with five people, unloading was easy.

Our married life seemed to improve as we spent more time together. Denise's brother moved with us was a good roommate, always considerate of our privacy.

Denise enrolled in a local high school and I took a job at another pizza chain franchise. Since I worked the morning shift, she drove me to work before going to school. When school let out, she reversed her travel to pick me up, and we drove home together.

January 28th, we were all at home when news came of the Challenger Space Shuttle explosion. Glued to the TV screen, we watched news coverage as the tragedy unfolded. The explosion left a big impression on us because it confirmed we were no longer kids. As young adults, it forced us to view life through a different lens.

I received calls at work from the school office. It seemed Denise had been skipping school again. I confronted her about the calls and her response was to accuse me of acting like her father. Experience caused my suspicion levels to rise again, and my trust fell faster than before.

My wife had a problem, one which plagues men more often than women. My reason for moving backfired. I thought I had removed her from an environment where temptation was a real thing with the networks she built. I took the fish out of the fishbowl and placed her into an ocean teeming with new opportunity.

The following month, adult life brought another challenge. As we prepared to start our day, I walked out to warm up the car. The car was not where I parked it. I searched the parking lot thinking my brother-in-law might have used it and had to find another spot when he came back.

I didn't see it anywhere, but I saw his truck so I reasoned he was still in his bedroom. I dashed back inside, woke him up, and asked if he moved my car. He said he hadn't, so I ran back out to check again, still no car. The space where I parked was empty and as I walked back toward my apartment, I noticed a wire coat hanger. Bent out of shape and lying on the pavement, it had to be the tool the thieves used to break into the car.

Although I had not customized this car as much as the former one, it held enough of my identity to feel violated. It's hard to describe the pain, but it's like being attacked on a dark street.

I ran back into the apartment and called the police. The dispatcher put me through to the grand theft auto division who said they had been trying to contact me at my last known residence. They recovered the car around 4am and tried to contact me back in Lawton.

The officer gave me the address to the impound yard and instructed me to bring proof of ownership so they could release the car. My brother-in-law took us to the impound yard and what I saw hit me hard.

Amateur thieves used a crowbar to pry the hood and the trunk open, crushing all four quarter panels. They were unsuccessful in getting either open. Dropped in a slot between two other cars, my once shiny pride and joy looked lifeless. A screwdriver used to start the car was still in the broken ignition switch. They ripped out the stereo, leaving wires hanging out of the dash. With all wheels removed, it rested on the pavement. The condition of the car was heartbreaking.

The insurance company sent a tow truck to take it to a body shop for repair. I watched the tow truck drag the car, without wheels, up onto the flatbed, destroying brake lines and ruining the entire undercarriage. The insurance company provided a rental as my car spent the next thirty-one days in the repair shop.

On top of the emotional trauma, we had to pay the deductible and the difference of the rental car not covered by the insurance. It was a major blow to our minor budget.

With only two payments posted, my loan balance hovered around $11,000. The repair estimate was staggering, at just under $10,000. My insurance covered all but the deductible. Suspecting the custom wheels attracted the thieves; I had the car refitted with stock wheels although I asked for the chrome version. It wouldn't be my car without chrome wheels, what can I say.

I then made another costly decision. Because we moved to the apartment sight unseen, I must have landed us in a bad neighborhood. For safety's sake, I decided to move. We broke the lease, which carried a financial penalty, and paid the cost of moving expenses and deposits on a new apartment.

My brother-in-law helped cover his share, for which I was grateful. Three days after moving into our new apartment, the body shop called to say my car was ready for pick up. I was eager to have my car back.

We turned in the rental car and drove the Cutlass back to our new place. Even though the car was already clean from the shop, I still gave it a wash and detail myself. It was like getting reacquainted. All polished up, and with a full tank of gas, I parked it for the night. A couple hours later, I remembered the repair paperwork I left on the front seat so about 11:30 pm I walked back to the parking lot to get it.

I stared at the car, marveling how the light reflected off the freshly painted surfaces. With my car back, life was normal again. In my review of the documents, I noticed all the equipment and parts which got replaced. Although the loss caused a huge disruption in our lives, the car was like a brand new one. I was trying to find something more positive to focus on.

I went to sleep around midnight, feeling more secure since we had moved out the "bad" neighborhood.

<u>2 6</u>

RING, RING!!! I THOUGHT I WAS DREAMING BUT REALIZED IT was my telephone ringing. As I reached for the phone, I noticed the time was 1:30 am. The caller asked for me by name and then identified himself as a member of the Tulsa Police Department.

I assumed someone was pulling a prank on me so I responded, "Yeah right, I suppose you're calling to tell me someone stole my car." "Yes sir," was the reply, "you need to come down to the impound yard to identify and claim the vehicle."

I didn't believe him. I let the prankster know I had seen my car just two hours prior. The caller insisted I go look for the car while he waited on the line. "Real funny!" I said. Fine, I'll play the game. The spot where I parked was visible from a long distance and I could see it was vacant.

I sprinted out to the parking lot to see if someone had moved my car as part of the rouse. The car was not there. I ran back inside and the caller, to my surprise, was still on the line. I let him know my car was missing, and he gave familiar instructions on where to find it.

How could that be possible? The car had been in my possession less than twelve hours. We drove down to the impound yard and met with the policemen involved in catching the car thieves.

The car was in worse condition than the last time, except it still had wheels and tires on it. We provided proof of ownership and the officers told us how they discovered my car.

An officer, along with his K-9 unit, patrolled a neighborhood on the north side of town. At midnight, he saw a car travel south carrying five passengers. About a half hour later, the officer watched the same car return to the area with only two passengers. The car was tailgating a white, late model Olds Cutlass which had three occupants.

Both cars sped away in opposite directions after they noticed the police car following. Suspecting car theft, the officer laid chase behind the newer one. The pursuit lasted a few miles, with speeds over ninety miles per hour.

The car thieves realized they couldn't outrun the police. They slowed the vehicle to approximately twenty miles per hour, and all three occupants bailed out of the car and took off running. With no one behind the wheel, the car continued its trajectory until a large oak tree stopped it. The front end of the car wrapped around the tree.

The officer chased the driver on foot with his K-9 partner taking the lead. When the officer caught up, the dog had the thief subdued. In the scuffle, the dog punctured an eyeball with its teeth. An ambulance took the thief to the hospital for emergency treatment of the puncture wound. The other two thieves got away.

More officers joined the chase and captured both accomplices. A tow truck took my car to the impound yard. The officer with the two escapees in his car asked if we knew them. We didn't, but what struck me was how young they were. The officer advised they were all brothers, ages thirteen, fourteen, and fifteen. The thirteen-year-old was the driver. All three wound up in jail.

It was 6 am before the police wrapped up everything. While waiting, I glanced over the mangled mess of my car. As the man at the impound yard wrote his report on the car, we discussed the auto theft business. He stated my car was number one on the list for theft in the greater Tulsa area. That was not good news to hear. I only had the car a few months, and I wondered if it would get stolen again.

I checked out a few other impounded cars. The one next to mine had a small hole in the roof. I asked the impound guy why the thieves put a hole there. That was not a stolen car; the police recovered it as evidence after a fatal shooting. Sensing I didn't understand, he told me the owner had committed suicide in the car, the hole was where the bullet exited the car. "Take a peek inside," he said, rather nonchalantly, "You can see brain matter all over the car. There's even a suicide note on the front seat!" As bad as I felt about my predicament, it paled in comparison.

My car got loaded onto a flatbed, bound for the body repair shop for a second time. The guys at the shop found the story amazing. The car spent another three weeks getting repaired. This time it had frame damage but the insurance company insisted to repair rather than total it out. The repair bill to the insurance company the second time was over $7,000.

When the car was ready for pick up, in jest, one mechanic suggested I should write a book about all my experiences with this car. "What a funny guy," I retorted.

2 7

WITH THE CAR BACK FROM THE REPAIR SHOP FOR A second time, we made plans to visit our families in Lawton. Spring break seemed a good time to go, so we packed the car, grabbed the dog, and set out on the four-hour drive.

Both sets of parents were glad we were still standing after all we endured over the previous few months. We spent our time rotating back and forth between our respective families. As a married couple with families living less than ten miles apart, it amazes me they never met.

We spent the better part of Spring break week in Lawton. The day before we were to go back to Tulsa, we visited my in-laws home for lunch. Her mother needed something from the grocery store and Denise volunteered to go get it. Being a picky eater, I'd have to prepare my food so it made sense for my wife to go. Always ready to go for a ride, the dog followed her out to the car.

More time passed than necessary for the grocery run and I got suspicious right away. We were back in her old stomping grounds and she may have arranged a secret rendezvous.

The phone rang. It was Denise, crying hysterically, saying she wrecked the car. My mother-in-law drove me to the crash scene. She examined her daughter, who was fine but frazzled.

A police officer arrived to investigate the crash. Denise stated she entered the street from the shopping center parking lot and was driving westward when her dog caught sight of a cat running across the street. The dog leapt from the passenger seat to her lap, in pursuit of the cat. Startled by the dog, she veered left to avoid the cat and hit a parked car on the opposite side of the street.

In the accident report, the officer estimated the rate of speed at impact at forty-five miles per hour. The distance from the point of entry onto the street, to the crash scene was less than one hundred fifty feet. There were other inconsistencies with her story.

The dog was a tiny Chihuahua and it would have been impossible for it to see over the dash to chase a cat crossing the street. Also, the posted speed limit was twenty-five miles per hour. There was no reason to be traveling forty-five miles per hour in a twenty-five zone.

I surmised there were crucial details being left out. I suspected my wife had run into affair number one; perhaps as he waited in the parking lot at the store, and when his girlfriend came out to find the two talking, a pursuit ensued. There were also tire tracks left by a car that came out of the parking lot at a high rate of speed. If there was a cat, swerving to avoid hitting it while being chased would make much more sense than the story she gave the officer.

Whatever the truth was, it didn't negate the fact my poor car was once again wrecked with major front-end damage. It was inoperable, as the impact pushed the front bumper back, wedging the tire into a permanent left turn configuration.

It looked like we were stuck in Lawton. As it was the weekend, we could not contact the insurance company. There was no way to pick up a rental car over the weekend, and we couldn't skip work and school on Monday morning.

I found a pay phone and called my mom. She came to the scene and picked us up. After discussing the situation with my step-father, they loaned us his car to get us back to Tulsa. He got my car to a shop he used in the past and handled all the logistics for us.

My step-father drove a 1982 Gold Chevy Camaro Z28. It was his "mid-life crisis" car though he was only thirty-one. Denise was excited about driving back to Tulsa. I suppose I slipped into father-mode when I burst her little bubble, telling her I would be the one to drive home. I know she would have pushed that car to maximum speed on the interstate, and the thought of her crashing was unnerving.

We made it back to Tulsa the next day. The responsibility for my parent's car made me apprehensive. I envisioned someone stealing it, or my speed-demon wife wrecking it. The added stress was unwanted.

To our amazement, the repair shop got my car back on the road in one week. My parents thought it would be nice to visit us so they drove my car to Tulsa and swapped it with theirs. That was a big help, plus it was fun to show them our apartment.

The weekend after my parent's visit, my in-laws came to see us. In the time since we were in Lawton for Spring break, someone stole my father-in-law's truck. After retiring from the Army, he worked as an apartment maintenance man. With his truck running, and the door open, he went into his office to grab a tool. When he came back out, just seconds later, the truck was no longer where he left it.

Police recovered the truck two days later after one of his sons spotted it across town. The only thing missing was the registration, which gave the thief their home address. Fearful the guy would return to steal the truck again; my father-in-law chained the truck to the carport in front of their house. He didn't wish to take chances while they were out of town.

During their weekend visit to our place, someone broke into their house, sprayed graffiti on the walls and set the house ablaze. They lost everything but the truck. They suspected it was the individual who stole the truck who started the fire.

After the insurance company settled their claim and reconstructed the house, my in-laws moved to Colorado. They purchased a little gift shop in a tourist town up the Ute Pass, west of Colorado Springs. It had a small one bedroom apartment attached where they lived.

Meanwhile, back in Tulsa, the logistics of one car was too taxing on us. I estimated with all the money we spent on fuel, we could pay for a second vehicle. I bought a little 1984 Nissan pickup for me to drive. It also seemed a good idea to get rid of my Cutlass because it was the number one stolen car in Tulsa that year.

We took the car to a dealership and Denise decided she wanted a Honda Accord. Hondas were more expensive than what I had paid for the Cutlass. The salesman brought out a used one, a 1984 model, burgundy, 4-door with manual transmission. The previous owner drove over 180,000 miles in less than three years. Sensing he had a sucker for a customer, the salesman figured he could make a great deal on a trade for this vehicle.

The appraiser ran his hand across the topside of the car, and without further inspection, asked if it had been in a rollover accident. I guessed the deal might be ruined if he knew the car was stolen and wrecked twice. I skirted on the edge of truth when I told him I was not aware of the car being involved in a rollover and that I was the second owner. We made the trade, but it resulted in me becoming buried in negative equity since I only had the Cutlass for about six months.

The following Monday, I contacted the insurance company to report the change of vehicle and my agent delivered bad news. I had ridded myself of the car model which was number one on car thieves' lists, but purchased the second hottest car on that list. Oh well, the car made my wife happy.

After I bought the truck, my father-in-law accepted me as his son. He said real men only drive trucks. Even though it was a mini-truck, it was a truck nonetheless. It was a nice feeling knowing he now accepted me.

<u>28</u>

THE STRUGGLES OF ADULT LIFE CONTINUED. I WORKED FOR another pizza chain; and Denise got a full-time office job after graduating high school, which gave us dual income. With two cars, our logistics issues improved, but little else did.

It remained a difficult task to keep up with her; but it proved more difficult to engage in conversation my wife without being labeled her second father.

One particular day, I received a call from my wife letting me know she wanted to talk after work. She left me hanging that afternoon, wondering what she wanted to discuss. I was always waiting for the other shoe to drop, so my assumptions ranged from disease to divorce.

After work, I detailed my truck as I awaited her arrival. It had to have been around 6 pm when she parked her car just a few spaces away from me.

As Denise approached, I noticed she had a friend with her. I knew none of her friends from school so she introduced the girl. In a persnickety tone, my wife started the conversation, right there in the open parking lot for anyone to hear. I felt I was being ambushed as her friend also had a look of disdain on her face. I had no intention of arguing in front of her friend.

Denise continued, saying she and her friend had gone to a women's clinic. They waited all afternoon for an appointment. Then she hit me with it. "I'm pregnant!"

My level of excitement was less than what either of the girls expected. For a long time I dreamed of having a child, and I had shared my dream with her several times throughout the course of our relationship. My mind flashed back to the last time she told me she was pregnant and the circumstances surrounding that event. I also considered the unexplained hours missed at work, late arrivals home, and how low my trust was for her.

All of that ran through my mind, in high speed, but my countenance must have showed something different. Her perception of my response was that of aloofness and a lack of support. Denise knew I wanted a child, so she expected exuberance in hearing the news. My last thought before opening my mouth was, "Oh no, here we go again."

"How far along are you?" was what came across my lips before both girls verbally accosted me. Her friend told me what an inconsiderate ass I was. My lackluster response confirmed Denise' opinion I was a jerk. I remember standing there as they spewed venom, but it was as if someone pressed a mute button and I could only hear the thoughts in my head.

The girls concluded their verbal assault and walked away disgusted. My wife said she was taking take her friend home and I should not to wait up for her. When she returned to the apartment, or where she had gone, was a mystery. We didn't communicate for days afterward. When we did, she asked if I wanted the pregnancy terminated. Not wanting to travel that road again, I said no.

I counted back the weeks of gestation on the calendar. I wanted to confirm the possibility the baby could be mine without being chastised for my lack of trust.

Like a time-release drug capsule, becoming a father slowly overshadowed the doubt, though it never went away. Harboring that doubt was torturous and it certainly impacted our relationship.

Our lease came up for renewal, which prompted us to make a decision. We were living in a two bedroom apartment with her brother as a roommate. Did we ask him to find other living arrangements, or should we consider moving to a larger place and keep the roommate to help offset expenses?

Somewhere along the way, we got the idea it might be better to move to Colorado to be closer to her parents. Her family vacationed there every summer, for years. I had never been, but the idea was worth investigating. I had my fill of living in Oklahoma and since both of my parents worked full time; it made little sense to go back to Lawton.

We decided to at least take vacation time to go explore. Since the age of eight, I had lived in either Kansas or Oklahoma where the topography was flat and mundane. When we arrived in Colorado Springs, I fell in love and decided it would be a great place to raise a child.

We toured several apartments to get an idea of living costs. We found one we liked with a great price. Excited about living in newer accommodations, in a beautiful community, and for less money, we were ready to pack up as soon as we got back to Tulsa.

The drive back to Oklahoma was fun as we talked about all the possibilities that lay before us. A fresh start loomed on the horizon, so it seemed.

We made it back to Tulsa and rested the following day. I worked the opening shift and was the first one to show up in the mornings. I opened the doors and got the daily food preparations started. My plan was to give a two week notice to the company that morning. I did not get that opportunity. When I placed my key in the lock at the front door, it did not turn. I peered inside the window to see if anyone else was there to open the door for me. No one was there. As I scanned the restaurant, I noticed the tables and chairs pushed to one side and stacked.

There was no sign or notice anywhere on the front of the building. I found a payphone and called the main office to inquire. The Corporation was forced to reduce the number of stores and mine was on the copping block. As I was on vacation the week prior, they had no way of notifying me. At the time it was a rude awakening but hindsight confirms it was a blessing. With our lease expiring at the end of the month, we now had the green light to move to Colorado.

29

AS COLORADO RESIDENTS, I HOPED OUR LIVES WOULD improve as the door to new opportunity opened. I got a job at JC Penney in the mall, a welcome change coming out the food service industry. Denise worked for a copy machine company. Her brother helped us move and then drove back to Tulsa where he continued his education. We chose a smaller apartment, with a short lease, to see if the neighborhood was a good fit.

While her older brother left to go back, her youngest brother, who still lived at home with his parents, was now hanging out with us often. By now, the baby bump had become very noticeable. Little brother Nick enjoyed teasing his sister, telling her she looked like a toothpick stuck through an olive. Nick was fun to have around our apartment, and the pair of siblings interacted well.

After getting our stuff put away, we drove to the store for groceries. After stocking up, we ran back home, excited to prepare steak for dinner in our new place. Steak was another sign of moving up the ladder as we often ate pizza and pasta from the restaurants in which I worked.

Work schedules in retail vary, which meant I worked most weekends, and many evenings. Denise worked in a business office setting and enjoyed the Monday-Friday, 8-5 schedule. Reminiscent of our days in Lawton, we didn't see much of one another because of our conflicting schedules. Rarely did we have time off together to go explore our new surroundings. We lacked critical time together to cultivate of fledgling marriage.

Part of the reasoning behind moving to Colorado was to give ourselves a fresh start to our marriage. There was so much darkness in both our pasts in Oklahoma and we thought it would serve us well, living in a new state. We hoped to build new friendships with other couples in similar stages of life.

Relationship building was difficult for me. After we left Lawton, the only friend I had was my wife and that relationship left a great deal to be desired. In contrast, Denise was social and outgoing. She got invited to many events, attending most without me.

There was a salesman in her office with seven or eight kids, and he rather enjoyed hanging out at the reception desk where my wife worked. He was quite the flirt, and Denise loved being flirted with. On one occasion, she shared a comment he made about her being beautiful. She was around eight months pregnant and like many women in that condition; she felt fat and ugly.

The salesman was skilled in manipulation tactics. He told my wife that a woman was at the peak of her beauty just before giving birth. He then mentioned her wedding ring. Pointing to it, he said, "Man, somebody must really love you to put a ring like that on your finger." He groomed, she responded. When Denise told me of the conversation, I knew I could not trust the guy.

I lacked the knowledge of how to properly "romance" my bride. She was my first real girlfriend, and I had no other frame of reference. What I knew was the slick salesman had a pregnant wife and a bunch of kids. He was also old enough to be her father as his oldest child was about fifteen. My wife was nineteen years old.

Within days, she quit wearing her wedding ring, which seemed a rather strange thing to do. When I questioned her about it she got defensive; saying her swollen fingers kept her from getting the ring on anymore. Denise had a way of making me feel horrible for questioning her on things. She always got angry and told me to get over my insecurities. She only fed those insecurities rather than help me overcome them.

I viewed the guy as a predator who loved to run his schemes on pregnant women, seducing them at their most vulnerable times. If any of the women surrendered to his seduction tactics, he could engage in extramarital sex without risk of fathering unwanted children. I never caught him with my wife, but I could never prove he hadn't slept with her. It was inappropriate for him to be rubbing her shoulders whenever I walked into the office.

When our apartment lease expired, my in-laws offered the apartment at the back of their gift shop up in the mountains. They had purchased a home a short distance away. Though it would add to our commute time, there were other benefits which made the drive worth it. When the baby came, grandma would be there to watch him while we worked, saving us money on childcare. The rent was less too. My father-in-law thought we paid rent but my mother-in-law always refused to take it.

Just before we moved, Denise checked into the hospital for labor induction. She had carried past term and due to her petite size, and the size of the baby, the doctor induced labor at forty-two weeks gestation. The nurse set up the Pitocin drip and the wait began. The wait for my son's arrival lingered on for hours. Sixteen bags of Pitocin later we still waited, and she had only dilated two centimeters before the doctor did a caesarean section.

Not allowed in the operating room, I could view the procedure from a side window. I remember hoping not to pass out at the sight of blood. To my benefit, I could see nothing graphic from my position behind the glass. The doctor lifted our little boy and spanked his bum to make him cry. He showed me the baby before nurses took him to get cleaned up. I think I counted fingers and toes five or six times, I wanted to be sure he had them all.

At the ages of nineteen and eighteen, we became a family of three. We took him home and the bond between him and I grew. Doubts still lingered in the back of my mind whether he was my biological child but I dismissed them and accepted the child, regardless.

I took him to all his well-baby appointments and vaccinations. I witnessed his first tooth, first steps, and many other firsts. This little one, of whom I dreamed for many years, captured my heart.

What I didn't comprehend, as my bond deepened with my newborn son, the wedge between my wife and I grew larger. There was something else at play. Denise experienced a deep postpartum depression. While it was normal for a mother to bond with and nurture her new baby, she grew to despise both the baby and me. Her disdain increased, making it obvious by saying she never wanted to have a boy child. It was my fault, I put her in that position, and the baby ruined her prized possession; her body. Regardless of how I responded, the result was always the same, more arguing.

As days unfolded, I shared stories with Denise of our baby's accomplishments, but her conversations always centered on work. A new guy got hired in her office, whose name was also David, and he soon became the dominant subject in her conversations. The new guy was a former soldier, and he drove a gold Trans Am, the license plate number I can still recite from memory. He loved to party and dance. "David used to be a Chippendale dancer!" she proclaimed with joy.

He had everything I lacked. Since I had known her, she had always acted as though I was her "Mr. Right (now)". She often talked about other guys in front of me, pointing out features she found attractive. After each episode of comparison, I felt less valued as a human being. The awesomeness of becoming a dad drowned out some of the many voices which told me how unworthy I was. With the proverbial writing on the wall, I focused more on the relationship my son than my wife.

30

THE SWITCHBOARD OPERATOR PAGED ME TO TAKE A CALL. at work less than an hour when I picked up the call, I thought it was a customer. It was my wife who called to say she would not be home when I got off work because she was leaving me.

There was no arguing, no yelling, she delivered her words in a monotone voice before hanging up on me. My shift had several hours to go, but I couldn't stay at work after that call. My world was crashing, and I had to stop it, so I asked my boss for time off from work for a family emergency.

I made it home about an hour after she called and found her gone. She had taken a bunch of clothes and other items, as much as she could fit into her car. I walked over to her parents' house to see if they knew anything. To my surprise, my son was still with his grandparents. I sat with my in-laws and tried to make sense of the situation. My wife told her parents what her intentions were, and they were less than pleased with her plan. Her father, in a fit of rage, got into a verbal fight with his daughter. He called her a whore, among other choice names, and told her he never wanted to see her again. She told them she had been dating a guy at work for several weeks and was leaving me for him.

My father-in-law may not have liked me in the beginning but he was on my side at that point. When the discussion ended, I took my son home and put him to bed. My mother-in-law told me to get some sleep too, and she would have a "heart-to-heart" discussion with her daughter about the choices she was making.

It was hard to sleep that night. I spent the night watching my baby boy as he slept, imagining the potential scenarios that could happen to him because of what took place that evening. He was just six months old when his home shattered. Someday, he might have to side with one parent over another, so I decided it would not be me who put that pressure on him.

I considered what I had lived through with my mom's divorce (s) and it terrified me. There was no peace that night, but I took solace in knowing my in-laws would testify on my behalf if Denise took me to divorce court. They thought the child stood a better chance with me than his mother. The thought of parents testifying against their own daughter was unfathomable.

Divorce is more than the dissolution of a covenantal relationship; it affects the extended family too, with children paying the highest price. Many couples fail to understand the full impact before resorting to it. Even in the most amicable divorces, the fabric of family is forever torn.

None of this I wanted for my son. Never did I want him to wonder where his mom was, or why he couldn't be with his dad. I purposed in my heart I would do whatever I could to keep this split from happening.

The next few days passed with no word from my wife. I went back to work, leaving my son with his grandparents.

About a week after she left, Denise knocked at our door one evening. To avoid an altercation with her father, she came to the house after nightfall, claiming she wanted to talk. Always open to a positive discussion, I let her in. As we talked, she collected things around the house and loaded them into a box.

At the risk of embarrassment, I share these next details because they are important to the story and will help you understand later events.

Before Denise walked out on our marriage, one thing she complained about was my lack of aggression in the bedroom. She would often say things like, "You need to put me in my place." She wanted someone who would resist her need for control in the relationship, someone who would dominate her into submission. That always sounded silly to me. I shouldn't have to lord myself over her to keep her in place.

Once inside her behavior was bizarre, even paranoid, but she also put off an amorous vibe. After looking outside to insure her parents weren't coming our way, she locked the door and led me into the living room. A warm fire burned in the earth stove as she attempted to explain what she meant by aggressiveness. "Take me, right now!"

The statement puzzled me. Take her where? She wanted me to be forceful with her when during times of intimacy. Being forceful reminded me of the times Robert forced himself upon me as a child, and it made me nauseous. My uneasiness resembled passivity, which killed the mood for her.

I became more confused by the minute as she described things her boyfriend did to her, things she wanted me to do. In the time it took to register her comments in my mind, she said I could no longer have her sexually. It felt like a tease, on one minute-off the next. Her motive was to have me rip her clothes off and have my way with her. To save my relationship, I tried to perform as requested, but my advances met with resistance. Did she want to have sex, or was this an act designed to accuse me of violence? When I backed off she hit me, further compounding my confusion. Only when she placed my hand in her private area, and said she wanted me to "rape" her, did I realize she wanted me to go ahead. Role play was what she wanted, so I acted out the role, but was uncomfortable with it.

In a role I never considered, for the sake of my marriage, I ripped off her blouse. She responded in favor and gave a little verbal indicator to let me know I was on the right track. When the blouse came off, I saw scabs on her back, long scratches that ran the length of her spine.

When we finished, I asked her about the scratches. With no reservation about sharing her exploits with other men, she let me that was how a real man loved his woman. Her boyfriend had broken a beer bottle and dragged the jagged edge down her back during intercourse, just hard enough to make it bleed. Disgusted by the thought, I said if she expected me to do those things to her, she could forget about it, because I never would.

As she got dressed, with disappointment in her voice, she said she expected me to respond that way. Our marriage, in her mind, was finished. Her final litmus test and I failed it. My refusal to take part in that kind of sexual activity meant I was rejecting her. I didn't see it as rejection; that behavior was a trigger for me based on prior abuse.

Denise packed several more items before leaving, and we did not see, or hear from her for another week. The next time she came over was during daylight hours. Not wanting her father to catch her there, she asked that I remove my truck from the garage so she could park her car in there. Her plan was to load more stuff into the car without being seen. There was just one problem. Her father knew if I was home, my truck was always in the garage.

I was changing a diaper while she packed more of her things. Our marriage shattered, I knew it in my head but my heart was not ready to let her go. I pleaded with her to stay. I may have begged her. She considered my behavior repulsive; she wanted me aggressive, not passive and codependent.

Nervous about seeing her dad, and packing at a feverish pace, she argued about silly things. When fueled by anger, it was easier to carry out her mission. My son in my arms, he got upset and cried as we continued to argue.

Knock, knock, knock! My father-in-law noticed my truck in the driveway rather than the garage and popped over to investigate. Between the doors to the apartment and garage, was a little covered breezeway. With the door to the garage propped open to load stuff out, her father saw the car, so he knew she was there.

We scurried around the apartment trying to figure out where to hide her. He knocked very hard on the door and demanded me to open it at once. My son cried louder. It scared me too, thinking my father-in-law would break the door down.

I left Denise in the laundry room to hide as I opened the door. Her father was angry I took so long. With a little white lie, I told him I was changing the baby's diaper.

"Where is she, where is the little bitch whore?" He was the maddest I had ever seen. "I know she's here so don't lie!" With no other way out, Denise walked out of the laundry room to confront her father, posturing herself in a defiance toward him. "What do you want?" she smugly asked.

"What are you doing here whore?" snorted her father. She replied her purpose was to collect more of her things and was just about to leave. "Besides, it's none of your business!" she yelled back. He looked through the box she packed, and pulling out a frying pan he said, "Get your own household stuff, your husband needs this to cook meals for your kid!"

Infuriated by her, he pulled a small pistol from his pocket, pointed it at her head, and ordered her to get out. "You made your nasty little bed, now go lie in it with your sorry boyfriend!"

For all intents and purposes, it looked like he intended to shoot her, right there in front of me. He allowed her to pick up the box she had packed and take it to her car, with the gun still pointed at her. "Give me your keys," he demanded of me, "and I'll move your truck so this little whore can get out of here." As she drove away, he yelled at her to never come back. As for him, he no longer had a daughter. "She's dead to me!" was the last thing he uttered before walking back to his house.

<u>3 1</u>

IT WAS ABUNDANTLY CLEAR MY WIFE HAD BURNED BRIDGES with her family, her father in particular. That only made her anger towards me more intense.

Not long after our separation, I received divorce papers at my job. My mom had already planned a visit to meet her first grandbaby, which should have been a fun time of bonding for us. Unfortunately, her visit coincided with the implosion of my marriage. Mom rearranged her plans and helped me find an attorney.

Denise cleaned out our bank account and charged our credit card to the limit purchasing clothing for her new stripper boyfriend. There were no funds left for me to hire a lawyer. I worked hard for everything we had, and though it wasn't much, it got taken from me. The material possessions were just the beginning.

Having been through two divorces herself, mom knew it was important I had access to a good attorney. While I was at work, mom interviewed divorce attorneys. After speaking with several, she chose one and set up an appointment for the three of us to meet. The attorney we met with was also the mayor of one of the suburbs, which made us think we scored a bonus.

The attorney listened to my story and agreed to take the case. With my in-laws support, he speculated it would be an easy case to win, to include full custody of my son.

To support my case, my attorney suggested we hire a private investigator to document Denise's actions. Mom paid the retainer fees for both. The private investigator recorded instances of late night partying, involving consumption of alcohol, which was unlawful. The legal drinking age was twenty-one, which made her thirty-eight-year-old boyfriend guilty of contributing to the delinquency of a minor as my wife was only nineteen. Armed with this information, I was confident I would win in court.

Mom could only spend a week with me but she felt good about our position, which made going back home a little easier for her. I can only imagine the thoughts mom had as she drove back to Oklahoma. I know she worried about what would happen to me, and her grandchild.

During that time, my sister started college and my brother his senior year in high school. Mom had a lot going in her own life and I felt horrible she had to help me. Since I had ignored her warnings, and married Denise without her knowledge, I didn't expect her help.

With the attorney and the PI on retainer, the waiting game started until our case went before the judge.

Meanwhile, I was still living rent-free in the apartment which belonged to my in-laws and my father-in-law found out. He was carrying two mortgages and trying to run a business. It was bad business to have non-revenue generating tenants, even if the tenant was his grandson. I had to find a different living situation.

I moved into a townhome on the far east side of Colorado Springs; it was the best I could afford. While it was close to my place of employment, I drove up the pass every day to take my son to his grandparents who cared for him while I worked. The commute added an extra three hours to our day, not to mention the extra gas.

Denise always knew our whereabouts. I ascribed to the notion she is the mother of our son and I would do nothing to hinder that. I remembered how my father had caused such strife in our lives with this issue and I vowed I would not do things the way he had.

As the months passed in our new home, my son and I settled into a new normal. I continued to experience many "firsts" with him. For his first birthday, I made a cake and we celebrated the grand occasion together, just the two of us. My wife may have thought she was punishing me in giving me what I wanted; to become a father, with all the stress that comes with being a single parent. It could've also been her way of avoiding responsibility; maybe it was both.

A letter from the private investigator came, informing he was removing himself from the case. There was no reason given, so I called his office. When I got the PI on the phone, he informed me he was extricating himself due to a conflict of interest in my case. He said he had been surveilling my wife on a recent Friday night when he made a disturbing discovery. The investigator tracked my wife to a gathering at a river where he noted "ritualistic behavior" taking place.

He moved closer for a better view of the action. What he said next floored me. I had been through some crazy stuff already but this revelation took the prize. He witnessed my wife, and my attorney, taking part in what he called satanic worship where people sacrificed chickens at an altar set up near a bonfire. The investigator said the potential political ramifications were more than he wanted to risk.

Based on this information, I hired a new attorney and asked him to relieve the other from the case. The chain of events, I hoped, would make my case even stronger. My new attorney was not willing to submit the incident as evidence because he had not arranged for the private investigator and could not confirm the validity of the report.

Not wanting to disclose my knowledge of her late night activities, I tried to get Denise to incriminate herself when she came to take stuff from the house. Not long afterward, she expressed a wish to reconcile, though she mentioned nothing about the activities at the river with my lawyer.

In the interim, with the divorce in process, my wife joined the military which didn't sit well with me, for many reasons. She wanted to join the Air Force, which was the better choice in my opinion, but after submitting the paperwork the recruiter called her into the office. The Air Force denied entrance as Denise tested positive for drug use. Disappointed in her for taking drugs, I was glad she didn't get in.

Serious about joining the service, we returned to the recruiting station the following week, only this time we met at the Army recruiter's office. As I was still her spouse, and we had a minor child, the recruiter needed signatures from me on some paperwork. As dependents, we had access to services offered to military family members.

I wondered how she could test positive for drugs one week, and join the Army the following week. It all became clear when I watched Denise sign documents while the recruiter massaged her shoulders.

Perhaps the same "transaction" took place with the sergeant, similar to what happened a few weeks earlier when she had a new clutch and tires installed on her car. Neither of us had funds to cover those expenses. Denise had methods for getting what she wanted. Never was I able to prove a trade for sex, but it made the most sense.

With orders from the Army, my parents transferred to Germany for a three year tour of duty. Not wanting to sell their house, they were reluctant to take on the challenge of managing the property from halfway around the world.

Because my wife wanted to reconcile, my mom presented us with an offer. If we returned to Oklahoma, we could live in their house rent-free, as long as we took care of the place. Mom felt it was the best she could do to help us financially, and she trusted me to take good care of the house while they were overseas. She also thought a rent-free place to live would be a good thing for me and my son, in the event the reconciliation failed.

With my wife joining the Army, she would be away for basic training, followed by tech school, lasting several months. There was a possibility she would get stationed at Fort Sill, so it seemed like a good choice for us.

Denise and I discussed the offer. Although I was not keen on returning to a place which held such bad memories, it was our best chance at saving our marriage. Once again, though, I was running, trying to get my wife away from inappropriate relationships. In my naiveté, I didn't understand that you cannot change another person, only they can change, and only when they are ready and willing to make the change.

We informed both attorneys to place a hold on the divorce proceedings while we attempted reconciliation. Our families approved the idea and supported us any way they could.

With logistics in order, the day came for us to leave Colorado. We quit our jobs and broke the lease where I was living.

Denise had an affinity for shoes and always kept them stored in the original boxes. As her storage facility, I had in my possession some thirty pair of shoes, most of which were still new.

After she arrived, one of the first things she did was dump most of those shoes in the garbage. The shoes represented a lot of hard-earned money wasted. While she made trips to dump the shoes, I backed her car to the door to load it.

I popped the trunk and what I saw there hit me like a ton of bricks. Strewn about the trunk were a dozen used condoms, nothing else. A clear message was being sent by her jilted lover. I got some paper towel and removed the semen filled prophylactics, dumping them in the garbage on top of the shoes.

After I discarded the condoms, I confronted her about them and she denied they were even there. My wife, in typical forum, tried to make me believe the condoms were a figment of my imagination. The mind games were still in play and it sickened me. Not only from the mess I cleaned up, but also from sensing the reconciliation attempt would end in failure. I had no better options. I stood at a precipice, waiting to fall into a dark abyss.

We continued loading, bumping into the pink elephant in the room in the process. Tensions were high for both of us. Inside me a war raged. The optimist in me wanted to believe what I had just seen was the end of a painful chapter in our relationship. The realist suggested the best thing was to cut my losses and let her go.

My decision was to continue with the move, taking my family back to Oklahoma to reboot, if you will. From the outside, most people say I made a poor decision in taking my wife back. The realist in me agreed, but the realist was not the victor of the internal battle.

<u>3 2</u>

ONCE WE HAD THE VEHICLES LOADED UP, WE DROPPED the house keys at the landlord's office and hit the road. The drive seemed as though it took several days. My son rode with me in the truck and Denise followed in her car.

It was after midnight when I pulled over for gas. With 45 miles to go, I wanted to insure I had enough fuel to get there. My wife's car did not need fuel, so she parked off to the side. After I pumped the fuel, I walked over to her car to ask if she was ready to go.

Denise rolled her window down, and I noticed she had been crying. When asked why, she said she missed her boyfriend. "That's funny, you didn't cry over leaving your husband!" I quipped. The last bit of hope I had slipped away into the darkness like a snake. I told her to turn the car around and go back to her lover. I did not want to be drug through the mud; I knew she could not remain faithful.

As I backed away from her car, I lost composure and raised my voice. "Go back to your stripper and leave us alone!" She gathered herself together and started the car. It was late; we had been driving for almost twelve hours with another one to go as we got back onto the highway. As my son slept next to me in his car seat, I thought about how sorry I was for what he would have to endure in his life because of his parents pending divorce.

Pressing on, we arrived at my parents' home after 1 am. I dove straight into bed and slept until noon the next day. Denise got up before me. My son awoke early too and had a great time playing with his grandparents.

My parents stayed with us for three days before they left for Germany. Having them there to babysit made it possible for me to find a job. I went to work for the same company I worked for in Colorado. Denise was to report for basic training in two weeks so it made little sense for her to look for a job.

We said goodbye to my parents. They drove their car to a staging point and shipped it to Germany along with their household goods. Mom was in tears as she blew kisses to her little grandson. I was glad they had that time with my son because they would be in Germany for at least three years.

After my parents left, the rest of the afternoon had a somber mood. The reality of the situation we faced set in. My wife had siblings in town, as did I, but we were on our own now. There would no longer be the safety net of our parents to help with our son, or anything else. It was make it or break it time and we had less than two weeks to work on our relationship before Denise shipped off to basic training. Still exhausted from our move, and the long drive, we all fell asleep early that night.

The next morning the baby crying out for breakfast woke me up. I remember thinking Denise had to be in the kitchen getting a bottle ready so I laid there in a semi-lucid state. The crying intensified, so I got up to check on the little guy. He was ready to get his day started.

We went to the kitchen to check on the bottle. Denise was not there. Thinking I passed her while in a sleepy haze, I retraced my steps to see if she was in one of the other rooms. Not finding her inside the house, I looked outside and saw her car gone.

"Did she go to the grocery store?" I asked my boy. We had plenty of baby food and formula. Maybe she went to get something else. I got the bottle ready and fed the little guy, then got him dressed before getting dressed myself.

After about an hour I got worried. We had no cell phones so I could not track her down that way. My suspicions kicked in, wondering if she had visited one of the two previous affairs. I had no addresses or phone numbers for any of them.

Three, four, five hours passed since I woke up and still no sign of my wife. After six or seven hours, the phone rang with the operator asking if I would accept the charges for a collect call. It was my wife, calling from the Colorado state line. She couldn't go through with reconciliation because she wanted to be with her boyfriend.

Denise admitted she never intended to go back to Oklahoma to work on our marriage. It was just a rouse she and her boyfriend had conspired to get me out of town, and therefore, out of their business. It would also get me away from the protection and help of her parents.

A week and a half later I got another call from Denise letting me know she parked her car in my driveway with the keys under the mat. She was at the airport, about to board a plane bound for boot camp. Since the car was in both of our names, she felt it was best to leave it with me.

She promised to send money to cover the car payment and insurance with a little extra to help with food costs. That money came only once.

After missing payments for a few months on her car, the repo man caught up with us. My brother had borrowed the car to run errands and when he pulled into our driveway, the tow truck driver pulled up behind the car. The driver gave the reason he was there and expecting this was coming, we gave him no resistance. Sympathetic to my plight, the driver allowed us to retrieve any belongings from the car, something he did not have to do.

The next time I got a call from Denise I let her know what happened to the car. She got irate and hung up on me. With no contribution of her money toward our expenses, what else could she expect?

My brother was a big help during that time and was a fantastic uncle to my son. He used to babysit for me until I secured actual childcare provisions. He would have continued to help, but he also joined the military and wound up stationed in Alaska. My sister was away at college, three plus hours away.

With all my family somewhere else, my son and I were now alone.

33

THINGS WERE VERY DIFFICULT FOR MY SON AND I OVER THE next several months. The economy was not great and although I worked full time, and paid zero for rent, we barely got by. The utilities alone consumed as much as two-thirds of my take home pay. Family Services denied food stamps because I was a man. I got a little help from the WIC program which covered formula for the baby.

Christmas 1988 looked bleak, but I figured we would be okay because my son was still too young to realize what it was all about, anyway. He wouldn't know what he was missing.

My wife called saying she had time off and wanted to see our son. She asked if we could meet halfway between Lawton and Colorado Springs. Regardless of how I felt about the woman, I never wanted to deny my son access to his mother. Since I had nothing else going on, I agreed to meet her in Dumas, Texas, a small town in the panhandle, about the halfway point.

We set out on Christmas day for the five-hour drive, just so my wife could spend some time with her son, something she never would have done for me.

We visited in the vehicle, on the shoulder lane of the highway. Denise had dropped off her boyfriend at a truck stop nearby so he could keep an eye on us. We stayed forty-five minutes before turning around to drive back home. That was a long day for a fifteen-month-old kiddo, stuck in a car seat for over ten hours.

Denise was a little hurt by the visit because our son was not receptive of her. It took a few minutes for him to warm up to his mom. Even though she made the choices which facilitated the situation, I still felt sympathy toward her.

Several people told me I should never have done that for her, driven so far just so she could see her son. Most would agree, but I didn't consider my desires to be above the needs of my son. I tried to consider the best interests of my child. He was innocent in the matter and it was not right to punish him for the mistakes of his parents.

<u>3 4</u>

AS MY SON GOT OLDER, AND PARENTING GOT A LITTLE easier, our relationship grew even closer. With an affinity for cars and airplanes, they were the toy of choice whenever he played.

He was an inquisitive kid. Like me, he enjoyed exploring how things worked in the world around him, mechanical things in particular.

Searching for somewhere to belong, I joined a Mini Truck club. Meetings were held once or twice a month and my son loved to go with me. He got a lot of attention at those meetings with all the girls taking turns holding him.

The eternal flirt, my boy loved to purse his lips at pretty girls. One lady would pick him up and at once he would pucker up for a smooch. A happy child, he never got fussy or caused disruption at gatherings.

As a club, we often traveled to various cities to compete in the car shows. Some guys had the latest and greatest aftermarket accessories which made their trucks stand out. Others, like me, just tried to keep up using items purchased on a shoestring budget.

That summer, I got a call from Denise asking where we stood with our relationship. She finished advanced training and waited to receive orders for her first duty station. Whatever I said would be wrong, so I stated the obvious. I told her I didn't think she could maintain a monogamous relationship, and it made no sense to prolong the inevitable.

She must have taken this as rejection, something she had never experienced. Her stories told how no one had ever broken up with her; she broke the hearts, a record of which she was proud. After all the damage done, I still wanted my wife back, but I knew she would never be faithful. My inability to trust her weighed down the relationship.

The "perceived" rejection infuriated her, and she got nasty. "You will regret this!" she screamed, slamming the phone down.

Within a few days her attorney bore down on me with his intimidation tactics. With my retainer long since used up, my attorney stopped work and removed himself from the case. At a disadvantage, as the only one who paid the bills, I relied on the military benefits available to spouses.

With a court date set, Denise's lawyer hastened the process, hoping I would not show up in court and lose everything. I got help from a military attorney, in the way of a drafted response to the Petition for Dissolution of Marriage. They could do nothing more than draft a legal response on my behalf, which thwarted the plans of my opposition.

A week later the divorce was final, but custody was set aside for later determination. During the late 1980's, there was a progressive movement to separate divorce from child custody/visitation/support issues. That separation of law required we go to court again to settle the custody issue.

We were both issued documents used to determine the parent more suitable for the child. The documents included a financial affidavit, character references, and a few others. The financial affidavit concerned me since I carried all the debt and expenses. She had all income because she lived in the barracks, debt free.

Car repossession had no effect on Denise, even with her name on the loan. The finance company explained they would not pursue collection efforts on a wife until the husband died. The department store credit card, also my responsibility because I had removed her name as an authorized user. I only did that to prevent her from maxing out the card but I was too late. She maxed out the $2,400 credit limit the night before leaving me.

Between the car and the credit card, I was legally responsible to repay all $10,000 of that debt, on top of all my own expenses. Even with explanations to the court, this did not help my case.

The character references document was my ace in the hole, I thought, because it would include her parents as references for my side. With passing time and the distance between us, my in-laws no longer backed me. Denise, I'm sure, fabricated stories to dissuade their support of me.

After basic training, Denise got stationed in Texas, a seven hour drive south of where I lived. She called to arrange a visit with our son. As always, I agreed to it. She came to Lawton and spent the day with our son, and as promised, she brought him back but she had ulterior motives. Denise returned our son that afternoon with a single bag of groceries, insisting the food was for the child only.

I found out later she took photos of the food in the bag, and the inventory of my refrigerator. That information got twisted to make me appear neglectful in providing for my son. For his sake, she provided the needed groceries. The result was more points lost for my side.

In August 1989, Denise called again to request our son visit with her for a week. Still, ever willing to show cooperation, I agreed but wanted to know her plan for certain things. First, she told the court she lived in the barracks, so where would my son sleep? Second, who would provide childcare? She insisted she had those bases covered though she would not divulge any details.

We set a date, and she made the drive once again. Upon her arrival, she invited me to meet with her at the home of one of her brothers. Denise presented an offer for me to consider before our meeting; an offer for joint custody with no need for child support or alimony. With the odds stacked against me, I didn't have to think hard on that offer. I figured it would be better to have part-time custody, without paying child support and alimony, than what I suspected the court's decision to be.

We met at her brother's home and she already had a handwritten document prepared, at the advice of her attorney. All that remained was for both of us to sign the agreement and have an unbiased third party sign as a witness. Denise would then forward the document to her attorney who would have it entered it into the court record closing the case.

We needed a third signature, from a non-family member. As fate would have it, an unbiased individual sat on the couch. This guy was a friend of my brother-in-law, who was willing sign his name to a legal document. It was all very convenient.

Isolated; from family, from legal counsel, from anyone who could help me with this decision, I trusted it was the right thing to do. I trusted since she was in the military, if she messed up, all I had to do was alert her commanding officer. I also figured that when the child grew to school age, he would spend more time with me to keep his schooling consistent. As a deployable soldier, our child would stay with me in her absence, should that occur. It appeared we had come to a reasonable compromise.

After we signed, we each got a photocopy of the document, the original forwarded to her attorney. After signing, I left there with my son, feeling optimistic. So much so, I got started with arrangements for moving to Colorado that evening.

I wanted out of Oklahoma; it was so depressing for me, plus there were no good paying jobs. Greater opportunities for a better quality of life awaited us in Colorado.

I contacted Denise to ask if she would like to take the first six month rotation with our child, instead of the week we agreed to earlier. If so, it would give me the ability to move away from Lawton. I thought she might enjoy reconnection time with our son while I set out to improve things on my end to prepare for his return. To surrender him to my ex-wife was no easy decision to make. Life without my son for six months was difficult to process. I kept telling myself it was a sacrifice for the greater good.

The next day, Denise came to my house, and we loaded our son's belongings into her car. I put his things in the trunk of her brand new Volkswagen sedan and then grabbed my boy and hugged him tight. I told him I loved him more than anything and I would see him soon, promising him we would live in Colorado again when he came back. A month shy of his second birthday, I'm sure none of that made any sense to him.

His mother was ready to leave, but my boy clung to me, unwilling to let go. I could tell he was very nervous. I know he didn't understand the full scope of what was happening, but he knew something didn't look right to him. He cried, which made the separation a thousand times harder. Frustrated, his mother pulled him away from me, placing him in the back seat. She plopped him in his car seat without fastening the restraints. Denise drove away and tears poured from my eyes as I watched my son leave. I saw him climb out of his car seat, screaming, with one hand outstretched toward me.

The pain from watching my boy leave is just as real today after all these years. It was horrible, the weight of guilt oppressive. As soon as he left, I questioned whether I made the right decision.

Life had to get better going forward. The worst part was now behind us, I hoped. The divorce was final and our custody agreement signed. With determination and motivation, I was ready to make a better life for my son.

3 5

A MONTH LATER IT WAS TIME TO CELEBRATE BIRTHDAY number two for my son, so I called Denise and asked to speak to him. The answer was an emphatic, NO! She explained I needed to respect her time with the boy and not call so much. She said she would pass along my message, though I doubt she did.

As fall gave way to winter temperatures, the cost of utilities skyrocketed. Even with working a full-time job, and not having the extra expenses of a child, I could not keep up with rising costs. The first thing to get shut off was the telephone service, followed by natural gas and water service. With a gas furnace and stove in the house, I lost access to heat and the ability to cook.

Without running water, I had no way to shower or flush the toilet. I had a five gallon bucket I would use to gather water from the neighbor's garden hose. I'm sure she would have been all right with it, but I was far too embarrassed to ask, so I would sneak over at night to fill the bucket. Second only to the molestation experience, this was one of the lowest moments in my life. The downward spiral continued.

A few weeks later it was my birthday. I had quit attending the car club meetings, fearing I smelled and didn't want to risk exposure to the shame. No one knew it was my birthday, so no one joined me to celebrate. With only electricity available, I microwaved a hot dog for dinner and climbed into my warm waterbed to watch TV until I fell asleep. Birthday number twenty-two was a blast.

The time between my birthday and Thanksgiving was grueling. I had been trying so hard to get my parent's house rented so I could move but no one was interested. Many of the troops had deployed for Operation Desert Storm, the first US war in Iraq. "Who are these guys running for office?" one radio personality joked. "One goes by the name *For Rent,* and the other *For Sale."* Out of twenty houses on a block, ten to fifteen of them had one of those two signs in the yard.

Thanksgiving passed without notice. As Christmas approached, I hoped my ex-wife would allow me access to our son. My brother came home on leave, surprised by the condition in which he found me. He tried to help with finances but I was drowning in debt. Together we called Denise to request a visit around Christmas. In what must have been a momentary lapse in her hostility towards me, she agreed.

My brother introduced me to two girls, who he had gone to school with, to encourage me to consider dating. While he was on leave, the four of us double-dated a few times. After learning of my situation, the girls suggested we all go together for the visit. They thought it would give Denise the impression I had moved on with someone new in my life, plus they knew I could use the extra support.

Denise agreed to let me visit the Thursday before Christmas. I got off work at 4 pm and my brother and the two girls picked me up. We took a few toys to give my son, one was an airplane. Tiffany had a t-shirt made with iron-on transfer letters which said "I love my daddy" on the front, and "My daddy loves me" on the back. Together, we drove straight through, stopping only to get drive through for dinner.

We arrived at the home where my son and his mom were staying just before midnight. Denise was not happy about the extra people with me. She had to wake up our son before letting us into his room. It had been four months since I last saw my boy. Shaking off the sleep, he recognized me and his uncle right away.

Elated to see him, but you couldn't tell by my countenance. The pictures I have of that night reveal a deep sadness on my face. I suppose I knew the visit would be short and it would be over in the blink of an eye. Another contributing factor was the difference in his environment.

When he lived with me he was a huge Donald Duck fan. His mother replaced Donald with Snoopy. It was as if Denise tried to wipe away every vestige of my influence, by creating a new identity for our little boy. Already very depressed, I didn't need to see hurtful stuff like that.

At 12:30 am, Denise returned to the room with a man, asking us to leave. I recognized the man as the same one who had signed our child custody agreement as an unbiased third party witness. She brought out the big guns with the psychological cruelty inflicted that night. "What's this?" I asked. "Who is this guy?"

"This guy is my husband and you all need to get out of my house, now!" she replied. The guy escorted us out the door. As we walked away, I heard my boy crying for me, asking why Daddy was leaving. We had driven over seven hours to spend less than forty-five minutes with my son.

Back on the road, my brother drove the entire way home to allow me to sleep. With no delays along the way, we arrived just in time for to start my shift at work. Sleep eluded me that night.

I don't know how I made it through my shift the next day. The end of the shift started a three-day Christmas weekend. I spent the day with my brother and the two girls at their apartment. We had a meal together, and they tried their best to cheer me up, to no avail. My brother left the day after Christmas to report back for duty in Alaska. With him gone, I sank deeper into depression, which worried my brother.

By Friday of that week, the darkness surrounding me was paralyzing. I asked a guy at work to loan me a gun. With a bogus excuse about people threatening me, I said it was for protection. I had never even touched a gun before so he showed me how to operate it and gave me a box of ammunition. It was a thirty-eight special pistol. "This pistol will resolve any problem you have," he said with a chuckle. Oh it would take care of the problem, all right, of that I was certain.

As I drove home from work, I stared at the weapon sitting out in the open on the passenger seat of my little truck. I recalled the name calling I'd heard as a kid; Captain Hook, one-armed bandit, four eyes, the gross kid with the robotic arm, and so many others. I thought about the abuse inflicted upon me by two men responsible for protecting me. The pain of divorce was still fresh and raw and weighed on my heart. As I drove, all the traumatic events which happened throughout my life took on voices. By the time I got home, the cacophony of voices, each one with its own distinct sound, blended into one. "You are WORTHLESS, YOU are WORTHLESS, YOU ARE WORTHLESS!"

In my mind, I agreed with those voices, I was worthless. I felt I did nothing right. Regardless of my attempts, nothing I did made people like me. Why would they, anyway? I didn't. The voices continued to taunt me, telling me I would actually do the world a big favor by taking myself out of it. It was obvious I was a failure, and it felt like everyone else knew it too. The one willing to verbalize it loudest was my ex-wife. For the previous couple years she made known her opinion every chance she got. I concluded there was no need to write a suicide note, no one would care anyway.

From the package of ammo I removed a single bullet. I rolled it around in my hand as I searched for the courage to bring to an end the pain which plagued me for so long. I slid the bullet into the chamber, gave it a little spin, and closed it up.

At rock bottom, I pulled the trigger.

Not true for every case, but many people often speak of the person who commits suicide as being a coward. As one who has walked that path, I can tell you there was no cowardice involved in pulling that trigger. Though tragically misguided, it took tremendous courage and strength to do it.

After lying on the living room floor for quite some time, I retreated to the warmth of my waterbed. Spent, I fell asleep after forty plus hours awake, having driven for fifteen of those hours, covering around 550 miles in the journey to see my precious boy.

Back at work in Alaska, and knowing the condition I was in when he left, my brother was concerned about me. He called the two girls to see if they would do a welfare check on me. They showed up on Saturday in the middle of the afternoon.

I responded to their knocking like a bear coming out of hibernation, all groggy and disheveled. They asked if I was okay and if I needed anything. Both suspected something was amiss when I didn't respond and asked if they could come in. With no words, I invited them in and we sat in the living room.

The gun and ammunition rested on the floor in plain sight where I had left them the night before. Untroubled by the sight of the gun, or unaware of its presence, neither said anything about it. They sensed the melancholy which emanated from me. Flanked between the two, Tiffany embraced me tight and whispered everything would be all right.

I fell apart in her arms, my body shuddering as I wept. No one spoke for quite some time. I gathered my composure and told the girls I was done, tired and done.

Tiffany looked in my tear-stained, bloodshot eyes, and asked, "If we pick you up in the morning, would you go to church with us?" Not knowing what purpose that would serve, I responded in defeat, "I guess so, what do I have to lose?"

The girls stayed with me a while longer that afternoon. They did not say much, or ask probing questions. It was the best thing they could have done. Had they pushed me to talk about the situation, I would have shut them down and told them to leave. Instead, they met me in the ugliness of my misery, with empathy and pure kindness, characteristics I was unaccustomed to.

After they left that afternoon, I went back to bed and slept through until Sunday morning. As promised, the girls came to take me to church. Uncertain of what to expect at a church service, if there had been a lightning bolt hit me when I walked through the door, I would have welcomed it.

I don't recall most of the service but I do remember a point the pastor made about strongholds the devil has on mankind. He suggested one of the most effective things a follower of Christ could do amid a spiritual battle was pray for someone else. "The enemy wants us to be so self-focused and self-absorbed that we become easy targets to take down," he proclaimed. To esteem others more than ourselves would frustrate the enemy, causing him to retreat and redirect his efforts toward some other selfish individual.

Something about that concept struck a chord deep within me. I speculated I had been looking at life from a selfish point of view. When the sermon finished, the pastor gave an altar call, to which I responded in surrender, and gave my heart to Jesus that day, December 31, 1989. It's not lost on me the irony of the date. The final day of the year, was also the final day of my slavery to sin. Jesus set me free, but I had a long road to recovery ahead.

If I said everything became as fresh as a bed of roses, I'd be lying. At home I attempted to pray for the first time, asking God to prove His existence by getting me out of the pit I was in. Proof came when I returned the borrowed gun. The hammer had jammed somehow, mere microns from the back of the bullet casing. When I handed the gun over, the individual I borrowed it from chastised me for my gun safety, or lack thereof. He said I was lucky the gun had not gone off, "What are you, an idiot? You could have shot yourself pal!"

After he said that, I swore an oath, that if God would just get me back to Colorado, I would serve Him for the rest of my life. I was unaware swearing oaths, especially un-honored ones, was not good to do. By His grace, and not because of anything I did, I signed a lease agreement with a couple from work. Finally, I had someone to rent my parents' home, and they wanted to move in as soon as possible. I agreed to a quick move-in date but had no place to go myself. Tiffany and Kimberly came to my rescue again, allowing me to stay with them in their apartment. I packed all of my belongings out of the house and moved in with the girls. I slept on the couch in the living room. It was nice to have access to heat and running water again.

I continued to ask favors of God with the promise I would serve Him. He continued to deliver, allowing me to return to Colorado Springs a short time later. In following the mandate prescribed by the court, I secured a two bedroom apartment, a job, and provision for licensed childcare for my son. It amazed me how things just fell

125

right into place. I didn't stay with the girls for long but I was grateful for their kindness and help.

Time ticked toward the return of my son so I had to hurry and get moved. I made that drive back to Colorado with all my earthly belongings packed like sardines in my little truck. In such a hurry to get back to Colorado to restart my life, I got a speeding ticket west of Dumas, Texas. I didn't see it then, hindsight always being 20/20, but I was still operating in my own will and strength, which led to making sloppy mistakes. The speeding ticket was one of the multitude I would make.

3 6

LIKE THE DAWN OF A NEW DAY, LIVING IN COLORADO AGAIN brightened my future. I met a neighbor who took a liking to my truck and offered to buy it. After I thought about it, it made sense to sell the truck and pay cash for decent used car. It would help with my financial woes.

We worked out a deal where he gave me $900 cash as a down payment and then gave me twelve postdated checks to cover the twelve remaining payments. Essentially, I carried the loan for him. I found a car which suited my needs and eliminated a monthly payment which brought a little reprieve.

I later found out the guy had taken the truck to a mechanic for some regular maintenance, only to find the mechanic had caught the truck on fire. It was a complete loss. As for the new owner, he received a settlement check to replace the vehicle.

Not so lucky for me, he used all the insurance money to buy another car. He had given me twelve checks, and per our agreement, I mailed them in monthly, one by one. None of those checks ever cleared the bank. After three months of not receiving payment, the bank issued an order for repossession. For the second time, a repo man appeared to take my vehicle. I directed him to the neighbor, who directed him to the mechanic, who then surrendered the burned out truck.

The bank was not happy about retrieving a destroyed vehicle and requested immediate payment of $980 to close out the loan. I had no money and the checks from the buyer were invalid. My ex-wife's brother and sister-in-law cosigned the loan and they ended up having to pay the money.

Part of me felt horrible about ditching the balance while another part felt it was poetic justice. I decided it was her problem to contend with since she stuck me with $10,000 worth of debt. Even though it was far from fair, it was like giving her a taste of her own medicine.

It didn't take long for Denise to contact me, demanding I repay her brother. I suggested when she took care of the $10,000; I would take care of the $980. After that incident, she changed her phone number, making communication with my son that much more difficult.

It was time to make plans with Denise for the return of my son. I tried several ways to contact her to set up the transfer but always met with dead ends. She had changed her phone number to a private line and my attempts to find her through the office of the Post Locator failed. A month into my visitation time with my son I still had no response from Denise.

Out of the blue one day, I received an urgent message from the receptionist where I worked. Marked "Important", it had a phone number with directions to call my ex-wife at once. I called as soon as I could that day.

The person who answered was her commanding officer. He said Denise had deployment orders to the Gulf War in Iraq. The protocol for deploying soldiers with children was to arrange for transferring their minor child (ren) to the other parent. Finally, it seemed someone would help get my son back.

The man identified himself at the start of the call but said his name so fast I didn't catch it. He requested my personal information, i.e., social security number (commonly used number in military circles), address, phone number, work address and phone number, work fax number. In my excitement, I questioned none of his requests.

Once he collected the info, I asked when I could meet with his soldier to transfer custody of my son. He placed me on hold. When he came back on the line, he said I would receive a subpoena in the mail within a few days. That got my attention, and I asked for his name again.

He stated his name again, and it was the same name I had seen on our custody agreement. The same guy who I met at the home of my ex-wife when I visited my son before Christmas. He informed me, in a rather hostile tone, that she was his wife and he acted on her behalf.

The deployment story was just a rouse to get my personal info for the purpose of suing me for alimony and child support. He told me what a loser I was and that I should be in jail for the way I abandoned my child without one ounce of support.

I figured he must have been trying to set me up and was recording the conversation to use in court. What popped in my head as a response was to inform him she could not get alimony payments from me because she had remarried. I asked again when I could come get my son. Angrily he responded, "We aren't going anywhere, and neither is the child! You will hear from our attorney!" He then hung up the phone.

I later found out he was her commanding officer, and he had married her (which was a violation in the Army known as fraternization). To top it off, they got married before our divorce was even completed. That, too, was a punishable offense (polygamy). As was always the case, none of these critical details helped me in court.

No one in the legal community wanted to touch my case. The only thing I had the ability to do was file a congressional complaint against Denise and her second husband through the military justice system. The complaint resulted in transferring Denise to another unit, outside of her new husband's command. No other disciplinary action happened.

I found the Army's course of action to be unsatisfactory. I wrote to and called more professional agencies related to fathers' rights. What a complete oxymoron. Fathers had no rights. I wrote to the Judge Advocate General of the US Army, the US Department of Defense, the Senator of Colorado, and even the President of the United States. All agencies responded, and each one said they could do nothing to help my case.

I called twenty-five attorneys specializing in fathers' rights and only one would even entertain the case. He wanted a retainer of $25,000 and then warned me there was no guarantee of victory in court, even with the "punishable offenses" committed by my former spouse.

He dropped the bomb when he told me I would be lucky to get two days per year visitation. I reminded the attorney I had a signed agreement stipulating joint custody, with the child spending six months with each parent. This was when a bad situation evolved into a horrible one.

He asked if I could produce a certified copy of the final motion regarding custody from the court. I had not received such a document. He asked for the case number. After a quick search, he found that the document we signed never entered the court record and was not even worth the paper it was written on. As for the court, the issue was still unresolved, leaving Denise with the upper hand. Possession was nine tenths of the law, and she had possession of the child for the previous eight plus months with no financial support from the father. He suspected that was how she would spin the story. His assessment was correct, that was the exact direction she took.

After all the hassle, my son did not come home. The last thing his mother did was promise I would never see him again. With the pain of continual loss, the urge to take my life welled up inside me again.

I remembered the One I found before, the one who had relieved my pain, so I searched for Him again. I had not been to church since the day I got saved after my suicide attempt. Admittedly, as someone who knew little about Christianity, I had been acting like God was a cosmic vending machine. After salvation, I expected life would get better and just by praying, and God would deliver.

Such was not the case. I prayed that God would return my son. My cosmic vending machine was out-of-order. I put in my token prayers but nothing came out. Maybe I was in the wrong church. I tried a few churches in the area but never regularly attended any of them. The only thing I saw was that I didn't fit in with church either. I saw Christians as hypocrites. They preached love and acceptance but I didn't see that in any church I visited. It felt lost, a lonely and desperately hurting person surrounded by a sea of people who didn't notice my existence.

3 7

L OOKING TO INCREASE MY INCOME, I TOOK A POSITION AT A sheltered workshop serving people with moderate to severe disabilities. The position was that of crew leader. In retrospect, it is clear to see how God was moving in my life; I was just unaware then.

The crew I supervised comprised twenty-five of the most handicapped people in the program. The average IQ of my team was thirty points. Not only were they dealing with mental challenges, many had physical ones too. Some of their challenges included severe deformities, Fetal Alcohol Syndrome, Fragile-X Syndrome, Down syndrome, Turrets, blindness, and crippling arthritis.

With no previous experience working with people in these conditions, it was intimidating in the beginning. The company had a difficult time keeping the position filled due to all the challenges, but the Lord knew exactly what He was doing placing me there.

The job developed characteristics such as perseverance, compassion, empathy toward others, and a love for details. I received a thank you award after my first month of service because no one lasted that long for quite some time.

It was a small token of appreciation, but it meant a lot to me. I felt like I mattered to someone. It also opened my eyes that there were people in far worse condition than me, and yet, they loved life. To have a job made them happy even if it was a piece rate position stuffing metal parts into a plastic bag. I soon grew to love my job, and my team responded well.

One of my favorites was a guy born with major deformities. His legs never formed in utero, his arms twisted like a thorn bush, blind in one eye, and had only 20% vision in the other. With no vocabulary, he used a system of grunts and noises to communicate. We were both in our early twenties but he looked like he was seventy years old.

I connected with him on a deeper level than previous crew leaders, and he loved to tease me with his work. As his production increased, he seemed to come out of his shell more. Although he never used words, we communicated well. I worked there for about eight months when he died in his sleep.

Andy's death was a huge loss for me. With no other friends, I was the only non-family member at his memorial service, and it was such an honor. He taught me so many things about life and the preciousness of human relationships. I will never forget him.

There were twenty-five people on my crew, each with their own story. Each life, each personality, had something valuable to teach me. I would never get rich working there, from a monetary perspective, but when I left I had amassed a great treasure from all the relationships I had built.

During the 1990's, the mall was the place for young people to hang out. I came upon a T-shirt shop where two artists painted shirts in an airbrush booth. In the evenings, and on the weekends, I hung out with the painters and we soon became friends.

I appreciate art and airbrush art was the rage then. My brain leans toward the artsy side, but I am also very analytical. I did a lot of studying besides hanging out and socializing. I studied people, shoppers, and wondered what made them tick. Why did they buy one item over another? What did their color choices say about them? I also wanted to see what attracted one person to another.

I discovered people with talent attracted others. For instance, there was a guitar shop across the hall from the T-shirt shop. The guys who worked there were not what you would call attractive, a couple were not even intelligent, but they had talent.

Most of the employees there could play multiple instruments. As a people watcher, I found it interesting how so many beautiful girls stopped to watch these guys play guitar or keyboard. The guys had such an air of confidence drawn from their talent, they drew a crowd.

The principle was also true for the airbrush artists. Neither of the two guys was anything special in the looks department but they always engaged people in conversation. This was fascinating, and I wondered if it would work for me.

My sister spent her summer break from college with me. One evening I took a pair of her white jeans to the T-shirt shop. Business was slow that night, so I asked if I could give the airbrush a try. Until then, I had only observed the other guys paint.

I slipped cardboard down one of the pant legs and sketched the outlines of letters and cartoon characters. With a couple test sprays through the airbrush, I set out to paint. I surprised even myself as I laid down the paint like I had experience. My artist friend could not believe he was seeing a guy with a hook, and no experience, paint those jeans. Thinking he found a prodigy, he taught me on the spot.

After a week of practice, I covered for the guys when they took a lunch or dinner break. Within a month I worked entire shifts so both guys could have some much needed time off. The best part of it all was I had opportunities to talk to people. It worked, talent draws people to you. These were the interactions I craved. It made me feel like I had a little value and the painting was fun too.

I wanted graphics painted on my car. It was a 1980 Buick Regal with faded paint. I paid $600 for the car at one of the many dumpy little used car lots around town.

If was never afraid of doing my own mechanical work. Armed with a little experience, I repainted the Regal a darker blue. Loaded with imperfections, the paint job improved the appearance slightly, and it would look better with airbrushed graphics.

My artist friend committed to painting the graphics, but he found multiple excuses to avoid doing it. Pro bono work was not motivating enough, I suppose.

After summer ended, my sister went back to college in Oklahoma. Since it looked like my son wasn't coming back, I wanted to downsize to a smaller place to reduce expenses. I found an apartment in the same complex where I lived when my son was born. After giving notice to vacate my current apartment, the new place let me know they somehow double rented the unit. Someone else moved into it a week earlier.

Rentals were difficult to find then, and unable find anything else; I tried to rescind my notice to vacate. The leasing office already rented my old unit to someone else and could change nothing. Within days I found myself with nowhere to go, so I slept in my car.

I rented a storage unit to paint the car in so I moved all my belongings into it and lived out of my car. At my day job, I would arrive early to use the restroom and sponge bathe to get ready for work. After a month of doing this, my supervisor approached me and let me know it was against company policy. An embarrassing conversation to have for both of us.

After asking how I found myself in the predicament, she offered a room at her place for a low rent. The price was right, so I agreed. An attractive lady, about twenty years older, I thought we would have no problem living together since we had a platonic work relationship. At the condo, we rarely saw each other as I was only home to sleep.

My car broke down, the transmission failed. While it was in the shop, I rode to work with my boss which was humbling. I'm not aware if anyone else in the office knew we were roommates, but I never discussed it with anyone.

Since I was homebound while my car got repaired, I didn't get to hang out at the mall much to paint. One Friday night after work, I ate an early dinner so I could get caught up on sleep. My boss/roommate had gone out to dinner with her sister. As I lay in bed, I watched a little television and fell asleep around 9 pm. Sometime around 2 am, I felt someone slip into bed beside me. I awoke to my roommate trying to have sex with me.

The average twenty-something single guy would have jumped on the opportunity, but I was not average. Though saved, I was not a practicing Christian. I reasoned I would only sleep with a girl if there was potential for marriage, but that was only half the problem. The other had to do with the damage caused by my mom's second husband. I had no intentions of marrying her, and she snuck into bed behind me, uninvited, and with one arm around my neck, she grabbed my genitals with the other. Her approach triggering as it brought back painful memories from the molestation I suffered as a child.

Resistance to her advances spelled the end of my housing situation, which meant I once again had to search for a place to live. As awkward as things became afterward, she allowed me time to find a place rather than booting me out to live in my car again.

I found a place, but I needed paperwork from the storage unit for the leasing agent. My car had come back from the shop so after the mall closed I drove over to the storage facility to look for the papers. As I rifled through boxes, it made sense to load things in the trunk to prepare for moving.

I packed the trunk with whatever I could stuff into it and placed a baseball bat in the front passenger seat. A comical sight, I remember how funny I looked that night wearing a pair of airbrushed white jeans and a long black trench coat. The movie "GoodFellas" came to mind, and I chuckled when I realized how much I looked like a character from the movie, ready to break someone's knee caps.

By the time I finished up at the storage unit, it was after midnight before I started back to my roommate's place. I was the only car on the road until I approached the last light before turning toward the condo complex. I stopped at the light, in the far right lane and a police car pulled up to my left. Without a second thought, I turned right.

I got about thirty feet down the road when I noticed the police car made a right turn from the center lane and sped after me. He turned on the red and blue lights as I turned into the condo's parking lot. The police cruiser blocked me in after I parked.

I didn't think I had done anything to attract his attention, but I was nervous just the same. The spotlight from the police car was blinding. As one who tried to avoid life's spotlight, the irony of the situation was almost comical. With all the bright lights, I pictured all the neighbors watching me like an episode of "Cops".

Just before the officer walked up to my window, I realized I was about to be in big trouble. After purchasing the car from the used car lot, I had been unsuccessful in getting the title to the car. It had Michigan plates and in the meantime, the tabs had expired. Without the title, or a bill of sale, I could not register the car in Colorado, or get it insured. To make matters worse, I had falsified the tabs on the license plate using electrical tape. I was just trying to extend the time on them hoping I would get the documents needed from the car dealership.

It was the poor job I did on the tabs that caught the officer's attention. He approached my driver's side window and his flashlight added to the intensity. Looking in the car, he noticed the baseball bat in the front passenger seat. My choice in clothing made him all the more suspicious. The next thing I knew, there was a service revolver pointed at me and the officer ordered me to get out of the car. He ordered me to lie face down on the pavement with my arms spread wide. The officer inspected my car and, finding no other weapons, removed the baseball bat from the car.

He asked what I was doing out so late. I gave him the truth and then he asked for my license, registration and insurance card. With only a driver's license in my possession, I gave him the details of the transaction and he was familiar with the particular car dealership. The problem was I could prove none of it.

The officer asked me to sit in the back of his police car while he rummaged through the rest of my car, including the trunk. It looked like I was about to find a new residence, and it wasn't the apartment I was trying to rent. I thought I would go to jail.

As it appeared to the officer, at least on the surface; no proof of ownership; grand theft auto, no proof of insurance; I would have to carry an SR-22 notation, my car was full of random items which looked like stolen property; theft, and I had on a trench coat and airbrushed jeans, with a baseball bat beside my seat. I knew it looked bad, but I also knew I was not a criminal. Unfortunately, I was not the one charged with determining my innocence.

After an hour in the backseat of the police car, the officer brought me to the front seat. He rattled off a list of charges he could press which would cause my immediate arrest. He seemed to believe my story but said there had been a series of recent break-ins, to both homes and storage units.

Convinced I stole none of it because I could list off all the contents of the car, the officer pressed no theft charges. He regarded me guilty of driving a car without proper registration, insurance, or a bill of sale. I had also falsified the vehicle tabs. He did not arrest me, but he had to impound the car. I could not remove a single thing from the car. The tow truck showed up a few minutes later and took the car to the impound yard.

The officer dismissed me with citations along with instructions on how to retrieve the car from impound. I would need to have the title, bill of sale, proof of insurance, and pay the impound fee of $150 to get the car out. After seven days, storage fees would be added at a rate of $7 per day.

The impound personnel, following standard operating procedure, contacted the last registered owner of the vehicle. The previous owner said he had traded the vehicle at the dealership from which I had purchased the car. They notified the dealership who then sent a guy down with the title to retrieve the car, to include my belongings in the trunk. The fraudulent car dealership found another victim in me. He had done this with thirty other people and after retrieving my car, he packed up and moved out of state.

These were details I learned when I went to court to respond to the traffic citations. During the court proceedings, my anxiety level reached maximum level as I saw people ahead of me stand before the judge.

The judge seemed in a rather bad mood because she handed down severe sentences. The worst case was a gentleman in front of me. His offense was "improper backing". He backed out of a parking spot at the mall and tapped another car backing out at the same time. There was only minor damage and his insurance covered it.

The man must have been in his seventies and I thought he had a heart attack when the judge gave his sentence. The judge ordered he pay a fine of $1,000, do 240 hours of community service, and spend ninety days in jail. Based on this, and the other harsh things I saw, I figured I would go directly to jail. It was now my turn to stand before the judge.

After reading the charges, the judge asked me several questions, one of which was the location and name of the business from which I had purchased the car. The judge was familiar with the scam this guy ran and considering that fact, she had mercy on me. Instead of jail time, I had to pay a $500 fine and serve 160 hours of community service. The district attorney asked if I would take part as a witness in a case he was putting together against the car salesman. I paid my fine and completed my service hours, but they never called me to be a witness.

After a rough few days of dealing with that mess, it was time to move into my apartment. With the city bus as my ride, it would not work well moving my stuff into the apartment. Another co-worker came to help me move with a truck.

At the storage unit, I saw my padlock was missing from the door. I opened the roll-up door to find most everything in the unit gone. Loose papers and remnants was all that remained. I stood there in disbelief, wondering what I would do next. I reported the theft at the office but the guy behind the counter pointed me to the sign that relieved the facility of responsibility for lost or stolen property. He said I could report it to the police but they would never find my stuff.

That move ended up being the easiest one I have ever done. All I had left to my name was the clothing in the closet at my roommates place. My co-worker helped me get my clothes, and I moved into my new place with nothing else.

Those dark thoughts of suicide reared their ugly heads again. Only this time, with my shallow knowledge of Christianity, I thought I would go to hell if I took my life. It sure felt like I was already getting a taste of it on Earth.

Rather than kill myself, I got the idea God would intervene and take me out when I turned thirty. I just needed strength to endure life another seven years and then I could say goodbye to misery.

3 8

IN THE INTERIM, AS I WAITED FOR THE DAY WHEN GOD would wipe me out, I continued to stumble along the path of life's journey. I found another part-time job as a waiter in a pizza restaurant. I worked three jobs, still trying to make ends meet.

My goal was to again meet the requirements imposed by the court to have my son live with me. One attorney said I must be able to prove I met all the requirements beforehand. If we turned the tables, and my son left my custody to live with his mother, he said those requirements would not apply to her. He said, "The mother could be homeless, living in a cardboard box under a bridge, and the judge would still grant custody to her over you. You must comply before your son comes back."

Though I stood in a deep valley, wanting relief from all the pain, I kept pushing for the pinnacle. Working three jobs gave me the ability to fill my empty apartment with furnishings. Since one job was at a pizza restaurant, I could count on a free meal most days. On my off days, I would eat biscuits with jelly, or if I wanted to spice things up, I made buttered noodles.

I knew eating this way was unhealthy, but I didn't care. The great depression continued though I would have argued with anyone who considered me depressed; oppressed for sure, but never depressed.

In Colorado Springs, I got involved in a couple different relationships. Both times the ladies agreed to join me at church for the first date. I thought my first relationship opened well, her not so much. I wanted marriage before sex. A fantastic girl though she was, she did not ascribe to the same beliefs. She believed in the doctrine of compatibility, especially in the areas of passion. Sexual compatibility was her prerequisite to marriage.

I thought the act of sexual intercourse between any male and female was the same, regardless of partner choice. What made it special was the bond the couple shared, but that was too old fashioned in her opinion and she ended the relationship.

The other relationship almost led to marriage. An attractive single mom, she lived at home with her parents, trying to make ends meet. Attracted by more than her physical appearances, she had a son about the same age as mine. The silent motive driving the relationship was to fill the void in my heart left by the loss of my son.

I tried to keep my standards on the purity issue but succumbed to the pressure. After we got engaged, the relationship ended, heaping more emotional baggage onto the pile. We both brought a lot of baggage into the relationship, and it would have been a marriage doomed from the start. Though it was a relationship I regret, my greater concern was the compounded misery it caused her son. I wanted a covenant relationship, not a convenient one. I was sick of getting dumped for asinine reasons; the hook, the glasses, my hair color, and the list goes on. I wanted someone willing to honor the classic vow, "Til death do us part."

Alone, I was in another new apartment. I had so many addresses I lost count. While living in this apartment, something shifted. For too long I tried to figure out my true identity, but had been doing so through the lenses of others.

In the new place, having avoided a train wreck marriage, I did a little contemplative self-reflection. Where did I fall short, what part of me wasn't good enough? I read books on anthropology to get a better understanding of human behaviors. If I could better understand others, maybe I would better understand myself. I was moving in a better direction, just not the best pathway.

While reading a book about anthropology, I fell asleep. Awakened from a bad dream by the ringing of the telephone, I noticed the time was 1 am. Who would call me at that hour? I answered the phone to a chipper sounding step-father calling from Germany. He apologized for the time but said he felt compelled to check on me.

It was odd he called at that moment, ending the nightmare I was having. I never shared the graphic details of my life because I didn't want my parents to worry, being halfway around the globe. We talked for a few minutes; pleasantries and small talk were the jist of the conversation. After the call, I resumed my slumber, and the dream reoccurred. At the same critical point in my dream, the phone rang again. It was my step-father, and this time it was after 3 am local time. He thought there was still something I needed to get off my chest, and he wanted me to know he was available if I needed to talk. After more small talk, I still couldn't discuss the dreams.

In those dreams, I pictured myself on a beautiful beach, lying face down on a towel, soaking up the sun. The sand enveloped me until all that remained exposed was my head. I fought hard to break free, but the sand paralyzed me.

I turned my face toward the ocean and something in the distance caught my eye. Whatever it was, it appeared to be moving in my direction. It looked like the head of a seal popping up above the water line. As the figure advanced, people in the area fled screaming, until I was the only person left. It continued moving toward me, rising as the water became shallow. Still a distance away, I struggled to see with the bright glare of sunlight reflecting off the water. The figure rose from the sea, silhouetted by the sun, and I could see it had a human form.

Scary enough was a human being walking up out of the ocean, but as it drew near, I recognized who it was. It was Robert, my mom's second husband, and he was naked.

As he stood over me, the sand spit me back up to the surface. I remained paralyzed, unable to move anything below my neck. When this monstrous man placed his body on top of mine, with intent to sodomize me, the phone rang and snapped me back into reality.

I never had the dream again, but the visual was so strong I never forgot it. Over the next few years, images from the dream popped into my mind like a random flashback. I didn't understand what it meant or why they kept coming to remembrance.

My parents spent a total of five years stationed in Germany. That one night was the only time my step-father ever called me at those hours. The dreams held a vital message, but it would take years to decipher.

I found a little success in gaining material possessions over the next couple of years. After having lost everything I owned, a few times, I re-established my home with furnishings. I had even purchased my first brand new car. As for personal relationships, that was a different story. I had a long road to hoe in that arena. After all that transpired since my wife walked out, I lost all ability to trust people.

I wanted to love and have someone love me in return, but found it difficult to believe people, especially women. I had been lied to, lied about, cheated, cheated on, and robbed so many times I had closed my heart to the outside world.

When my parents transferred back from Germany, they found their home ransacked. The couple I had rented the house to only paid rent a few times, and it took two years to get them out after serving them with an eviction. They took the ceiling fans, put holes in the walls, stacked a bunch of used tires in the house, and broke the toilet.

I felt so guilty about what happened there since my folks had entrusted me with their home. It was a major failure in responsibility on my part. It took half the original cost of the home to restore it, resulting in a second mortgage.

My mom called to say how the repairs were going, and I wished I could be there to help them get the house back to normal. My parents never held that over my head, but I beat myself up over it for years. They always expressed that I was welcome to come back home anytime and during a random conversation one day, my step-father told me I should just do just that.

He told me to get packed and ready to go in ten hours because he was coming to get me. I dismissed him thinking he was joking. I was two months into a one-year lease agreement. Ten hours later, he and a good friend were at my doorstep ready to load my stuff. I thought he was kidding and had packed nothing. Did I even want to do this?

"What about my job and my lease?" I asked. To these two guys none of that mattered, they were on a rescue mission. I'm sure they sensed something wasn't right with me. Had they known the full scope of my experiences, I'm certain they would have been there sooner. The polished version of the story is what I gave to my family because I wanted them to see me as successful and be proud of me. I felt like a constant failure, and if they knew the truth, it would disappoint them.

I called my work and left a message stating I was leaving town and provided an address to send my final pay. The leasing office got the same message, but their response was not kind. They sued me and ended up collecting the rest of the lease, plus attorney fees, by way of garnishment.

Once again my parents allowed me to stay in their home rent free. That was helpful since my take-home pay was garnished to pay for the apartment I no longer lived in.

Back at home in Lawton, I found work on Fort Sill at the Post Exchange. I started as a part-time cashier at the main branch with a weekly schedule of 2-19 hours, not even a livable wage. They always gave me the full 19 hours per week which allowed me to keep my car. I worked in that position for two months until a full-time position opened in the customer service department. I applied for and got the Customer Service Supervisor position.

Pouring myself into my work impressed my superiors. I worked hard to prove myself.   A little character trait which had been festering, manifested. To others, it looked like a strong work ethic, but it was more deep-seated than that.

Everything I attempted had to be perfect. If I didn't feel it was up to the high standards I set for myself, then I felt like a failure again. It was a vicious cycle that sometimes seemed like a war raging inside of me. All my co-workers saw was a real go-getter of an employee.

A couple people took exception to my behavior, thinking I was just being a show-off or trying to make others look bad. That has never been my motivation. I have never thought I was better than anyone else; it had always been an internal struggle trying to prove myself worthy.

I took every elective training course the company offered. After two months as the Customer Service Supervisor, I applied for another open position and got it. The position was Night Supervisor at the fueling station. One perk of that position was a set schedule, a rarity in the retail sales world.

Meanwhile, my brother and sister came home for a family reunion. It had been six years since we lived in the same town. My brother had married, and they were expecting their first child. He moved his family back to Lawton a few days prior, and they were staying in our parents' house too. My sister lived in Minnesota where she started her career as a Veterinarian.

The dream I had back in Colorado kept coming back to mind. I had pondered the dream's meaning many times since it occurred a couple years prior. Mustering the courage, I asked my brother and sister to meet me on the front porch as I had something personal I needed to discuss with them.

As a means of survival, I repressed the memories of what my father and first step-father had done. I knew my siblings endured many of the same things and I wanted to bring the issues to the light.

We met on the porch, and not wanting to beat around the bush, I dove straight in. I shared the dreams involving Robert, and how I awoke twice, at the exact point in the dream by Charles, who we now referred to as our dad. By interrupting the dreams dad was coming to my rescue, the way he had when he came into our lives.

The discussion stunned both siblings. They, too, had repressed memories. Neither of them had discussed the issues with anyone since they occurred. As I shared, they both recalled similar details and events.

Something I learned when dabbling in the study of anthropology, for healing to take place, one has talk about the pain to work through it. If we keep wounds bottled up inside, at some point we will explode.

We all agreed these things happened and that we should broach the subject with our mom. We asked her to join us on the porch. No one knew how to start the conversation so I blurted it out. Mom listened as her three grown children described the terrible things we endured. Blindsided by this revelation, her first response was common in situations like these - denial.

To think her husband molested all three of her kids must have hit her like a ton of bricks. After telling our stories, mom acted like we had been mean to her. I realize today it was a coping mechanism. For another twenty years no one discussed it. We crammed our "skeletons" back into the closet, with no intentions to open the door again. For myself, I returned to what I knew how to do, bury the pain.

39

FOUR YEARS HAD PASSED SINCE LAST I SAW MY SON. EVERY year, on his birthday I would bake a cake in his honor. As I celebrated his sixth birthday with his grandparents, there was still no sign of him. Determined as ever to provide a good life for him if/when he returned, I continued to pour myself into my work. I took every online course the company offered to improve my chances of upward mobility.

One manager noticed all the effort I put in and recommended I apply for the fast track program. After I got accepted, someone from the Dallas headquarters invited me to appear in a training video the company was filming about diversity in the workplace. After the video production wrapped, an opportunity came along I couldn't pass up.

A promotion to management level was the next move, but it involved relocation. Living in Oklahoma was never my idea of fun. When presented with an opportunity to transfer, I was more than interested. I took a promotion to Assistant Manager at Thule Air Force Base, in Greenland.

The adage, *"Be careful what you wish for..."* had a new meaning with that transfer. My car and belongings stored with my parents, I set out on a new journey. Serving at such a remote facility was a career jump starter. If a person could spend a year in a remote and isolated outpost and not go crazy, then they were all but guaranteed to become a facility manager.

I packed a couple suitcases and boarded a plane. I flew from Oklahoma to Philadelphia, and then caught a bus to Fort Dix, New

Jersey. From there I flew to Thule on an Air Force C-141 cargo plane, a six-hour flight, cruising at 35,000 feet with no heat in the passenger area. The plane carried cargo, so it had no standard airline accommodations and to top it off, the seats faced the tail of the plane. With so little information provided before traveling, I was ill prepared.

The first week of January 1994 the temperature was eighty-five degrees Fahrenheit, below zero. With the wind chill factored in it felt like one hundred ten degrees below. A slight wind blew as we got off the plane to begin the three hundred fifty yard death march across the tarmac to the terminal building. The plane ride was cold enough.

I had on a pair of tennis shoes, blue jeans, a t-shirt, and a suede jacket. When we landed, I was cold to the bone and nauseous from flying rear-facing. The first stop on the agenda was to pick up cold weather gear; Arctic necessities such as muclucs (fur-lined boots) and a parka (fur-lined hooded coat) helped take the bite away from the cold temperature.

The next order of business was lodging. On the bottom floor of a three-story barrack was my room, home for the next year. It was across the hall from the community room, which included table games, a TV, and a complete kitchen. At first I liked the location but soon found out why no one else wanted it.

The community room could get loud and rowdy, especially if folks were drinking. It was difficult to get any sleep due to the noise. While I appreciate diversity, the culinary delights prepared in the kitchen took getting used to.

Our store closed on Mondays so the staff could rest. Not long after arriving on base, perhaps within the first few weeks, I had slept in on a Monday when my sense of smell came under full assault. An unknown delicacy was being cooked, or burned, in the kitchen. The aroma woke me from a deep sleep.

I have experienced stinky food in the past but that odor surpassed anything I had, or have since experienced. It was so overpowering I had to open the windows in my room and take deep breaths of frozen arctic air. When I opened the door and stepped into the hallway, the intensity multiplied tenfold.

I poked my head inside the room to find several people waiting to enjoy whatever was cooking in the kitchen. Someone invited me to join them. Not wanting to appear disrespectful, I asked what was on the menu. With twinkles in their eyes, and saliva dripping from their mouths, together in unison they said, "SEAL BLUBBER!"

A picky eater most of my life, it's always awkward when others offer me food. I never want to offend anyone so it's always challenging to decline. For most, eating is a near magical experience. People come together over a meal. For me, eating is

145

nowhere near magical; it's almost like a chore. While so many live to eat, I eat to live.

I avoided eating the seal blubber while maintaining good relations with my new Inuit and Danish friends. They tried again to get me to sample a different delicacy, whale skin. It was fascinating to watch folks munch on raw skin an inch thick, but there was no way I would eat that either. I am grateful for those who always included me, but even more so they didn't take offense when I declined.

There were so many exciting things I experienced in Greenland. A tough assignment for certain, but the experience will last a lifetime.

One highlight was when a civilian crew came to retrieve an old World War II airplane which had gone down just north of the base. The B-29, known as the *Kee Bird*, had crash landed in 1947 after running out of fuel. Frozen in the ice for forty-seven years, a group from the United States attempted to retrieve the plane.

Five of the eight original crew members flew in to witness the plane's escape from the ice. One man gave me an autographed copy of a narrative he had written about the crash.

The day had come to fly the plane back to Thule, and the veterans waited in the Base Exchange listening to the radio traffic. Then the news no one expected came across the air, the plane caught fire and burned to the ground. What a sad moment that was. So much time, money, and effort wasted as the engineers watched it burn. Tears streamed down faces as we heard the devastating news.

Each of the five veterans returned home just like they had forty-seven years prior, without their beloved airplane. For more information on the Kee Bird, Nova produced a great documentary in 1996 called "B-29 Frozen In Time".

Few people ever get the pleasure of reaching into pristine arctic waters to grab handfuls of giant shrimp. Fewer still experience the thrill of flying a small plane over the ice covered bay at Thule, or circle the North Pole in the cockpit of a C-130 airplane. I also spent a day at the Canadian outpost, known as RFS Alert, the northern most tip of land before the solid ice cap which covers the top of the world. If we felt isolated with 1,500 people at Thule; imagine the Canadians, who operated their base with a crew of ninety.

Perhaps the greatest thing about enduring the isolation of a remote outpost was I learned how to trust people a little more. I learned how to build genuine relationships with others. My interactions with other cultures taught me to see the beauty of humanity through different lenses. My paradigm shifted.

40

THE RESULT OF ALL MY HARD WORK IN GREENLAND WAS A promotion to store manager at a little place known as Rock Island Arsenal. On a tiny island in the Mississippi River, 2-1/2 hours west of Chicago, RIA is a small Army installation with few active duty troops stationed there. Most of my business came from the retired community, predominantly World War II veterans.

I had on my dream sheet of desired duty stations a couple assignments on tropical islands. I got stationed to two islands, both were anything but tropical. The area surrounding Rock Island is called the Quad Cities.

The weather in the Quad City area proved far worse than Thule. In Greenland snowfall was rare, mostly ice crystals blowing from the glaciers, but it was not uncommon to see twenty inches of snow accumulate overnight in the Quad Cities. I spent fourteen months at that duty station so I was unlucky enough to go through two winters during my stay. I have never been a fan of snow but that assignment created within me a disdain for the stuff that has endured to this day.

When I first arrived in town, I rented a garden level apartment. The floor was about four feet below the surface of the land. It was a noisy place to live. Cars would back into their parking spaces, pumping carbon monoxide into my windows. The tenants above wore concrete shoes and danced across the floor, maybe even pirouetted. At the end of my lease I looked for a house to rent, but finding one available proved difficult. A customer of mine was trying to help his mother get her rental home occupied. He had trouble finding tenants due to the property being next to a large cemetery. I didn't have a problem with living next to a cemetery, so long as the residents remained six feet under. To seal the deal, they offered the place for only $200 per month. I moved in on that deal, and though I sometimes played my music loud enough to wake the dead, I had no visitors from the grave.

I got through the first winter to enjoy the warmth of summer temperatures. My store closed at 6 pm daily so after work I spent a lot of time at a little park facing the river. Without a social life I went to the park to read and watch the river traffic.

With reading a new pastime, I investigated books on Christianity. At twenty-seven, and five years into it, my faith had grown a little. I had gone to church a few times but never studied the Bible much. What began as a curiosity that summer, turned into a hunger for knowledge, and I spent many hours at the river reading books on faith. With the long hours of summer days, I would sometimes forget about dinner in my quest to learn.

It must have been a Monday evening, while reading in the park I sensed an urgent need to be in church, at that instant. Odd because I did not attend church then, and it was difficult to even think of a church location nearby. I dismissed the urge and continued to read. I don't recall the title of the book I was reading but the longer I read, the more I sensed an urgency to be in a church. The impression was strange, and very foreign, but it persisted as I headed home to make dinner.

As I turned onto the street where I lived, it was just a straight shot of about twelve blocks to my house. About three or four blocks from home I slammed on the brakes to make an immediate left turn. Some force other than my own caused me to alter my course. I pulled into the parking lot of a tiny church and walked up to the front door.

Pulling on the handle of both doors, I found them locked. I stood there thinking to myself how crazy it must look for me to be trying to get into a church at 7:30 pm on a Monday night. I didn't see service times listed anywhere on the front wall so I peered through the stain glass window next to the doors. The doors opened, and a man asked if I needed help. I told him I needed to be in church at that moment. "You are being washed by the Holy Spirit right now," he stated. He may as well have been speaking another language as I didn't understand what he meant. He invited me in and said I could sit in any pew, for as long as I needed to.

I chose a pew in the back of the sanctuary. All alone in the room, I felt the most amazing peace wash over me. I stayed for ten or fifteen minutes, waiting to see or hear something, but nothing came. A skeptic by nature, even though an unknown peace came over me during those few minutes in the quiet sanctuary, I got up and walked toward the door. As we crossed paths, the minister invited me back for service and gave me the schedule.

At home, as I reflected on the day's events, I decided it must have been a fluke experience I had visiting the church. The more I thought about it, the more concerned I became thinking I had experienced something occultist. The issue moved to the back burner, I returned to being me; a broken individual unaware of his brokenness, striving for perfection and purpose.

I continued to read religious books but never darkened the door of another church the entire time I was in that area. In my mind, the church was full of hypocrites anyway, and I thought it would be best to find God on my own terms. My experiences with the church had been people acting nice and welcoming on Sunday, but ignoring me any other day of the week.

My struggle with perfectionism blinded me to the reality of being a very broken person, in deep need of healing and restoration. I continued on the well-worn path I had always traveled. Along the way, I crossed paths with a girl I found attractive and we dated. The relationship had many problems, the main one was me. My brokenness contributed to the pain in her life. The relationship soon ended, a good thing for both parties. After it ended though, the defeated feeling persisted, and I longed for my situation to change. I needed to get away.

At work I applied for a position on the Contingency Team. They were a group of managers available for deployment anywhere in the world to support the troops in "hot spots". Accepted to the team, I had hopes of going to the Dominican Republic to support "Operation Uphold Democracy". I thought I would finally make it to that tropical island assignment I dreamed of. It was not to be. The company had that operation staffed, but a few weeks later I received deployment orders to the Former Republic of Yugoslavia to support "Operation Joint Endeavor".

President Clinton announced to the American people he was sending US troops into the area on a joint peacekeeping mission for a twelve month duration. My deployment orders were for thirty days, returning to Rock Island to resume my post afterward.

The protocol going into this deployment required I prepare for an extension of up to one year. Preparation for long term deployment included placing all my stuff in storage, vacating my residence, and storing my vehicle.

As I prepared to go, the newspaper back in Lawton named me in a blurb about the deployment to Bosnia. One of my former brothers-in-law read the article and alerted my ex-wife. Out of the blue one day, I received a collect call from Denise asking about the article. After years of silence, I hoped to speak with my son and wish him a happy belated birthday. His birthday never passed without me celebrating him even if it was just a party of one.

I told my ex-wife I was due to ship out in the next few weeks. She insisted I was lying. Based on her experience in the actual military, she said civilians never deployed into war zones with troops. I changed the subject to avoid arguing with her and asked to speak to my son. I had not seen my boy, or heard his voice, for over six years. She claimed he was not available, but she provided me with a long list of items he needed for Boy Scouts.

I purchased all the items from the list. It was near Christmas so I included a few gifts too. I took the stuff to work to have one of my co-workers inventory the box. We wrote out a list and she signed it as a witness. I wanted proof of my provision to use in court if that became necessary. I had the package sent with a signature required, return receipt request, as another means of proving that I did what I said I would.

A neighbor of hers received the package, signing for it with his name, so proof of delivery was worthless. I'm positive my son never knew the package came from me.

Denise called again to discuss my deployment. When asked, she would not confirm receipt of the package. Again, she refused to let me speak to my son. She delved into another rant and ended the call by threatening to sue me again for alimony and child support. She continued to trample my rights to visitation with my son.

I was down to the final preparations for deployment, which included getting the series of vaccinations required for international travel. Once that was complete, all that remained was to lock my belongings up in storage and park my truck. I left my truck with my parents in Oklahoma for safekeeping. From Lawton I took a flight to Fort Benning, GA where I would go through a mini basic training course, an abridged version what actual soldiers do.

Once on the plane bound for Georgia, all I had in my possession was a couple sets of clothes, and that was only temporary. At Fort Benning, I was issued military gear and uniforms. From there I had to send all my civilian possessions back home.

For the entire trip, I remained glued to the television as news reports came in about the deployment. Christmas 1995, I spent learning what our brave men and women go through when called to overseas duty. It was both exhilarating and frightening, and it all happened so fast.

41

I T WAS SURREAL TO BE AT FORT BENNING AGAIN. MY FATHER
transferred there after returning from Thailand. As I look back
from my current vantage point, it's easy to see God at work in my
life, even then.

Fort Benning, twenty-three years prior, almost to the date, my
family came together after losing my hand in Thailand. It was there
I met Desmond, the kid who brought me out of my shell through his
accepting friendship and Big Wheel racing.

My biological father found out I was at Fort Benning so he came
for a visit. He arranged a surprise I could never have expected. As
my father and I discussed all things deployment, someone knocked
on the door.

It was my old friend Desmond. Together again, after more
than twenty years! When a connection happens with a true friend,
time and distance between are irrelevant.

A visit from this special friend encouraged me the same way he
had all those years ago. If my father did nothing else for me, he had
done something good in organizing this reunion.

I could not leave the base and only had limited free time before
training started; so we stayed in the room and talked about our life
experiences. I pray for the opportunity to cross paths again
someday. Maybe we can race big wheels again, the adult version.

On to basic training. While at Fort Benning, the goal of our military
hosts was to weed out those they felt wouldn't do well being
deployed. The mission of IFOR was one of keeping the peace, but

the risk of danger was high as the civil war had been going on in Yugoslavia for decades. To make things more difficult, it was near impossible for Americans to discern the differences between warring factions. We needed to protect ourselves in the event of a hostile situation.

As an amputee, I have faced discrimination over the years, from individuals and employers alike. It's ironic to think, as a civilian, I was taking part in something the military denied ten years earlier. I remembered the Army recruiter who laughed at me when I attempted to join right out of high school. Let's see, what was the comment he made before I left his office? Oh yeah, it was "Don't tell me you came in to sign up, because you'll never make it in this man's Army!"

His comments fueled my desire to prove to him, and everyone else who ever doubted me, just how wrong they were. I would show them all. If formation was at 5:30 am, I was there at 5:15. If asked to do twenty pushups, I did thirty. Whatever they asked, I gave more. Every challenge I passed without issue.

Like the recruiter, one soldier viewed me as nothing more than a liability to the mission. He noticed I was passing the tests, and whether someone told him to, or he wanted to do so, he became my permanent drill instructor. He was a man on a mission, to disqualify me and send me home. It wasn't hard to pick up on his vibe but I used it to increase my motivation. I had nothing against the guy but he personified every person who ever picked on me or treated as garbage. The guy was relentless.

Determined he would not beat me, I passed every challenge, every hurdle, every test he pushed at me. I didn't always score in the top but I passed.

Next on the docket was weapons qualification. By that point I was feeling a lot of rage. I wanted to get my hands on an M-16 rifle and let loose on the targets. I wanted to feel the power which comes from blowing stuff up with a machine gun.

Because my civilian rank was GS-7, the equivalent rank in the Army was that of an O-3, or Captain. As an officer, I had to qualify on the 9mm pistol rather than the M-16. That bothered me for a couple reasons. First, I wanted to shred stuff with a machine gun. Second, I was nervous this would be the one test I failed because it involved reloading ammo clips while firing non-stop at pop-up and moving targets. I had only handled a gun during my attempt at suicide six years earlier.

Walking onto the range was nerve racking, especially when I saw my drill instructor waiting for me with a big Cheshire cat style grin on his face. This was the event he had been waiting for, the one where he could send me packing after I failed to qualify.

There was no practice. It was go big, or go home.

I got into position and listened to the instructions. There were several scenarios I would have to tackle but the one I most recall was the final one. It involved hitting fifty enemy targets in two minutes. I would have to change out clips and pull back the slide, a maneuver no one suspected I could do.

I picked up the weapon. When he gave the signal, I chambered that first round with ease. I amazed even myself when I dropped the clip and inserted a new one, pulled back the slide, and continued firing. When it was all over, I missed only one target, which qualified me at the level of an expert.

With my drill instructor reeling from his loss, he asked how I pulled it off. In jest, I replied, "Simple; I pictured the faces of people who had hurt me on the targets." With that comment, he sent me to get a psych exam.

I passed that test too and got back into formation. When he saw me return to the group, the drill instructor stood there shaking his head in disbelief. He thought he had me. Medical evaluations were all that remained.

I marched through those with no problem, including the test for AIDS. After everything my first wife put me through, testing negative for HIV was a relief. In relation to Denise, it was the only time something negative meant something positive.

The final item on the checklist was a visit to the dentist. The dental exam showed a small cavity in need of a filling. At first glance, the dentist flagged my record "Non-Deployable", which made my drill instructor do the happy dance. Another doctor looked at the record and informed my dentist the deployment order was for a term of only thirty days. The recommendation was to have a filling done within six months. The dentist retrieved my file and scratched through the word "Non", giving me the green light to go ahead with the deployment.

The drill instructor had no choice but to give the final signature approving me to go. Early the next morning busses shuttled our team to the post office where we packed our civilian clothes into boxes and shipped them home. From there the busses took us to the airport in Atlanta where we boarded a flight to Frankfurt, Germany.

In Germany we received gas mask and cold weather training. We also trained in land mine safety. Land mines were the greatest threat. The instructor explained that the estimated time to remove every land mine in the six states making up the Former Republic of Yugoslavia was thirty years.

After two weeks of training in Germany, we received our post assignments. There were several incidences of sniper fire around Tuzla, Bosnia so I was glad to know I wasn't going there.

There had been reports of a camp flooding due to heavy snowfall, followed by warmer rain. That was the site selected for me. While those in charge worked out the logistics, I hoped to fly into my post on a Blackhawk helicopter.

Some people flew in by Blackhawk, others by C-130 cargo plane, and still others by land convoy, which was the mode of travel selected for me. I wasn't pleased about it but I had no say in the matter.

Life's pathway is less about the destination, and more about the journey. Such was the case for that deployment. A nearby post needed a vehicle, so it made sense to send my colleague and me by land.

We had seven vehicles in our convoy, each with a driver from facilities in Germany. The drivers returned home by air once they delivered the vehicles and personnel to their final destinations. Each person in the vehicle carried four full duffle bags. The bags contained our military gear; canteens, boots, Kevlar vests, helmets, gas masks, and clothing.

For all intents and purposes, we looked just like a military convoy, except not a one of us had a weapon. We set off from Germany bound for Hungary. AAFES operated two stores in the area to support the troops stationed there. The main branch at Kaposvar was a staging hub of sorts. The second facility at Taszar, a few miles east, housed an airstrip.

Passing through Austria during the day, it was beautiful to see the ski slopes and watch the skiers go downhill, passing under the autobahn as we drove by. After driving several hours, we arrived at the border checkpoint. It surprised us to learn we were at the border of Austria and Slovenia, instead of the Hungarian border.

In the dark, somewhere along the way we had missed a turn which would have taken us east instead of south. Slovenian soldiers at the checkpoint were not aware of a convoy of Americans passing though. Language was a barrier but my driver, being a German citizen, could communicate. Many people across Europe speak German.

Unaffected by the civil war, Slovenia functioned in a state of high alert. Try to imagine how we looked to the Slovenian soldiers, a group of twenty-eight people dressed in American Battle Dress Uniforms, traveling in seven vehicles loaded with military gear. Our leader explained the team's mission was to provide potato chips and Beenie-Weenies to American soldiers in Croatia. They bought none of our explanation.

With orders to exit our vehicles, we stood off to one side, guarded by soldiers with machine guns pointed at us, as other soldiers searched our vehicles for weapons. After waiting so long, several of our team requested use of the restroom. Armed soldiers escorted everyone, including the ladies, in and out. No one had privacy.

Several hours later, the Slovenian soldiers granted entrance to their country, by permission of the President of Slovenia himself. Our team huddled together to hear the update and though we had access, the directions given did not lead us to Hungary.

Our leadership felt we were being set up for an ambush so they devised a quick plan. We got back in our vehicles and entered Slovenia. We drove a couple miles until we were out of sight of the checkpoint. Our convoy made a U-turn and passed back through the Austrian checkpoint without incident, as we headed northward to find the road we had missed. The Slovenian soldiers just glared at us while the Austrians stamped our passports and waved us through.

We finally arrived in Kaposvar in the wee hours of the morning. The company had rented a house for us to use but it was already full of people. We had to step over sleeping bodies to find places on the floor to sleep. We lost several hours of critical time due to the little side excursion into Slovenia.

After only a couple hours sleep, we boarded a bus to the air base. Some people in our convoy were due to board flights within the hour so we had to hustle to get everyone to the staging area. In quick order, people dispatched to their posts. Only Janice and I remained, with a final destination Camp Harmon.

This is when we realized Harmon was the camp featured on the news which flooded before Christmas. I questioned my decision to volunteer for this mission. Janice and I stayed another day or two, waiting to go by helicopter, but inclement weather kept us grounded. Old man winter pounded the area something fierce.

The crew chief sent us by car as flight conditions remained unsuitable. We gathered our things and loaded back into the Jeep Cherokee with the same driver who had driven us to Hungary.

As we traveled, we engaged in casual conversation about our families. Helga, our driver, worked at the Baumholder Exchange. I found that interesting because Baumholder is where my mom worked when they lived in Germany. When asked if she recognized my mom's name, Helga said she was her supervisor. What a chance encounter!

After leaving Kaposvar, we stopped in Pecs, Hungary for lunch at none other than McDonald's. I have never been a huge fan, but after several weeks of starving in Europe, the golden arches were a sight for sore eyes. We placed our order in the drive-through and when I heard the total, I almost fell over. Our order totaled more than eight thousand Forint; the equivalent of $30 in US currency. I wondered how it was for Hungarian children to learn math using such large numbers for so little merchandise.

Leaving Pecs with our McDonald's food, we continued the journey to Camp Harmon. The whole trip was supposed to be a three to four hour drive. After four hours without reaching our destination, we figured we got lost. Helga used the road atlas provided but there were not many signs along the road.

The clouds low, it was rainy and cold. No longer traveling on the autobahn, the country roads were just wide enough for one car, and some were unpaved. Helga tried to stay calm. On a straight open section of road, I noted her constant mirror checking. We had seen no other cars for a long time, and out of curiosity, I inquired as to our status.

Helga admitted to being lost, but that was the least of her worries. She checked the mirrors with more frequency. We were being followed. She pulled over to the roadside to glance at the map. The car following us also pulled over, stopping a short distance behind us. We rolled forward anther twenty yards, and since the road was not matching the map, she pulled over again.

The car behind also pulled over, close enough we could see their faces. The car was a red Yugo carrying five rather large men. We continued in the same direction another half mile before pulling over a third time. As I glanced out the passenger window toward the field, I noticed something very disturbing.

The sky was gray and fog was setting in across the fields, enveloping the little barns and farmhouses across the landscape. As I focused on the foreground, something caught my eye. Human body parts projected out of the soil as if reaching for help; a hand here, a foot there. We had stopped in front of a mass grave. The ugliness of war, specifically ethnic cleansing, was staring back at me, not from a television screen but an open field. It was a gut-wrenching sight.

Lost in Europe, in a car with two ladies and no weapons, and a carload of ominous looking dudes following us, we needed help. I suspected the men guarded the area we stumbled across by accident. It was obvious we did not belong there, and they wanted us gone.

I suggested Helga make a U-turn and blaze past the little red car. It was impossible for an overloaded Yugo to catch us. I thought it was best to backtrack, determine our location, and figure out how to get to our destination.

Any deployment can get chaotic. We expected hiccups, but that experience was worrisome, both for ourselves, and the others who waited to receive us.

After turning around and passing the thugs who had been following us, we backtracked until we found a place to ask for help. Croatia was our destination, but we had strayed into neighboring Serbia. We got help with directions and finally made it to our destination at Camp Harmon.

4 2

WE WERE SO GRATEFUL TO ARRIVE AT OUR DESTINATION, safe within the confines of a US military installation. As we entered the camp, the equipment and firepower already on site amazed me. Camp Harmon was outside the city of Zupanja, Croatia, a few miles from the Sava River.

Following the signs to the "PX", Helga parked the car next to the tent that was our place of work. After more than eight hours of driving, I was ready to stretch my legs. As I stepped away from the vehicle, I sank in the mud until it spilled over the top of the combat boots I had on. A local potato farmer agreed to lease the land but didn't mention that his field flooded every winter. Flood waters had receded, but it was still very muddy. The Army had truckloads of large crushed rock delivered to build roadways inside the camp. The rock was as deep as three feet in wetter areas.

I cleaned the mud off my boot as best I could and then followed our colleague into the store. Janice and I were there to relieve this guy as his mission was to open and run the facility until we could get there from the United States.

We gathered our duffle bags from the Jeep and said goodbye to Helga. She continued the journey to deliver the vehicle in Bosnia before flying back to Germany. Gene briefed us on post protocols and locations of showers, latrines, and the mess hall. He also gave us the lay of the land about our facilities. We operated out of a 16' x 20' Army tent. Shelves lined the perimeter of the tent, with the cash register by the front door. A bank of shelves down the center served a dual purpose, to hold product, and divide the sleeping areas. Soldiers entered the tent and used their helmets as a shopping cart.

With the crude surroundings, it looked I had stepped onto the set of the TV show, M.A.S.H.. When the store closed, Gene showed us our fancy sleeping quarters. Janice chose aisle two, next to the cash register, Gene, and I slept in aisle one. Only the merchandise on the center row of shelves separated us from Janice.

We received Army issue cots to use with our sleeping bags. Every morning we moved all our gear from the tent to one of the two 20' storage containers we used for warehouse space. Every evening we had to go retrieve all that equipment before going to sleep.

January 1996, the cold temperatures were brutal in Croatia. Each tent had a propane space heater but just before our arrival, an unattended heater sparked a blaze in a tent full of sleeping soldiers. A new rule prohibited space heater use during the night unless a dedicated person stayed awake as a fire watch. With no heat during the night, once you bundled up in your Gore-Tex sleeping bag you didn't want to come out, even to use the bathroom facilities.

The shower tent was 100 yards away with a row of portable toilets in front. The shower tent used the same 16' x 20' configuration and had about two dozen shower heads around the perimeter. There were no private stalls. Because of my past, a phobia about being naked in the presence of other men prevented me from using the shower facilities. I made a deal with the guy tasked with supervising the shower. I bought him a case of soda every week in trade for the shower after-hours, an arrangement which served me well.

As for food, the mess hall served basic hot meals three times per day. Also available were MRE's, pre-packaged Meals Ready-to-Eat. As a picky eater, my food options were more limited than in Greenland. At least in Greenland I could get pizza and hamburgers. There was none of that in Croatia. My typical diet comprised day old rolls from a local bakery and MRE peanut butter packets to make a sandwich. I also had access to the junk food we sold in the PX. With so few choices besides junk food, I lost a few pounds during that deployment.

Upper management soon discovered the cost and logistics of rotating people through on thirty-day assignments was unjustifiable. After my second week at Camp Harmon, an email came through asking to extend my deployment from thirty days up to one year. It was a great opportunity, so I agreed to stay.

I spent January and February at Camp Harmon before re-mobilizing to Kaposvar and Taszar, Hungary for a couple weeks to fill in for those who rotated back to their permanent bases. When their replacements were on site, I returned to Croatia with a new assignment. Camp Harmon supported a group known as the *River Rats*. They operated a floating pontoon bridge spanning the Sava River. The Sava divided Croatia and Bosnia/Herzegovina. The original bridge, blown to bits during the war, was part of a major supply route.

My new assignment was fifty miles west of Zupanja, along the Sava River, at a place known as Slavonski Brod. Our troops had taken over a factory which had been manufacturing weapons during the war. To reignite the economy after the war, the factory resumed production of farming equipment. Our troops established this camp on the factory campus to monitor production activities.

My store started, at that post, in a forty foot semi-trailer. Shelves lined both sides front to back. Soldiers entered the rear of the trailer via metal steps, made their selections, and paid for them at the front of the trailer. A side door to their right was how they exited my snack food emporium.

As the sole employee, the store was only open between the hours of 9am and 6pm. There were exceptions. On occasion, a high ranking officer would fly into camp at 10 pm, wanting to buy chips or cigarettes. A couple times an aid woke me at 2 or 3 am to open the store for a General who wanted chewing gum. It's the price you paid to be one of the most essential people in the camp.

After about a month in the trailer, the operation moved inside a big warehouse. The warehouse served as the post hub and included amenities such as a barber shop, post office, game and community areas, military police (MP's), and the Post Exchange (PX). The space allotted to my facility was 30' x 40', which we filled with various sundries and other merchandise.

We brought more American comfort to a war zone. I wondered how the locals perceived our American affluence, especially when soldiers complained about not having the greatest choice of televisions. We graduated from selling just sodas, chips, and cigarettes, to various types of tobacco products, hygiene products, satellite dishes, even Rolex watches. One customer, an Italian General, purchased three Rolex watches at $20,000 each, in cash.

Built by a civilian contractor, the camp included lighted wooden boardwalks to keep us out of the mud. We also had wood framed tents, with plywood subfloors and interior walls. There were electrical outlets and florescent lighting. Our prefabricated bathroom facilities had toilets with stalls and private showers, and to top that off, they were heated.

Conditions were much better than Camp Harmon. It's the times in life, with all distractions stripped away, when you learn to appreciate everything you have. As I look back on my experiences in Croatia, I see how God used every situation I endured to get my attention. That deployment exposed my idols, my truck being the chief one, my electronics, even the idol which plagues many - busyness. I didn't have to worry about paying bills, keeping appointments, or running errands.

With nowhere to go after work, I had free time to contemplate life. The war we were there to end revolved around religion; Islam versus Christianity. I had questions about the 1,500 year struggle between the two faiths. As I read the Bible, layers peeled from my eyes like an onion, and I could see the world around me through better lenses.

As the guy holding the keys to all the comforts from home, I garnered a little popularity and developed friendships, some genuine, others just because of my position. I became friends with many of the MP's (Military Police) across the hall.

Many times at night, opposing factions would fire bullets and mortars at each other, trying to engage in the other in battle. Both sides were trying to garner American support for their respective causes. The MP's would dispatch patrols in Humvee's armed with 50 caliber machine guns, and their presence in the area settled things down. On more than one occasion, a patrol set out to calm hostilities and returned with one of our own in a body bag. Sometimes caught in the crossfire between opposing factions, other times they had stepped on a land mine.

If not for the deployment, I would never have met and befriended the brave guys who died. Their deaths were a tragic end to a friendship just begun. From ashes to beauty, through loss I found a deep respect for the men and women who volunteer to serve our country in the military.

I thought back to the two young draftees who caused the loss of my hand. They were so young and placed in an environment of hostility beyond their limited understanding. I realized war can have such an impact on a person's soul they would do irrational things and make illogical choices to escape the hellish situations they were in.

My experiences on this deployment were many, some great, others less so, but all valuable. I could ramble on about them, but the greatest included the opportunity to work with individuals from many other countries. Operation Joint Endeavor was a multi-national peace keeping force with soldiers from the United States, Italy, Hungary, Poland, Bosnia, Serbia, and even Russia, to name but a few. It was the single greatest display of unity I had ever seen. Perhaps the greatest moment was when we gathered to dedicate Camp Slavonski Brod. The American flag raised to our national anthem as soldiers from many nations stood in respect. It was a real tear-jerker when the Lee Greenwood song, "God Bless the USA", followed the anthem. As I scanned the crowd, I saw many non-American soldiers singing along, a beautiful moment indeed.

Another awesome experience involved people I hired to work in the store. Wonderful people, they were grateful for the opportunity to work and earn money to support their families. Of the several hired, I only remember the names of two, Gabi and Alan. Gabi and I have remained friends for more than twenty years. Someday I hope to return to Croatia to visit my friends. It's a lovely place for anyone who enjoys travel, history, and cultural experiences.

Perhaps the pinnacle of my experience on this deployment was learning how to forgive. Because I lived with the troops 24/7, I saw firsthand what soldier life is like in the field. I carried the heavy baggage of anger, resentment, and bitterness, toward our military in particular, for over twenty years because of the loss of my hand. Not only did I learn to forgive, but I also learned to empathize with others. Later in life I came to understand how critical those two virtues are, and how important they are for navigating the Christian walk.

43

OUT OF THE BLUE, I RECEIVED A PIECE OF MAIL FROM THE Sergeant who ran the post office at Slavonski Brod. It was a registered piece that required a signature. This was not a typical classification of mail handled there so it carried a bit of mystique. The Sergeant handed the letter to me and said she hoped everything was all right.

I opened it there in the middle of the community area with many onlookers waiting to see if it was good news or bad. It was a legal summons to respond to a complaint filed by my ex-wife. The complaint indicated I was a deadbeat father who fled the country to avoid paying alimony and child support.

The summons allowed thirty days for a response, from the date of issuance, not the date I received it. If there was no response to the petition within those thirty days, the court would accept the complaint and enter it into the record. I received the document on the twenty-seventh day, leaving just three days to act.

Calling in a favor, the base commander allowed me to use the military satellite phone to call home. I needed an attorney to respond to the summons. My mom called the state bar association and took the recommendation given. Twenty-four hours later, she hired an attorney who responded with two days to spare.

Since I was not an active duty soldier, I did not fall under the *Soldier Relief Act* which protects a soldier from legal actions during overseas deployments. With no other choice, I had to return to the United States to fight in a civil court.

My deployment was ongoing and my company was not yet ready to move me. If I had to leave, for any reason other than a company ordered transfer, it would be my responsibility. Leaving required I resign my position.

I was absolutely furious about being placed in that position!

How was it possible for my ex-wife to continue ruining my life, and with the help of the legal system? As a result, my career with AAFES ended. I resigned, said farewell to friends, and set off to hitch hike out of the war zone to Frankfurt, Germany, where I caught a flight home to the States.

The process of travel took ten days so by the time I made it back to my parents' home in Oklahoma; my case had already gone before the judge. Mom had relayed as much information as she could to my attorney while I was en route.

The attorney, amazed by the "injustice" I had suffered as a father, told my mom he would dedicate himself to "righting the wrongs". Based on what he had seen and heard, he planned to go after full custody, not to the arrangement we had signed seven years earlier. Relieved by the news, I finally had an attorney willing to fight for me. He offered hope to see my son again.

When I arrived in Oklahoma mom filled me in on the details surrounding case. Denise was getting divorced from her second husband at the same time our case went on the docket. Theirs was not a No-Fault divorce state which meant her husband had to prove grounds for divorce, such as marital infidelity. The second husband hired a private investigator who documented several cases of extramarital affairs. Labeled an unfit mother for the two girls she had with her second husband, the court ordered Denise to pay him child support.

My attorney requested the PI's investigative records to use in my case. Those records contributed to the victory of the second husband over my ex-wife so my attorney assumed they would secure mine. With confidence, he boasted of certain victory. That was good news.

After mom briefed me, I called the attorney to let him know I was back in the US and available to help any way I could with the case. The receptionist took the message and assured me of a return call.

The following day passed without a call. Several more calls I made, but he took none of them, nor did he respond to messages. I pretended to be someone looking for a divorce attorney, referred to him by a friend. My plan worked as the receptionist put me through to him right away. I dropped the rouse after he picked up the phone, demanding to know why he had not taken or returned any of my calls. I had a right to know the result of my case hearing.

In a belligerent tone, my attorney, once a champion for my cause, suggested I should be happy with the results. He had not filled me in on the results of the hearing, so what reason did I have to be happy?

He informed me the joint custody agreement was worthless. The new agreement, decided by the judge, was that I would have two days per calendar year of supervised visitation. That visitation was to occur on a Saturday and Sunday between the hours of 8 am and 5 pm. I had to coordinate the visitation with both my ex-wife and a county social worker with at least a thirty day advance notice. Both parties were to be within eyesight of me with no greater than one hundred yards between us at all times. "Deadbeat Father" and "Flight Risk" were monikers entered on record due to my being in Croatia at the time of the court hearing.

The court awarded Denise almost everything she requested, including mandatory child support payments. Not granted were alimony and backdated child support for my son from the age of two to nine years. Denise had to pay her second husband $75 per week to cover both of their daughters, while I had to pay her $95 for my son. It was obvious what my support payments would cover, and it chapped my hide.

The "injustice" my attorney spoke of before the hearing evolved into a travesty of justice after, if only in my eyes. Once a judge gives an order, that order stands, whether right or wrong. Back to square one, or whatever comes before that even.

Back in the States, with the legal mess behind me, I tried to visit my son. My attorney was a useless source of information. He refused to give the address of my ex-wife, citing it would violate her civil rights to do so. I called the Child Support Division to make plans with a social worker, hoping they would help me contact Denise. They also required I give an address for the child before they would assign a social worker to chaperone. When I asked if they had an address for her, the response was yes, but they could not give it out for legal reasons. Without an address, I could do nothing.

My sole choice, according to the court clerk, was to take my ex-wife back to civil court and sue her for violating my visitation rights. A summons had to be served by the Sheriff's department, followed by another hearing. Everything hinged on me providing a current physical address to initiate any legal proceedings.

With persistence, I called every agency I could, multiple times, hoping to gain a sympathetic ear, with no such luck. I called so often, the people just hung up when they knew it was me on the phone. Once again, the legal system failed me.

I had a little savings at that point but I needed to find work soon because I had child support payments to make, on top of all my other expenses. There was no reason to stay in Oklahoma any longer. My brother had retired from the Navy and moved to Reno, Nevada. I had never been there but having been a part of his wedding in Las Vegas, I assumed the geography was similar. With a lot of my time spent in the snow and ice over the past several years, moving to the desert sounded good. A bonus would be living near my brother. My niece was three then, and since the legal system wouldn't allow me to be a dad, I tried to be a great uncle.

I made it to Reno toward the end of summer 1996. I found work and after my second paycheck the child support division garnished my wages. The amount of money garnished made it impossible to sustain basic living standards, so I took a second job. My work schedule at the primary job, being in the retail industry, varied from week to week which made it difficult to keep a second job. After a couple months of balancing schedules, I let go of the second job.

It wasn't long before my truck became too great a financial burden as I could no longer afford the payments. The cost of living was higher in Nevada than Oklahoma. When I left Oklahoma to move to Reno, I was complaining about the high cost of fuel at $0.88 per gallon. Two days after leaving Oklahoma the price of gas in Reno shocked me at $1.89 per gallon. Housing was also a lot more expensive.

Once again, I lost any material gain I achieved. The bitterness I harbored toward my ex-wife consumed me. A gradual process, it didn't register in my head as it happened. I was sinking in the proverbial quicksand, and in desperation I clawed at people like a crazy person, trying to make somebody care.

Others saw me as needy and negativity oozed from my pores. Rather than reaching out with the helping hand I needed and wanted, they pulled back. At a high level of mental toxicity, I repelled as opposed to drawing people closer.

Any progress made in my spiritual walk vanished.

My income improved after taking a new position at work. The new job required traveling to customer homes to take measurements for floor covering installations.

A good fit, the job better aligned with my natural talents. The biggest drawback was the extended periods of "windshield time" spent driving to the various homes. There are seventeen counties in the large state of Nevada, and I covered sixteen of them.

The increased alone time further isolated me, and my animosity toward the general public continued to grow. Even now, it's scary to consider how far away from society I drifted. While the desire to end my life diminished, I had a big list of others whose lives I wished would end by some tragic means. A silent rage filled the depths of my soul. For every person who ever hurt me, I dreamed of mysterious boulders falling from the sky. They needed to feel my pain.

I saw a movie, starring Michael Douglas, called "Falling Down". As I watched, the movie hit me on a deep level because I recognized myself in Douglas' character. The movie terrified me because I was dangerously close to slipping into the same abyss as the character in the movie.

I was angry, wildly mad, at the entire world. Everyone was on a mission to destroy me. Injustice was everywhere. For years, I struggled to be everything society expected, but regardless of what I did, it never measured up. I knew something had to change, and soon, I just couldn't understand how to bring about said change. I prayed God would hasten my demise.

4 4

NEGATIVE EXPERIENCES PERSISTED. THE HIGH COST OF living, plus the child support and ongoing legal debt put me in need of a roommate to keep up above water. One roommate was from the old days of airbrushing back in Colorado. I drove out to Denver to bring him to Reno for better opportunities. His life had spiraled downward, and he worked as a bagger in a grocery store to support his family while airbrushing t-shirts at the swap meet on weekends.

The guy had so much talent and I thought he could open a little air brush business in one of the casinos. Together, we rented space in the Circus Circus hotel and casino. He was there all day, painting, while I worked my day job. After my shift ended, I covered the booth to give him a dinner break. I kept any money I made for any t-shirts I painted so it was a win-win for both of us.

Painting t-shirts gave me that interaction with people I wanted, but I knew it was only a mirage. There was no depth to the interaction, it was a business transaction. Unless I was behind the counter, no one knew I existed. I took whatever I could get though; I was desperate.

After a short while; however, our relationship soured. I had driven back to Denver to retrieve my roommate's girlfriend and two small kids. She was pregnant with a third. Once she joined us, my expenses rose as I now had to cover things like diapers for the roommates. Meanwhile, they stopped paying their share of rent and utility costs. His girlfriend ran up a long distance phone bill, in the neighborhood of $300 every month, calling her family back in

Denver. The relationship between my friend and his girlfriend also deteriorated as she suspected him of cheating. I suspected it too when the casino management called to say there were many times when the booth was unstaffed.

It was time for them to leave. It was a difficult to do but the toxicity of the relationship had reached the critical stage. I gave them a week to find another place. They had the means, and if they did the right thing, I would have helped them move. They chose otherwise, refusing to leave, insisting they had squatter's rights. I checked into the laws, and to my chagrin, they did. Since I accepted payment towards rent, to get these people out of my house, I had to work through legal channels and serve them with a thirty-day eviction notice.

Never having had any success with the legal system, I was fearful that in the process of eviction, they would somehow end up with my house, evicting me from it.

One evening they went out, so I loaded all their belongings out to the edge of the property. When they returned to find their things outside, a confrontation ensued. My dad was working with the county Sherriff's office and he and his partner were on patrol in my neighborhood.

They arrived just as my roommate got belligerent with me, making threats and yelling. Since none of their property was in my house, and they could not produce any signed lease agreement, the officers asked them to leave the premises. By morning, all the stuff I moved outside disappeared. I hoped no one stole it, but I couldn't allow them to continue taking advantage of me.

After that fiasco, I decided I would no longer take roommates. The thoughts I had years earlier of my life changing at thirty occupied my mind again. The change I desired most, leaving this life, was not far off but that change eluded me, again.

My sister-in-law introduced me to a girl she worked with, hoping we would become a couple. We did, and in rather quick order.

Tina was a divorcee with a four-year-old little girl. We got married within months of meeting. As a husband and a step-dad, I had a renewed sense of purpose. Her little girl confirmed that purpose after the wedding when she asked to call me daddy. That was such an honor. I promised her I would never attempt to replace her biological father. He would always be her father and I intended to honor him in that, but she was welcome to call me whatever she felt most comfortable with. "Then it's settled," she said, "I'm calling you daddy!"

An issue I was hypersensitive to because I had a child somewhere in the world who thought I was dead and his step-father was his daddy. I never wanted to place undue pressure on this beautiful little girl. Marlee, and my niece Taylor, became the bright lights in my life, illuminating the way out of the darkness.

Not long after I married the second time, I started a business. Our financial situation improved fast. My success also facilitated a move to the Pacific Northwest. I spent a six years in the Reno area and was long overdue for a change. I welcomed the opportunity to move.

Tina exhibited the same telltale signs of marital infidelity as my first wife. If I questioned anything, such as her unplanned emergency trips to San Francisco for the weekend, she would shame me for my insecurities and say I was acting ridiculous.

Just before we packed for our move to Oregon, Tina asked for a divorce. Why? What wrong had I done to warrant divorce as the only option?

Not one to drink, I did not use drugs, and I did not forsake my family every weekend in the name of TV sports. I worked very hard to provide, self-sacrificed, and rarely ever purchased anything for myself. I didn't flirt with women or cheat on my marriage. Everything I could do to be a good husband I did, so why was I so horrible that my second wife wanted to get rid of me too? I asked myself that question often but the answer never came. I asked Tina, but she always said the problem was with her and not me. That made little sense.

To save my marriage, I would "buy" her love through gifts. I suppose I had already started down that path but I shifted into overdrive. Somehow, I convinced her to stay, and we packed the house into a rental truck to move to our new home in Oregon. I hoped things would get better there. Both of us had grown to despise the Reno area, so I thought a change in scenery would do us good.

I had been getting calls at home where the person just breathed into the phone, saying nothing. Dismissed as a prank caller, I would just hang up on them. On moving day, the last item loaded was our home telephone.

I went to my bedroom to grab the phone just as it rang. I answered the phone and it was the breather. Since we were leaving town in minutes, I thought I would play along. When the person breathed heavy, I did the same in response. Then silence. After a while I said, "Don, I know it's you." Don was a former boyfriend of Tina's who just couldn't let her go.

Outed by my comment, he asked, "Why don't you ask your wife how many times she's cheated on you?" I told him to grow up then disconnected the phone and set out on the road to Oregon.

When I shared the context of the phone call with Tina, she did not refute the claim he made of cheating. She said nothing and got in her car to follow behind me.

Once again, I found myself in a marriage racked with adulterous affairs. What to do? The long drive gave me lots of time to think. I got angry, I got sad. I felt used and abused, and lower than pond scum. My reaction was to pretend nothing happened. Tina was still *my* wife, and we were moving further away from her former boyfriend. And, we were moving into one of the most affluent communities in the Portland metro area, close to the exclusive lake from which the suburb gets its name.

After we settled into our new home, it wasn't long before the road trips to San Francisco happened again. With my business doing well, Tina quit her job and helped by scheduling appointments for my clients. I'm certain being a stay-at-home mom got to be boring for her. She tried to combat the boredom by hanging out with other wives in the neighborhood, taking walks around the lake, and spending lots of money in coffee shops.

Each year, like a flu strain, the divorce bug infected my wife, and each year, the remedy was to outdo the cure of the previous year. It wasn't enough to live in the affluent suburb; we had to move into a larger home across the street from the lake.

The next remedy was to elevate from one German made vehicle to another. Who would drive a Volkswagen when you can drive a Mercedes, a brand new M-class selected from an interior showroom and delivered with a massive red bow on top? That, I thought, would surely make her happy enough to quit trying to leave.

In trying to buy her affection, I had not been paying my child support or income taxes. A fact she well knew. The main reason for stopping child support payments was to lure my ex-wife out of hiding. Denise was great at hiding her whereabouts though she always knew mine.

If I quit making support payments, Denise would surface and I could sue her for violating my visitation. In my ignorance, I discovered that as a mother, all she had to do was notify the court and the court would pursue me on her behalf. My plan backfired, and then I found myself in deep trouble with the court over support arrearages.

I also got into deep water owing taxes on my business income, to both the Federal Government and the State of Oregon. Another perfect storm brewed, and I wasn't sure how best to deal with it. I decided procrastination was the plan but in the meantime, it seemed best to move across the river into Washington. There was no state income tax there and the property taxes were lower. Housing was also less expensive so moving there would put me in a better position to deal with other issues.

After the terrorist attack on 9/11, Tina wanted to attend church. I did too, so we joined one. We were both baptized in that church and befriended the pastor and his family. We even attended small group Bible studies in his home.

Because of the relationships we formed, I felt secure enough to ask my pastor's brother-in-law for help in getting a mortgage to buy a home in Washington. Paul had brokered loans for a few years and seemed knowledgeable enough to help us. With challenges to overcome, child support and taxes, some random broker with no concern for us as people, would dismiss us right away. We met with Paul and he agreed to work with us, assuring us he could get loan for us.

We found a great new construction home and put down an earnest money deposit while we awaited financing. Paul told me he would need to open an escrow account and needed $3,000 to do that. It sounded legitimate, so I gave him a check. He came back twice more stating he needed another $2,000 each time to buy down points on our interest rate. With the challenges we faced that too seemed reasonable, so I didn't hesitate. Paul now had $7,000 of my money and our closing date was coming up.

Paul assured us underwriting was finishing up their process and he would make the date. The date passed with no loan. The builder gave us two—one week extensions without penalty. During that time, I had purchased a stainless steel refrigerator and had it installed in the home.

We had also moved out of our current home in preparation to take possession of the new home. Our household goods were in storage and we stayed with my mother-in-law in her tiny one bedroom condo in downtown Portland.

Paul quit taking my calls and stopped responding to voice mails. I circumvented him by calling the mortgage company direct, only to receive bad news. Paul had opened a file for us but did nothing else. He had not even done a credit check. There was no loan started, much less one in the final stages of underwriting.

Faced with this quagmire, my builder informed me he could no longer hold the home without more earnest money. As a result, I lost the home, the earnest money, and the brand new refrigerator.

Paul was still unresponsive and my $7,000 was missing. I reached out to his brother-in-law, my pastor, and asked for help in getting Paul to refund the money. The pastor refused to get involved.

In need of a place to live, I first checked with my previous landlord, hoping to move back in. Another family already signed a lease agreement. We remained stuck, and cramped, in my mother-in-law's little place.

That was the final straw for Tina. She had been waiting for confirmation on how to proceed; the home her deciding factor. In her eyes, since I failed to deliver on the home, God had now given her the freedom to divorce me. I had reached the end of my ability to purchase her love. She insisted on a separation and asked me to move out. That was a heavy blow. Once again, everything was stripped away and I couldn't understand why.

Within a few days, I moved into a townhome in Vancouver where I would sit and lick my wounds. This time, I decided life would not defeat me.

4 5

I MOVED INTO THE LITTLE TWO BEDROOM TOWNHOME WITH little more than my clothing and the few items I used to conduct my business. My hope was Tina would come to her senses and realize she overreacted to an unfortunate situation and join me in Vancouver.

It didn't turn out quite that way. She got her own place, and together with her daughter, moved forward without me. To add insult to injury, the place she chose was just six doors down from my unit.

Since separation seemed to be our destiny, I got our things from storage and divided them up. If I couldn't be with my family, I the material items meant nothing. She took whatever she wanted. Most everything we owned was brand new and as she had chosen it all, it made sense to let her have it. To look at that stuff, reminders of the family I lost, was not appealing.

For the better part of six months, I sat around my desolate little place after work, which looked more like a squatter lived there. From my front bedroom window upstairs, I could see cars come and go. It was painful to sit there, as I completed my paperwork in the evenings, and watch other men come visit my wife just six doors down.

Regardless of what happened between us, I tried my best to remain a stable presence in the life of our daughter. My provision for her continued and Tina allowed me to maintain my role as a parent. I continued paying school tuition because I wanted her to have as much continuity as possible. Though we did not share a blood bond, my commitment to my daughter did not waiver. When she called me daddy that was serious business and I wanted to honor the trust and love she placed in me as a father figure.

It was time for me to pull myself out of the self-pity pool. Since Tina was not coming back, I bought new furniture. I also furnished the second bedroom in case our daughter ever needed to stay the night.

Since possessions were a means of gauging success for me, having a few motivated me more each day to get up and attack the world. For more inspiration, I attended a large church in the area. One thing I liked about the church was I could disappear in the sea of faces. I wanted answers to my problems and this time I searched for them in church.

Pastor Bill had an amazing way of teaching the Bible. In his sermons, he painted amazing word pictures making the stories come alive.

Based on my experience with the previous church I attended, I was skeptical of the congregants. I trusted no one. Content to be a fly on the wall, if you will, I kept going. I would calculate my arrival to coincide with the end of the worship part of the service. Not knowing the songs, I assumed people noticed my lack of participation and judged me for it. To ease that problem, I came late, sat in the back row, and left early so I wouldn't have to associate with anyone.

I thought I should continue my effort to buy a house if for no other reason than tax relief. I returned to the same builder to find they were closing out the development.

He sympathized with my situation and offered to try again if I was interested. The builder agreed to sell the model home, which was larger, include the refrigerator, which was nicer, and, to seal the deal, he contributed $5,000 towards closing costs. His generosity overwhelmed me.

With a mortgage broker willing to work with me, I needed tax returns to prove income. My accountant terrified me with the results. Between the Federal and State, I owed almost $100,000. Penalties and interest only added to that figure.

Initially, it seemed like a hopeless situation, but I got approved for a mortgage. The loan offered was a 2 year fixed, 28 year adjustable rate mortgage. After twenty-four payments I planned to refinance and take out a second mortgage, using the money as leverage in negotiating tax settlements. I knew it was a risk, but it seemed the only opportunity to correct my mistakes.

With the financing secured my estranged wife offered to have her office handle the closing transaction to save money.

The loan closed, I got the keys, and moved in on Thanksgiving Day of 2003. After all the struggle, it felt so good to achieve the American dream of home ownership. I wanted to dedicate my home to God in thanks for His provision. With all the space in the house, I thought a home Bible study was a good way to steward the awesome gift God gave me.

Tina said she too had received a divine sign. Since I had achieved the goal of home ownership, it led her to believe she made a mistake in asking for a separation. She paid a visit one evening to discuss her revelation from on high.

She confessed to having the affair with Don for the duration of our marriage. Since she was "coming clean", she confessed to another affair established during our separation. She cheated on the guy she cheated on me with.

A lot to process, I told her I needed time to think about her coming back. I thought long and hard about it. There was a fifty percent chance she was genuine in her repentance and willingness to work on rebuilding our marriage. There was also a fifty percent chance, with a high probability, that she plotted something else.

To reconcile after the infidelity was risky. After careful consideration, I erred on the side of trust, but with a stipulation. She had to rebuild trust, which included marital counseling and attending church with me. She agreed and a few days later we reunited as a family just in time to celebrate Christmas together in the new home. Our separation lasted just under one year.

As the new year progressed, Tina attended church with me a few times. Sundays, she claimed, were the only days she had for just herself and catching up on sleep was of the utmost importance to her. By summer, she only attended once every three or four weeks.

I signed up for a marriage retreat the church offered which took place at a nice resort in Central Oregon during the summer. Since there was a trip involved, she agreed to go. At the retreat, we attended group sessions during the day with couple exercises assigned for "homework" in the evening. The homework was a means to reopen lines of communication and foster renewed connectedness for the couples. Tina was not interested in any of that, but she allowed me to take her to the shopping district and spend large sums of money on her.

On the way home, there was next to no conversation as she slept most of the five hour drive. The retreat was a failure, and it was the only marriage building activity we tried.

Because I wanted to honor God by using my home for ministry, I signed up for an event the church organized that summer called Backyard BBQ's. The premise was for a host to open their home to anyone in the church looking to connect with others. The host provided a meat offering, and the guests brought a side dish or dessert to share.

Our name and address were made known to congregation through the bulletin and website. Not knowing how many to prepare for, I barbecued chicken for thirty people, provided a big side dish and drinks.

As the day progressed, no one showed up, not one person. Disappointed, I had hoped we would meet some new friends. To add insult to injury, Tina said, "Well, I guess it wasn't meant to be." Maybe she was right; maybe I wasn't supposed to have friends. Never again did I host an event at that house."

I forgot it was God's gift, and I worshipped the house instead of the Lord. My attendance at church slipped too because I was busy improving the house on the only days I had to myself, those being Sundays. I put a lot of sweat equity into that house, determined to get my back taxes caught up when I refinanced at the two year mark.

Meanwhile, Tina and I drifted further apart, becoming more like roommates than spouses. She would put our daughter to bed at night and fall asleep with her. Other times she slept in the guest room. We saw little of one another after dinner most days.

I was disappointed and regretted my decision to take her back. I had tried my best to make things work, but it was a one-sided effort.

Frustration I released through working in the backyard, moving a lot of dirt by shovel and wheel barrow to level it off. A benefit to having a hook was not getting splinters. My neighbor used to tease me saying he could have the work completed in one afternoon using a Bobcat loader to move the dirt. Hard labor was cheaper than therapy and it relieved some of the stress brought on from my failing marriage. The yard was beautiful when it was all said and done, to include a unique wooden fence.

Time ticked toward the two year mark in the home, the time when I could refinance, drop my interest rate, and pull out the equity to pay my taxes. At twenty months, the other shoe dropped.

Tina decided she could no longer remain married. She asked for a divorce, saying I could do nothing to change her mind. Trying to ease her guilt, she told me it was not anything I had done, that it was all her. She struggled with the concept of a monogamous lifestyle, and could not imagine waking up beside the same man for the rest of her life.

She moved out and suggested we get the divorce proceedings under way as soon as possible. To her credit, unlike my first wife, Tina did not seek to destroy me. Washington, as she informed me, was a community property state which meant the court would divide the couples' assets in half. She had done her homework in the legal realm.

We divided the personal property and rather than moving furniture to her new place, she sold it all. She planned to buy everything new once she collected half of the proceeds from the sale of the house.

Once Tina moved out, from the confines of a big empty house, I questioned the perpetual loss. Was I not meant to have anything in this world? Every time I amassed earthly treasures, they got taken away.

Material possessions, I concluded, contributed to my lack of true happiness and peace. My truck, the house, financial status; these things became gods in my life. With every purchase, hoping to find validation and self-worth, I bowed the god of materialism. I needed to find the Creator and quit chasing His creations.

Under counsel from the church, I tried everything I could to save the marriage. I supported my wife during our separation, knowing she carried on extramarital affairs. I took her back, despite the betrayal, and had been willing to accept counsel and do the hard work of reconciliation. Through it all, I never strayed from my vows.

Since we chose to work together towards an amicable divorce, there was no need to waste money on attorneys so we handled the paperwork ourselves. With fees submitted, paperwork completed, the divorce was final a short time later.

In the interim, I had to sell the house because the law entitled Tina to half of everything. I hired a real estate agent who turned out to be worthless. He would schedule an open house but not show up to take prospective buyers through the house. I did all of that work for him.

As I loaded the last of my personal items, a couple parked their car and asked to see the house. They toured the house while another couple arrived asking to see it. Neither couple had been working with an agent. Within hours I had two offers in hand and I accepted the one offering the full listing price.

Realtors, who had done nothing to earn it, received $17,000 in commission from the proceeds which chapped my hide. The remaining proceeds of $50,000 went to the Internal Revenue Service to pay back taxes owed.

After the closing reconciliation was complete, the amount of money Tina and I each netted was $0.00. She always talked about Karma. I am not a believer in that philosophy but our situation bore a resemblance to it. The outcome pleased me because the federal tax debt reduced by 70% from the sale proceeds, and I didn't have to take out a second mortgage. It also felt a little like sweet revenge when Tina received no money out the house. She got decorations and furniture, furniture she sold, which left her with mattresses on the floor and little else. The part which hurt most was that our daughter had to suffer though it all.

I continued to pay her tuition through private school for the rest of the year because I wanted her to have the best foundation for life possible. Although her mommy divorced me, I would never divorce her. She would always be my daughter. Her mother and I agreed upon Marlee staying with me one night a week. I picked her up on Tuesdays after school and dropped her off at school on Wednesday mornings. The arrangement continued until the distance of travel made it impossible. We kept in touch and it got a little tricky for a while due to some other business between her mom and I which put a strain on the relationship. My daughter and I remain close to this day. A daughter to me she will always be.

46

THE BULLETIN AT CHURCH READ, "WHAT DO YOU DO WHEN things don't work out?" A question I had struggled to find an answer to. Intrigued by the thought, I read the rest of the blurb. It was an advertisement for the Singles Ministry regarding an event scheduled for the following Friday.

With two failed marriages, I had no desire to get involved in another relationship. My purpose in attending the event was to learn the answer to that question, nothing more.

I had never been part of any structured group outside of a Sunday morning corporate worship service, so I walked into foreign territory that evening not knowing what to expect. Instead of my normal position at the back, I sat in the front row wanting to know if the pastor had the answer.

That night's overall message I do not recall, but a couple scriptures he referenced left an impression which guided me toward a place of healing and hope.

The first was from Hebrews 12:1-2, "Therefore we also, since we are surrounded by so great a cloud of witnesses, let us lay aside every weight, and the sin which so easily ensnares *us*, and let us run with endurance the race that is set before us, ² looking unto Jesus, the author, and finisher of *our* faith, who for the joy that was set before Him endured the cross, despising the shame, and has sat down at the right hand of the throne of God."

That verse helped me to realize life was a journey, or a race, if you will. Like any race, endurance is what the runner needs to succeed. That means never giving up. I had almost given up, several times, but I was still in the race. That realization gave me strength to continue.

The second was Colossians 3:1-2, "If then you were raised with Christ, seek those things which are above, where Christ is, sitting at the right hand of God. Set your mind on things above, not on things on the earth."

The writer of that passage encouraged followers of Jesus to turn away from their carnal ways, to seek only things from above, where Jesus is. I concluded I had spent a lifetime searching for happiness, peace, even validity, from material things here on Earth. If a car could bring me happiness, wouldn't a newer car bring more happiness? If having a home could make me happy, wouldn't the model home send me over the clouds? That night, I discovered the answer to my own questions was; not exactly.

I learned there was a distinction between happiness and joy. Happiness is fleeting and based on circumstance. The new car gets old, and no longer produces feelings of happiness, especially when you get repair bills. Joy comes from the heart, not circumstance. Even in the darkest of situations, one can be joyful.

Soon after that meeting, I came across a hymn which solidified what I learned that night. Written by Helen Lemmel in 1922, the hymn brings me joy every time I hear it.

O soul, are you weary and troubled?
No light in the darkness you see?
There's light for a look at the savior
And life more abundant and free.

Turn your eyes upon Jesus,
Look full in His wonderful face,
And the things of earth will grow strangely dim
In the light of his glory and grace.

The answer to the question, according to Pastor Dave, was turning to Jesus. Everything I ever needed, Jesus waited to give. I wish I could learn things the easy way, but there is no easy way. Jesus grabbed me and showed me He had a purpose for everything.

I can be stubborn, perhaps too stubborn, and I turned elsewhere most times instead of Jesus.

The first meeting with the Singles Ministry left me wanting to return for more. There had to be others in the room who had divorce experiences similar to mine and I wanted to know how they overcame them.

181

By the second or third week of attending meetings, a certain someone caught my attention. She seemed to enjoy helping people get set up for game night. There were different games going on, including volleyball. This lady was setting up tables for a game called *Bunco*. It was a fast paced dice game I had never played, so I decided to sit at the table where she was.

After the game started, she left to assist other tables with first time players like me. I was a little disappointed when she didn't come back to sit with us.

A singles retreat was coming up at a beach resort on the Oregon coast. Several others asked if I was going. It looked like it might be fun but I was in no position to afford it. My business had gone under and the company I worked for didn't pay well.

I made friends with several people in the group who spent a lot of time together outside of the church. They enjoyed doing life together. This young lady named Shelly was part of that group. Shortly before the deadline for reservations for the retreat, many folks gathered to discuss the event. When someone asked if I was going I said no.

Someone found out the reason for my "no" was due to a lack of funds. They approached me and said if I could come up with half the money, they would cover the other half through gifts. That was a foreign concept. I knew how to give but had difficulty with receiving.

Their offer embarrassed me. The group encouraged me by saying true Christians give and share with others, and it was a blessing for them to share with me. Intrigued by the concept, I filed it in the back of my mind.

The retreat was great fun and just what I needed. The people surrounding me were a loving group and demonstrated that love and care over and over, in many tangible ways. The teaching sessions were great but the fellowship afterward was awesome. Our core group gathered in the community area of the resort and enjoyed each other's company, talking and laughing into the wee hours of the morning.

I continued to feel drawn to Shelly though a relationship was not what I was looking for. I had decided to never put my heart out there and allow someone to treat it like a door mat. Marriage was a trauma best avoided, and yet it seemed as though God himself told me Shelly was who He had for me.

More opportunities to get together with the group came about, with dinners out, movies, and pot-lucks. Shelly caught on to the Lord's lead and noticed me as more than just a friend. We started dating, with other couples at first, as we explored whether there was something to this attraction.

After a little time, and prayer, we made our relationship exclusive. As we both made mistakes in former marriages, we wanted to do our best to honor God in our relationship. We asked friends to keep us accountable and sought counsel, from both people and workbooks. We took time to become friends first. The study workbooks we used helped us to explore our likes and dislikes, our weaknesses, strengths and hot buttons. We discussed future goals and dreams to see where we aligned and where we differed.

We agreed to do the hard work up front, before marriage, before families, before responsibilities, as neither of us wanted to commit to a marriage doomed to fail.

I found myself with a growing hunger for more knowledge about God. I wanted to know how I contributed to my two failed marriages. The summer of 2004 I spent a great deal of time doing research. I read sixty-six books in less than four months. Most were Bible-based, geared toward marriage and relationships. Some were testimonials while others were by well-known pastors about specific books of the Bible.

As I studied, scales fell away from my eyes. The Bible once had been a collection of strange riddles and thou-shalt-not lists, but over time it became easier to understand.

Almost fifteen years had passed since my salvation experience after hitting rock bottom. I got a taste of what a relationship with Jesus was like as opposed to a religion wrought with the fallacies of man's vain attempt to please God. I had a long journey ahead, but sensed I was on the right path.

The singles group produced couples, and while some celebrated the unions, others became jealous. Shelly and I, as we progressed in our courtship, thought it would be a good idea to serve together in ministry. I was teaching a third grade Sunday school class, and she joined me. Shelly has a teaching background, and I thought it was great to have her critique me, as a way of developing my teaching skills. You can also learn more about a person when you labor together, so it seemed like a win-win situation.

Driven by jealousy, someone complained to pastoral staff we were a couple, and it was against church policy to have couples teaching together. Shelly and I got called into the office of the number two pastor to answer the charge. He informed us the policy was to prevent someone from abusing their authority with the students. The church did not want to enable a situation where a male teacher could do anything to violate the children and have his partner protect him against any allegation.

The rule made sense, but it hurt that someone thought I would abuse a child, and second, why would someone conspire against me/ us? I was cordial with everyone to but someone had an ax to grind with me. I was not prepared to accept that behavior happened in church.

I suppose I suffered from a disillusion many people experience, thinking people who attend church are above all of that. Snitching and gossip make a Christian a hypocrite, right? Hypocrites were one of the biggest impediments to my faith journey. Something changed in me though. Sure, the accusations stung, but they did not define us, and, rather than retaliate in typical human fashion, I learned, and applied the words of Jesus; "But I say to you, love your enemies, bless those who curse you, do good to those who hate you, and pray for those who spitefully use you and persecute you." Matthew 5:44.

Hard to believe one could have enemies inside the church, but I realized church is more like a hospital for broken and wounded people than a palace of perfect ones. So began my understanding of grace. I heard a pastor say *Grace* is receiving that which we do not deserve, while in contrast, *Mercy* is not receiving that which we do deserve. Shelly and I learned a lot about how to receive grace and give mercy.

Another test on these concepts came shortly thereafter. Based on the complaints, we could no longer serve together in a classroom setting teaching children. We continued to serve together in the singles ministry. I believe it was from the singles group where the accusations were coming because we got called to the pastor's office again to answer to more allegations.

Someone had informed the pastor we needed correction because we were not following God's will for marriage. The accusation was both of our former spouses sought reconciliation and we denied them the opportunity.

Wow! I didn't know if the same person made the allegations but it was getting out of control. In the process of my healing, I had purposed in my heart to focus on one attribute to serve as a core principle of who I am; integrity. Someone appeared to be on a constant mission to challenge that principle.

Without challenge, there is no growth; another concept I picked up in my research.

The pastor asked us if either of our former spouses sought reconciliation, because if so, we should pursue reconciliation through prayer and forgiveness. We both replied no. Called into the pastor's office twice in two weeks didn't make us look good. The pastor decided the appropriate thing for him to do, in due diligence, was to contact both former spouses and speak to them directly. He asked us to provide telephone numbers, and he called them both, in our presence to ask the question. Both former spouses acknowledged they were the ones who sought the divorce and had no desire to reconcile, which exonerated us.

Shelly and I have shared that story with others who have said we should have walked away from that church after being falsely accused. We disagree. Both of us are grateful pastoral leadership cared enough about their flock to seek the truth. It was an act of love and too many churches forego discipline these days, for fear of losing congregants, specifically those who donate money. It ought not to be so.

47

FORSAKING ALL ATTEMPTS OF OTHERS TO DERAIL WHAT WE
sensed God calling us to, we pressed onward. We watched God
at work through it all. He was teaching us crucial lessons, and we
both sensed there were specific reasons we had to endure all the
tests though we had no clue what they were.

Propose to her. I sensed in my heart I should, but so soon after
my second divorce? I feared what people might think. *Propose to
her.* Was God telling me to propose to Shelly? As a skeptic, it
seemed rational to question this God I had been following to
understand if it was providence directing me or my selfish wants.

Since we were trying our best to do things right, there were
certain things which needed to happen before any proposal. The
first was a ring. I barely made ends meet with the job I had and
there was no money in my budget for a ring, let alone a wedding.
The second was I intended to ask for her father's blessing to marry
his daughter.

If God was directing me to propose, then He would have to prove
it. An idea came to have Shelly's best friend help me in selecting the
perfect ring. If I picked the same ring Shelly did, then it would be a
confirmation. I asked her friend to take Shelly shopping and direct
her toward the jewelry counter, and in a dreaming way have her
select the ring she liked the most. It was all in fun. The friend was
not to share my plan with Shelly.

Oblivious to my plan, Shelly chose her dream ring. Next, I
arranged a trip to the same jewelry counter with the same friend.
Our friend was gracious as I looked at almost all of them. I selected

the three I thought best represented Shelly and we discussed the reasons behind each choice.

Our friend mentioned I got three of the five selections right, but which was the right one? I eliminated one right away. How she kept such a straight face during the process I don't know, but she gave nothing away.

When I made the final choice, our friend exploded with excitement. Of all the rings in the cases, my number one choice matched Shelly's. Not proof enough for me though. Shelly and I agreed we would not incur any more debt going into the marriage, we already had enough. "Lord, please confirm your will is for me to propose, by providing the funds to pay for the ring without credit cards."

Within a week I received an unexpected check which covered the ring. Still, I needed further confirmation. I needed to ask her father for his daughter's hand in marriage. That part would be tough because Shelly and I had not known each other long. Her family didn't know much about me except I was a two-time divorcee, had an estranged son, and an unusual connection to a step-daughter.

How could I blame the family for their suspicions? It was understandable as I would have been suspicious too. I placed the call to her dad to arrange the meeting. I drove to his home, with the ring, and asked for his blessing. I acknowledged my past was cause for his concern and promised I would do nothing to hurt his daughter. At thirty-eight years old, it was as if I was sixteen and asking to take his daughter to the prom. After saying my piece I waited for his response.

To my surprise, and relief, he gave his blessing. I was so glad because I planned to propose that evening. I left his home to make the forty mile drive back home, hoping to get there in time to set my plan into motion.

It was a Tuesday night, and we were to meet at the church to attend the men's and women's ministries. I arranged for someone to let me into the main sanctuary and had another friend guide Shelly into the darkened room using a bogus excuse. She was to pick up materials a ministry leader left on the stage. Only a couple lights illuminated the large wooden cross standing in the center of the stage.

I only wish I had arranged for someone to film it for me. As Shelly entered the sanctuary to look for the mystery materials, she was unaware of me hiding behind the piano. She stepped up onto the stage and I walked around the piano, startling her.

In front of the cross, I bowed before her on one knee and asked her to marry me. I presented her with the ring, the same ring she had picked out, and she said yes. I shared with her the story of how the plan came together and we knew we were doing what God wanted us to do.

The holiday season was approaching as we planned for the wedding. The logical place to hold the ceremony was in the church where we met. Much to our disappointment, we could not get married there. None of the pastors would officiate a service for us, even off campus. Their primary reason; my second divorce was not even a year old, and they felt we were moving too fast.

Was this another test of our faith? We decided to have the ceremony elsewhere and looked for options. A dear friend of Shelly's offered their lovely home, but that choice didn't work due to a schedule conflict.

Discouraged by all the doors that closed, we changed gears to look for a wedding dress. Shelly had already experienced the extravagant style wedding. With our lack of money, we decided it was best to look for a practical dress, something she could wear more than once, perhaps to another wedding or formal event.

That mission also failed. The least expensive dress we found was around $350 which was more than we could afford. As a man that was frustrating. In my previous marriage, I provided expensive cars, a giant sized home, and a coffee allowance of $900 per month for my ex-wife. This time, as we followed God's statutes, nothing went the way we expected.

What were we doing wrong? We prayed about whether we followed His will or, in our own strength, tried to assert our own. The answer to both of our prayers was to wait. To wait on the Lord is one of the toughest things I have had to learn in my Christian walk, and I am still learning to this day.

We wondered if we would have any luck finding reduced prices after Christmas. Shelly's friends joined us at the mall. After she tried on the first choice, she knew was it was the one. The dress was a deep purple color and full length. Marked originally at $300, the dress had several reduced price stickers. The lowest sticker showed a price of $80. A good price for the dress, but it was still more than we could afford.

We decided we would continue looking at other stores to see if we could find something less expensive. As she finished up in the fitting room, her friends asked if she liked the dress. Shelly told one friend it was out of our budget so the friend grabbed the dress and took it to the register. I feared she intended to pay for it. While a nice gesture, it would have hurt my pride if she did.

I followed the friend to the cash register, hoping to intercept her if she tried to pay for the dress. Our friend asked the cashier to scan the tag and the sale price came up as $35. Overjoyed with that news, I yelled across the dress department to Shelly, still in the fitting room, "Yep, that's the dress!"

We perused the men's department to find something for me. We found a dark purple shirt that was almost an exact match in hue. For the same price as the dress, I got a shirt, slacks, and tie. Coincidence? I think not.

What's next God?

Looking at the calendar, Shelly and I both landed on March 25th as the wedding date, and it worked for everyone invited. We received confirmation in several ways the date was correct; one was finding someone to officiate the ceremony on the sands of Cannon Beach.

We had decided on that location because it was where we first realized our attraction to each other, plus, the beach is Shelly's favorite place. The difficulty with that location was March is the peak of the rainy season. That was another great opportunity to exercise our faith muscles. With the logistics falling into place, we prayed we were on the right track.

The last major task was designing the order of the ceremony. We knew we wanted a unity candle as part of it. I suggested we write our own vows, but Shelly resisted the idea. She didn't feel confident in her own ability to write and looked for pre-written vows to use.

None of those seemed to express her feelings, which frustrated her. I had written mine already which increased her frustration until one day, as she drove home from work, the words poured into her head. She pulled the car over on the side of the road and wrote out her vows on a napkin.

All that remained was awaiting the date.

Shelly stayed the night with her aunt and uncle so she had a place to get ready for the wedding. On the morning of the wedding, my daughter rode with our friend and her daughter to help Shelly with hair and makeup. Rain had been falling hard all night, but as she got dressed that morning the sun split the clouds over the beach. Since we had no plan B, she trusted God, despite the weather.

Months earlier at the singles retreat, we met a guy from the Tacoma area and he drove me to the venue. He was also our photographer. We drove over the mountain pass and with the windshield wipers at full speed; we still had difficulty seeing the road. Like Shelly, I trusted God had arranged everything, and all we had to do was show up. That faith was in stark contrast to the weather.

Carlos and I arrived at the hotel and joined other friends who had a room I could use to get dressed. The rain still fell as the clock showed one hour to go before the wedding. After getting dressed, I glanced out the sliding glass door across the room. The rain had stopped, and the clouds rolled back to a beautiful blue sky.

We all walked out onto the beach, with me in flip flops. A few people walked the beach, picking up trash and debris, as if their job was to make sure the area was beautiful for us.

Other guests arrived, also amazed by the change in the weather. It was a balmy fifty-four degrees and windy but the rain and the clouds vanished. To best describe it, I would liken it to the parting of the Red Sea for the Israelites during the exodus. There was no sun forecasted so we took joy in the Lord's handiwork.

My bride arrived, also donning flip flops, walking on the arm of her father. With the famous "Haystack Rock" as our back drop, the ceremony began. The minister read the service I had written and then we read our vows to one another, followed by the lighting of the unity candle. In a clear glass vessel, sand taken from the beach secured the candle. After touching both flames to the wick, the candle remained lit, even with the wind. It was a symbol to us, representing the flame of our union enduring windy storms of life.

After the ceremony, we gathered at one of our favorite restaurants for lunch and then went back out to the beach for photos. The sky remained cloudless for the duration of our activities with our guests. After the guests left, we checked into the honeymoon suite for our two night stay.

We decided we would change clothes and go walking through the shops before heading to dinner. As we walked out of the restaurant to go back to our suite, rain pelted us once again falling hard and sideways. It continued to rain that way for the duration of our stay.

What a gift though. To have our faith strengthened, in such a tangible way, to begin our new journey as a couple, was more than we could ask.

4 8

NOW MARRIED, WE MOVED SHELLY'S THINGS INTO THE little house I rented. Two weeks later we held a reception there, and many people blessed us by coming. It was great to have a bunch of people to journey through life with. To feel loved rather than despised was a welcomed feeling.

We settled into our new life as a couple. We plugged into ministry, with activities at church filling our schedule six days per week. It is difficult to describe with words the exponential growth I experienced, both as an individual and as a husband. By honoring our commitment to God, and each other, we got it right this time. We delayed intimacy until the wedding night. We were also successful in adding no new debt to our finances. Through the process we learned that if we wanted the Lord to honor and bless our marriage, then we must honor and bless the Lord by following His commandments.

That concept never crossed my mind in my previous marriages, but I could already see the benefit, and it was worth it. What some see as an outdated list of rules, protects the couple of faith. Not following God's statutes, on courtship and marriage, is one of the greatest contributing factors to the number of Christians getting divorced. Christian divorces are rivaling those who do not ascribe to the faith.

For the Christ follower, tests of faith are part of the sanctification process. Each test serves a purpose, to build strength, perseverance, and character. After the joyous high of what the Lord had done with our marriage, our next test was just around the corner.

Within two months of getting married, I got laid off from work. I knew something wasn't right because three consecutive paychecks bounced due to insufficient funds.

I had never experienced a job lay off. It was a new loss to handle. About a week after the layoff, we discovered that Shelly was four weeks pregnant. That was yet another shock. First, because I wasn't sure I could produce children as none were born in my previous marriage. Second, Shelly worked two part-time jobs as a nanny and her income alone wound not carry the two of us, let alone adding a child to the equation.

In our pre-marital sessions we also discussed; if we were to have children, whether biological or adopted, Shelly would become a stay-at-home mom. Our family values dictated that we raise our children rather than babysitters and daycare facilities. No disrespect toward anyone who uses those options, we just felt having Shelly stay home was best for us. To keep our modest lifestyle, I would have to earn at least the sum of our combined income.

We got excited about the amazing gift of a coming child but I needed to find a job. Two weeks later I landed a great new position. My starting salary decreased a little from my previous job, and I also had to commute to Oregon, thirty-five miles each way. Morning commute time was less than an hour but the trip home often took three hours, sometimes four.

In faith, I took the job and endured the extra fuel expense and commute time. My new boss noted my work ethic and waived the ninety day waiting period, providing medical insurance coverage so Shelly could get the prenatal care she needed. That was a huge blessing for us.

The next paycheck I had expected having less take-home pay because of the deduction for insurance premiums, but it seemed the amount was higher than I predicted. I asked my HR manager to explain. She said I had a garnishment taken from my check.

She didn't think it was fair the way the writ of garnishment for child support was processed. She knew the government agency responsible for the garnishment had not followed its own rules and she hated having to do what they asked. The standard operating procedure allowed for a thirty day notice, but they required my company to take immediate payroll deduction without notifying me.

Two pay periods later, I went back to HR for another explanation of short funds. I had taken a couple personal days and wondered if those hours got missed by mistake. Just like the child support garnishment, through clandestine means the Department of Revenue executed another writ of garnishment for back taxes owed.

I did a little investigating. It was my understanding that a person's wages could be garnished up to twenty-five percent. I found out the rule does not apply to governmental agencies, who could take up to twenty-five percent each.

A jagged little pill to swallow, but running from my problems would solve nothing. I faced the music and asked God to see us through. Besides, I had found a job I enjoyed. We had to rely on our faith at that point.

A few months into my tenure, I took a promotion to a project manager position. It was a move which carried a modest, but much needed, increase in salary. By the seventh or eighth month on the job, the boss asked if I had an interest in the chief estimator position. I loved my job as a PM and told him I would take the estimator position only if he would allow me to keep my PM responsibilities. He agreed, since he could cover two positions with one person. A fair man, he provided a salary increase which exceeded our needs for Shelly to be a stay-at-home mom, even with the two garnishments. It was an answer to prayer, and a dream come true for her.

I worked eight hours per day and commuted four. Shelly would be home with our baby all day, and I would only spend time with him on weekends.

We decided it would be best to move back to Oregon to be closer to my office. Our search for rental homes was futile. Every time we looked at one, someone outbid us on the rent. We found a home out in the country which exceeded our expectations, in terms of square footage and amenities, and the landlord accepted our offer. He mentioned he had turned down others who offered more, which we counted as yet another blessing.

We signed a lease to move in on January first, just four weeks before the due date of the baby. Shortly before the move, we had a Christmas party at the office and I received an envelope from a raffle drawing. I was disappointed to find four tickets to a Portland Trail Blazers basketball game. I was not a sports fan, so I figured I would just give them to someone who would use them.

The vice-president's wife leaned over and told me to list them for sale online. I took her advice and sold them for $500. That money made it possible for us to buy a crib and dresser for the baby's room, yet another unforeseen blessing. At that party, I also received an award for the employee of the year which included a small stipend. We could not deny the Lord's provision.

Our new landlord allowed us to have the keys early and did not charge us for the last few days of December so we moved the day after Christmas. So many friends and family graciously helped on both ends.

After the move, Shelly began the nesting process to prepare for the little one. Early in the pregnancy, we bought a little Christmas dress as we believed the baby was a girl, but the sonogram showed the baby was a boy. After changing our mindsets to think boy, instead of a girl, we began the process of choosing a name. I already knew what I wanted to name him; it was a name with deep meaning for me. In the Bible, Jacob had twelve sons, one of them he named Asher. The name means happy in Hebrew. Jacob named his son Asher because the child brought happiness to the man in his old age. This little boy definitely brought joy into my life. I was thirty-nine when Asher arrived, twenty years after the birth of my first son, Gerrod.

Given a second chance, I had a brand new baby boy who bore such a striking resemblance to his older brother. My heart filled to overflowing, with a love I didn't think was possible. Not only did God show me I could love again, He also opened my heart with a capacity for limitless love.

Watching my baby boy sleep, I thought about where I had been, and how far I had come. This gift of new life was double sided, new life I held in my arms, and new life I held in my heart. Once I was a broken and wounded soul, desperate for love, but now I basked in a joy so glorious, so amazing, so wonderful, all I could do was rejoice. My sense of purpose revived; but, I did not know the full extent of that purpose other than to be the best husband and father possible.

At the behest of my bride, I went to the doctor for a physical. In the past, I looked forward to leaving this world, so it never made sense to visit a doctor.

It seemed like a reasonable thing to do since I turned forty that year. I agreed to get checked out to make sure everything was in good working order. I had a brand new wife and baby to provide for, not to forget my older son whom I still longed to find.

The physical part of that first exam was no problem. The doctor ordered a blood draw to check for various things and the results showed a severe cholesterol problem. My numbers surprised the doctor because they were so out of whack, he said it was miraculous I hadn't suffered a heart attack.

The doctor prescribed medications to reduce triglycerides and bad cholesterol and increase the good. He suggested I change my lifestyle or I wouldn't be around long enough to see Asher grow up.

That wake-up call was motivating, but it posed a dilemma. My picky eating habits were the biggest contributor to my condition. I had pizza almost every day, for twenty-five years. If not pizza, it was burgers, or chicken nuggets, and lots of sweets.

All the way back to when I was seventeen and moved out of my parents' house, that was my diet. My only claim to eating vegetables was the lettuce and pickles on my burgers, which I thought counted for something.

I started with the medication and then addressed the dietary issues; cutting out a majority of the fried food, sacrilegious for someone from the South to do. I also discovered a new beverage; water. Growing up in Oklahoma where the water quality was poor, you had to flavor it with tea or kool-aid, and copious amounts of sugar to drink it. I always opted for soda, consuming two or three per meal, every day, for years.

The doctor ordered that I come in every three months for a blood draw to check my numbers. Each time I came in, the numbers showed improvement, but every time the doctor increased the dosage on the medication. No fan of taking pills, I did not like the way they made me feel, especially the high dose of niacin (3,000 mg/day) which caused almost unbearable flushing.

The meds also seemed to make me irritable, a feeling I was all too familiar with but one I no longer wanted. The increase in dosage, coupled with my growing frustration with my own moodiness turned me into a hyper critical person. This idea of grace, which I had learned about in church, faded and I lost patience for others, especially in traffic.

I also felt very isolated where we lived. I had never lived in a rural area before. Many people dream of the peace and solitude of country living, but that lifestyle didn't work for someone longing for connection with other people. I had a taste of connectedness through church and I missed it. With a newborn and a bride suffering from mild postpartum depression, living out in the country was not all that fun.

After the first two blood draws, I met with a different doctor each time. Whether the insurance provider changed, or the doctor moved, there was no consistency in the doctor/patient relationship and that also made me grumpy.

Our lease came up for renewal and the owners considered selling the house. Their decision put us in a bind, forcing us to search for another home, in a boiling rental market. My perceptions of injustice grew again, reminiscent of my "Falling Down" days, if you will. Only this time, I recognized the shift within. Lost in a fog because of the medicine, I didn't know how to rectify the situation.

God's hand was upon me but I couldn't see it. Shelly had another aunt and uncle who had purchased a new home and kept their old one as a rental. Stained by pets from a previous tenant, the carpet needed replacing. Her uncle wanted to install hardwood flooring instead. They let us rent the place for the budget we could afford, and I agreed to install the new wood flooring to return the favor. That house was only a four minute drive from my office.

We finished the floor and moved in just before celebrating Asher's second birthday. It was nice to be close enough to ride my bike to work which helped with my exercise regimen. A downturn in the economy loomed and my boss sold the building and moved to a smaller facility. A strategic move for the company, but it put an end to cycling to work.

The time came for another quarterly blood draw at the doctor's office, and as usual, I had a new physician assigned. When I arrived for the appointment, I was in a crabby mood. The nurse took my vitals and left me to wait for the doctor.

After several minutes, perhaps fifteen, in walked a very peppy, short statured man of Asian descent, who asked the purpose of my visit. My mood was foul by the time he walked in. After making me wait so long, he had quite the nerve popping into the room in such a jovial manner. Who did he think he was, anyway?

I explained to him why I was there, and why I was not happy about it. I insisted he get on with it and send me to get my blood drawn so he could raise my dosage yet again. Even after I dumped on him, his bedside manner remained chipper and pleasant. He angered me, but I noticed he had something I wanted, a joyous spirit.

He left the room, and another nurse escorted me to the lab for the blood draw. Once that was complete she brought me back to wait for the doctor to discuss the results.

Another fifteen minutes of waiting in a tiny exam room, with nothing to do but sit and marinate in my misery. The doctor returned without the nurse and asked me to stand.

With a Cheshire grin on his face, he looked me in the eye and said, "I know exactly what you need." He caught me off guard as he leaped up and planted a giant bear hug on me. I pushed him away, telling him I definitely did not need that. I was a married man, thank you very much!

Unbothered by my rejection, he asked me to count my male friends. I informed him that was none of his business and I was not interested in any homosexual encounters.

"I'm not talking about homosexuality; I'm talking about male friendships. How many guys do you consider a friend, could you call at 3 am to ask for help, who would be there for you no matter what?"

Still reeling from the hug, I insisted there were several, but as I thought about it, I realized they were only male acquaintances. Most were only connections because they were the husbands of friends my wife had. I never wanted to attend social gatherings because I would watch everyone else interact while I sat there, invisible to everyone.

The doc was right; I had no one who fit that description. He told me how critical it was to my physical health, and my mental and spiritual health, to foster deep relationships with male friends. He also suggested I heaped an unfair burden upon my wife by expecting her to meet needs that weren't hers to meet.

The prognosis he gave that day was to find a friend or two and then finish the prescriptions until they ran out. He was confident that if I were to form genuine friendships with other guys, I would no longer need the pills. He was correct.

On my way back to work I thought I had just been through the absolute weirdest doctor visit ever, but it caused me to ponder everything he said. All afternoon, I thought about the profoundness of my experience that day. It was a pivotal point in my life.

I could tell God was teaching me something as I had an epiphany. One effect of my molestation experience was a lack of trust toward men. That lack of trust built a wall which prevented me forming normal relationships with other guys. I was subconsciously fearful of men. That fear led to homophobia. The homophobia manifested itself when the doctor sprang a bear hug on me. God had been revealing Himself since my second divorce; that He was real, and that He was my provider, through many miracles and blessings. With the incredible experience I had at the doctor's office, the Lord showed me He was my healer.

I could not wait to share this revelation with my bride but it was too personal to do over the phone. I decided I would hold off until after we had dinner and put Asher to bed. To my dismay, Shelly fell asleep when I was reading bedtime stories to Asher. Tired after a long day of "momming", I didn't wake her.

I did the next best thing. Not wanting the day to pass and forget any details, I wrote her an email, thinking she might read it the following day during Asher's naptime.

She indeed read the email that next day and replied to it with her own letter of revelation. Shelly misunderstood the intent of my letter. In fact, her perception was that I intended leave our marriage for someone else.

I have learned something on my journey. Many couples marry with the assumption their spouse will complete them. No one person can complete another. One person completing another is a fallacy which leads to disillusionment, opening the door to extramarital affairs and divorce.

My wife's misguided assumption, opened my eyes to the fact we are all just broken people, going through life trying our best to hide our brokenness from others. As wonderful as she is, my bride is a broken person too. She brought her invisible baggage into the marriage. I had a choice to make, react negatively to her lack of trust by responding in haste, or, I could wait and try to help her better understand my intention. I waited until I got home. It would be several more years before the wounds of betrayal, inflicted by her first husband, scabbed over enough to allow her to begin her own healing process.

Friends, the process of healing sometimes takes years to come to fruition. There are many factors at play, but one of the greatest is a person's unwillingness to admit to brokenness. We want to believe we have it all together, but coming to terms with our imperfection is the first hurdle to leap on the journey toward healing.

In my humble opinion, people wounded by molestation or marital infidelity, have more difficulty understanding their own brokenness. Their refusal to acknowledge their own sin leads them to becoming judgmental and hypercritical of the sins of others, which was the case for Shelly and me.

What neither of us understood then was the power we held onto as a "victim" in life, was the same power that kept us ensnared as victims. For myself, perhaps there's a reason the road to healing is so long, it might just be that it takes time to make my courage strong. To overcome, it takes great courage, great strength, perseverance, deep faith, and a willingness to heal before one can walk in victory.

The Lord, in His grace, had shown us some amazing things, but it was a small sample of what He would do next.

49

MY POSITION AT WORK AS A PROJECT MANAGER PROVIDED opportunities for travel. I worked on high rise condominium towers in Los Angeles, San Diego, Seattle, Portland, Las Vegas, Hawaii, and Austin, Texas. I got to visit all of them except Hawaii. My boss always volunteered to visit those projects himself, go figure.

I had three towers in Las Vegas which required my presence on-site for a week at a time, over ten straight months. It was fun having my family join me on two of those trips.

I had been sensing in my spirit that the Lord wanted to use me as a chain breaker in my family. A lot of destruction and wreckage exists but I couldn't see how anything I did would rectify any of it. During my time in Reno, mom's oldest brother Larry spent an evening with us when he came through town on business. It was great to see an actual family member, and I looked forward to more reunions.

I traveled to Austin to inspect the sixty story tower in progress. I discovered mom's younger brother Steve, and his wife Anne, lived in Houston. Shelly and Asher joined me on that trip and I hoped to visit with my aunt and uncle while we were in town.

To my delight, they agreed to a visit and drove all the way from Houston to Austin. We spent the better part of two days together and it was fantastic. Since I had reconnected with both of my uncles, the dream of locating my son reignited.

I searched for my oldest son often, and the internet made searching easier. Since the legal system failed me multiple times, I had resigned myself to waiting it out. I thought once my son reached the age of emancipation, his mother would no longer keep him from me by hiding behind the law. He was a grown man when I visited Austin but I didn't know where to find him.

On a somewhat regular basis, perhaps every two to three months, I would enter both my ex-wife's name and my son's into a search engine. More often than not, the result of said searches was links to sites requiring various amounts of money before providing basic information. Only one time did I surrender any hard earned cash to one of those sites. I paid $19.95 (that price point should have been a clue) for a full report that listed N/A for all items other than names. Those sites proved they were nothing more than scams.

One day, while searching online, I hit pay dirt. I found two sites listing my son's name, one of which was Facebook. There was no picture on his profile page but there was a partial email address listed. The other site had an article showing someone with my son's name being promoted to E-5 in the Army.

With a wild guess, I filled in the rest of the email address after the "@" sign. I expected it to get rejected so the only thing I wrote was "HI" in the subject line. I assumed the worst that would happen was nothing, and the best would be a return response showing it was an undeliverable e-address.

The next day there was a response and before I even opened it, I suspected it was the undeliverable response. I almost fell out of my seat when I read the words, "It's about time you found me". At once, I set up a Facebook account and sent him a friend request. He surprised me when he accepted.

Was this real? Had I found my son?

We communicated through electronic means. In the beginning, there was a lot of anger in his tone and he asked only a few questions about the divorce. He didn't ask much about my current life but I volunteered it. I told him he had a step-sister and a little brother. Both kids knew of their brother's existence and always wanted him in their lives as much as I did.

Rarely did he respond to those types of messages. He spoke of his endeavors as a soldier, of being deployed to Afghanistan and Iraq several times. At a new post in Alaska, he was adjusting to the snow instead of the hot desert.

It took a while before he shared a few pictures of himself. Because of things which happened in my relationship with his mom, there was always a slight bit of doubt whether he was my son. Any doubts I had fell away when I saw one particular photo of him with his dog. That photo might have substituted as better proof than an actual DNA test as the resemblance was so strong.

We continued an electronic relationship for several months until one day I received a voicemail from him. The battery on my cell phone had died while I was out with my family. By the time I got home and charged the phone it was almost midnight. I could tell by the message my son was in distress, and figuring he was in a time zone one or two hours behind mine, I called him back right away.

He was actually in Texas, on leave, in a time zone two hours ahead, when he answered the phone. His relationship with a girl had dissolved, and he wanted to talk to someone who could relate to what he was going through. As much as my heart hurt knowing he was suffering the pain of a broken relationship, it was bittersweet to speak to my son again. Twenty years had passed since I last heard his voice. It was the first and last time he called me. I tried to call him on other occasions but always got his voicemail. Sometimes he responded on Facebook, or via email, but never the phone.

Shortly thereafter, he let me know he was deploying to the Middle East again, and could not share the location or the duration of the deployment. Gone for close to a year that trip, I was so glad to receive a few messages from him during that time. Each message received broke the silence and let me know he was still alive, but the silence lingered on.

Meanwhile, little brother Asher was growing like a weed. We could tell Asher would be a social kid from a young age. Shelly and I considered adding another little one to our family so Asher would always have someone close in age to grow up with.

We soon discovered Shelly was pregnant. We went to prenatal appointments, and the excitement grew as we prepared for a little sibling. Everything progressed well until the ninth week appointment. Being in her mid-thirties, the doctor wanted to see Shelly more often than usual in the first trimester.

On this visit, the doctor checked Shelly's vitals and everything looked good. She then placed the monitor on her tummy to listen to the sound of the baby's heartbeat. We watched the doctor's face as she moved the probe around and her expressions gave cause for concern. More adjustments, more pressure on the abdomen as she searched for that unmistakable sound, but there was no heartbeat.

Without speaking, the doctor left the room in haste and returned with an ultrasound machine. The room was completely quiet as she searched for the visual heartbeat. We saw the embryo on the screen but it was clear there was no movement. The diagnosis was miscarriage; the treatment was an immediate Dilation and Curettage, or D & C.

Shelly said the procedure was more painful than giving birth. There was a sadness we felt during recovery, mourning the loss of our second child. The impact of loss resulted in a slow recovery, for both of us. Our families knew about the loss but we chose not to share it with Asher as he would not have understood as a toddler.

Several months later we discovered Shelly was pregnant again. We did our best to avoid things which might jeopardize the pregnancy, but we settled down and trusted God had the situation under control.

In the first trimester we could test the baby for certain birth defects. Would-be parents could decide whether to terminate the pregnancy if they discovered the baby had Down's syndrome, for example. There was no need for discussion, we both agreed to accept whatever baby we got and love it, regardless.

In my experience working with people with disabilities, I learned that all people have value, regardless of any defect or flaw. In fact, some of the most beautiful people I have met have Down's syndrome. It was a no-brainer for us to decline that blood test.

For a second time, the home we rented got put on the market for sale. Our landlord gave us first right of refusal. Unable to get a mortgage due to the financial burdens I carried from two divorces, we were back to searching for a place to rent.

The search for rental property continued to be very stressful. We found a property which was having an open house the following day. The listing agent would not accept any applications or deposits unless the potential tenant walked through the unit beforehand. Without even seeing the inside, I downloaded the paperwork from the property manager's website, filled it out, and wrote a deposit check.

The open house was at 11:00 the next morning, and I was at work just a five minute drive away. Shelly called at 10:30 and said I should get to the house quick because fifteen cars full of people waited to view the home. She had already walked through the house, so when I got there I was the first to turn in my paperwork and deposit. The angry look on people's faces, and the hostile complaints, made me nervous that someone would start a fight. The rental market was just that hot.

They approved our application for the home and we signed a two-year lease. We gave notice to vacate our current house and buttoned up all loose ends to prepare for the move. One week prior to moving, we had all the utilities switched over to the new address, changed our address with the post office, and rented the moving truck.

A few days before moving day, the property manager called to share some "bad news". The home owner decided to sell the home rather than lease it and they canceled our lease agreement.

I wish I could say I smiled and said, "No worries, we trust that God had a better plan." What I did was panic. Were there legal recourses we could have taken? Maybe, but without money and time to deal with it we pressed forward.

Another member of the family had a client who wanted to lease their home but were not looking forward to bringing in destructive tenants. Not aware that we had found something, Shelly's aunt gave her clients a background story on us and asked if they wanted to meet us.

The couple agreed and passed along their contact info. This happened the day after we lost the other place. Excited about the lead, we planned to view the home that evening.

At first sight we loved the house, and the owners liked us. We had another property to view afterward, so we told the couple we needed to see that one before deciding.

Before leaving, I realized we had not discussed the rent amount. Our budget, already stressed with a rent payment of $1,100 per month, and the asking price for that house was $1,700. I shook the man's hand and apologized for wasting his time. There was no way we could afford the extra $600 per month. I also knew he would not have any trouble renting it for that amount.

As we thanked them for the tour, the couple whispered something between themselves. They suggested we go look at the other property to see if it worked better for us while they considered their options.

We left in low spirits. After viewing the second home, the decision was easy to make because it fit our budget. As promised, I called the couple back to thank them for their time and consideration, but we could not afford more than $1,100. I wished them well in their endeavors and said goodbye.

Before hanging up, the gentleman asked me to return that night to discuss a potential option. I didn't want to appear rude by telling him no, I felt the least I could do was hear him out since he was so gracious to us earlier. I knew the visit would be futile.

Minutes later, we knocked on the door and Asher ran inside to claim his bedroom. Embarrassed by his behavior, Shelly chased after him and whispered we would not get to live there. She could not convince our three-year-old otherwise, he had already staked a claim on his room.

Shelly took our boy outside to redirect his attention, and while she was outside, the couple told me how much they enjoyed meeting us earlier. They loved watching Asher as he delighted in walking through the house.

I expected they would extend a counter offer, perhaps reducing the rent by $100 to $150. We were astounded when the man offered the home at $1,100 to meet our budget, with the stipulation I finish a few projects they had yet to complete.

The house got all new plumbing and the walls which had sheetrock replaced needed new texture and paint. There was a well pump that needed replacing and a ceiling to install. If I would complete those projects and email pictures of the work to them, they would love to have us rent their home.

That was an absolute God-send. They didn't even want a security deposit from us. They asked what our target move-in date was and surprised us again, agreeing to move out earlier than expected. There was one stipulation. They needed use of half the garage for short term storage until other family members could retrieve the last few pieces of furniture. That was no problem.

God had a better plan for us, despite our small faith.

Banned from helping with the move, Shelly was eight months pregnant and had experienced symptoms of preeclampsia, resulting in bedrest. The stress of moving, and the events leading up to it, took a toll on her.

The evening before the big move I took a trailer load of stuff to the new house to get a head start. On the way back, I received a call from the property manager of the house we lost. She called at 8:30 pm to give me the "good news" this time. The property owners changed their plan to sell the house, and it was available to lease again. We had first dibs but there was one change to the deal. The rent had gone up to $1,600 per month.

I thanked her for thinking of us and informed her we had secured another home, for $1,100 and it was 800 square feet larger. She responded by saying it was impossible for us to find such a deal. I said, "I know, thank you for calling," and hung up.

God had not only provided a miracle by giving us more than we hoped for, but He also saved us from doing business with an unethical company. There never was a plan to sell; they realized they had left money on the table by offering the place for less than market value.

With many helping hands on moving day, we finished sooner than I expected. We set up the bedrooms first so my family could come home before the weekend was over.

As is often the case, the Lord, in His perfect timing, makes things happen right on time. The weekend after we moved in, we welcomed our little Princess Amelia into the world three weeks early. We like to say she came early because she didn't want to miss out on anything, but her early arrival was likely instigated by the stress of the move.

We got to the hospital, and the doctor said three weeks early was close enough, so she admitted Shelly into a birthing room. After several hours on Pitocin, the nurse broke the water membrane to encourage delivery. Thirty minutes later, without time for an epidural, Shelly delivered our little girl after just two pushes.

All was not bliss and joy, however. Our little six and a half pound baby girl was completely purple, almost eggplant purple, from head to toe. My immediate thought was that she was stillborn because she looked dead. Within seconds she moved a little, followed by the cry that said "I'm alive!"

The sight of a little purple baby shocked us. It was difficult to process the image. The nurses seemed unbothered by it and assured us everything would be all right. They explained it was a common occurrence. The purple was bruising which takes place when babies make a rapid evacuation from the womb.

The nurses took baby Amelia for a bath and did all the normal things they do for a newborn. Asked to lie back in the chair beside Shelly's bed and remove my shirt, they placed my daughter against my chest, skin to skin. The suggestion was for Shelly to sleep while I held they baby.

Over the next several hours I watched the scary little purple raisin of a baby turn pink, and then on to her normal color. In retrospect, it was a beautiful moment of bonding with my little girl which I will never forget.

50

THE EXCITEMENT OF A HAVING A NEW BABY WAS SHORT lived. Sleepless nights are normal and expected. This was not our first rodeo, enduring the one, three, five o'clock feedings, but something was different. Baby Amelia did not go back to sleep after nursing. We received a baby co-sleeper as a shower gift which allowed Shelly to keep Amelia next to her in bed.

The first appointment with the pediatrician showed Amelia's bilirubin count was too high. Perhaps jaundice was to blame for the fussiness. The doctor ordered a light blanket wrapped around the baby while she slept. The emanating light was to help with the jaundice. We also had to take Amelia to the hospital every day for two weeks for a heel stick to check the bilirubin count. Our poor baby's foot looked like a pincushion. The jaundice faded, but the fussiness got worse. In fact, her cries graduated to screams, and she screamed inconsolably for hours at a time. Even though managing high rise tower construction was stressful, I was lucky to get a break from the screaming when at the office.

The housing market bubble had burst a couple years prior, resulting in a complete halt to new single family home and multi-use high rise construction. Our business took a hit but survived a couple more years through attrition.

As the crisis worsened, layoffs occurred. I filled the role of two people which added a level of job security for me. By early 2010, I was the last estimator and project manager on staff, with the last project. The sixty story tower in Austin neared completion when we encountered delays caused by other trades, finishing our scope in May instead of January.

For lunch every day, I drove the few miles home to give Shelly a break from the kids. On the day the Austin project received the Certificate of Occupancy, I was excited because it meant the project was complete. It was my greatest accomplishment with the company.

I took the project at the 20% design development stage as the estimator, and carried it through to completion as the project manager, a duration of four years. Also cause for celebration, as it was the only project I had full control of from start to finish. We wrapped up the project with a record gross profit margin. I was the guy who ran projects underbid by others, requiring damage control to mitigate losses.

It was a great feeling of accomplishment I couldn't wait to share with my bride. A sleep-deprived, postpartum depressed mommy of a rambunctious three-year-old and a fussy newborn, she did not share the same level of excitement. On that day, she didn't even want to take her usual lunchtime shower. A nap was all she wanted.

I hated waking her, but I had to get back to work. It took a few minutes to snap her back from her power nap, which made me late getting back to work. Upon my return, the boss called me into his office. Was I in trouble for being late from lunch? Ever punctual, it was strange for him to get upset over being late one time, by ten minutes.

The purpose of the discussion had nothing to do with my tardiness from lunch break. He had to lay me off. Because of the downturn in the economy, we had no more projects on the books and he could no longer afford my salary. To his credit, he delayed the inevitable as long as possible to make sure we had insurance coverage for the birth of Amelia. I have great respect for the man, and could fill chapters with stories of how he took care of my family.

Faced with this new reality, I now had to break the news to my bride. I decided I would wait to tell her until after 5 pm. My plan was to go apply for unemployment benefits to offset the news we no longer had any income.

As fate would have it, driving away from the office, she called my cell phone. I pulled over to talk, and she figured out I was in my vehicle from the sound of the turn signal. Unable to lie to her, I had to give the news over the phone.

Out of fear and insecurity, she reminded me of our freshly signed two year lease, not to mention the two car payments. We also had a sick newborn, with no solution for her constant screaming. She wanted to know my plan for the immediate future.

We wept together on the phone, and I wanted to run away and hide at that moment. I didn't want to face my family. As sole provider, with three people depending on me for their survival, I had let them down. As I sat in my truck, on the side of the road, I felt the weight of the world upon my shoulders. "Just come home," she said, "I need you here to help with the baby."

Amelia was a happy baby during the day, but like clockwork, every day from 4-11 pm she screamed. Those were not just the cries of a colicky baby, they were blood curdling screams. She looked us in the eyes, her beautiful blues glazed over with tears, begging for us to help her. We took her into the pediatrician's office at least once a week, trying to get help, to no avail.

Since I was home more than usual, I helped lift the burden from Shelly. We assumed Amelia was born with the same condition Asher had, Gastroesophageal Reflux Disorder (GERD). Our pediatrician was not willing to diagnose that condition for Amelia, citing her belief it was just colic.

We took baby girl for walks to distract her with sights and sounds, always keeping her in a vertical posture to reduce reflux. Sometimes I would walk for blocks around the neighborhood and Amelia would cry and scream the entire way. One time it got so bad a neighbor from behind came to our house to see if we were abusing the child.

After several months of constant screaming, there were times of desperation when being older and wiser parents was a life saver. If Amelia was born in our early twenties, one or both of us could have gone to jail for shaken baby syndrome.

Shelly and I developed a code word for one to let the other know to take over if we felt ourselves losing control. A few times the time lapse between volleys was as little as twenty minutes. Sleep deprived, unemployed, stressed out parents, frustrated by the lack of answers, we were ready to go crazy.

The job market was terrible and I could not find work anywhere. Employers required master's degrees for positions once requiring only a high school diploma. With the aid of a federal grant, I could go back to school; with hope the added education would increase my chances of finding work.

In trying to decide the best field of study from the choices available, I looked for a field not likely to get outsourced to another country. I settled on Bioscience Technology. It had been twenty-five years since I last attended school. On the first day of classes we jumped right into it, performing DNA extraction from a strawberry. Taking college courses after all that time made my brain hurt. It was quite a juggle to balance school, work search, and family but we made it.

I was unemployed for eight months. Unemployment compensation was only thirty-five percent of my previous income, but in that time I never missed a payment. Our family helped by providing groceries and medical necessities. Our church also helped with money and groceries. On one occasion, a couple from the church stopped by to deliver thirty-five paper bags full of groceries. The Lord's provision was definitely clear to see.

We continued to lead small group Bible studies in our home. I took a full course load of sixteen credit hours plus studied to lead the small group sessions. I was so busy during that season I longed for a job just to get a break.

Toward the end of the semester I found a job, though it was not in the Bioscience industry. It was closer to the construction field I had come out of. Two weeks from graduation and though it meant delayed financial recovery, I asked my new employer if they would hold the position until I finished classes. Thankfully, they agreed to let me finish. To my amazement, I completed the program with a 4.0 grade point average and had made the President's list. It was also an honor when one of my instructors asked to use my personal resume as part of her curriculum.

I started the new position on December 20th, just five days before Christmas. With a 40% pay cut at the new job, we had no money to buy presents for anyone. On Christmas day, our kids had to take naps mid-way through opening gifts because they had so many. Blessed by so many family members and friends, I couldn't believe.

5 1

ONE SUNDAY MORNING, WHILE LISTENING TO THE SERMON in church, I had an experience which made me feel as though I had gone deaf. I could see the pastor speaking but no sound made it to my ears. Closing my eyes and bowing my head, trying to reboot my ears, I heard an internal voice. The message concerned my son, who was still overseas in a war zone.

"You shall soon realize that I have a purpose for your pain. You will need to prepare your heart as your son will lose a limb."

Never had I heard God's voice, but I was certain it was a direct message from Him. With my head still bowed, I sobbed. When I realized I was crying, I tried to suppress the tears, which invoked choking sounds, drawing my wife's attention. She asked if I was all right, confused by my behavior. "The sermon is great but why are you crying?" she queried.

In hesitation, for fear she would consider me looney; I shared the experience with her. In response, she said all we could do was pray. She was right; there was nothing else I could do.

I prayed every day, "Lord, please, no, please don't allow this to happen to my son. What can I do to prevent this?" I am all too familiar with the pain of traumatic amputation. Never would I want one of my kids to endure what I had. My soul was so troubled by this, and the more I prayed for it not to happen, the more haunted I felt.

Then something inside me changed. I don't recall what instigated the change, but I surrendered. My prayers changed from asking God to do what I wanted, to Lord, let your will be done. Whatever redirected my prayers, it was not something I decided on my own. Once I surrendered my will, the turmoil in my soul faded away. It didn't matter if my son lost a body part, I would just be thankful to have him come back alive.

Several weeks later, I got the message that my soldier son resumed his post in Alaska. The weight of the world lifted because that meant he had come home in one piece.

More relief came a few months later when he informed me he was leaving the Army once his enlistment was complete. Grateful and extremely proud of him for his service to our country, it was good knowing he would no longer be subject to deployments, which made me a happy dad.

When he got out of the military, he chose a school in Arizona to finish his degree in a diesel mechanics program. He made the move and started school, picking up a nighttime position as a bartender. As a concerned dad, I kept thinking he would soon graduate and leave that job.

We continued chatting, albeit through electronic means. He connected with my bride on Facebook and some of my other family members. His anger toward me reduced to the point the four-lettered words tapered off.

One day, I noticed a post on his Facebook page that was just a random set of letters. Initially, I thought it must have been a code he was using with his Army buddies. The following day, the random letters formed random clusters resembling words, but no real language. His friends posted things like "What's Up", and "Where are you". It still seemed like a game he and his friends were playing.

On the third evening, after the kids were in bed, Shelly was checking her Facebook account while I watched television. As she scrolled through her feed, she came upon a post that grabbed her attention. "David, you have to look at this post from your son!"

"Has he lost a limb?" was my response on my way to the computer screen. She looked at me with confusion on her face, wondering why I asked such a question. She read the post aloud. "Went to work, woke up in the hospital missing a leg."

She had forgotten about the prophetic message I had received several months prior so it seemed to her like a strange question for me to ask.

At once my mind flashed back to that tear-jerking Sunday morning when the prophecy about my son came to me. I tried dismissing it afterward, thinking the prophecy resulted from a bad meal from the night before. Several months later, the prophecy had come to fruition!

DL BOOTHE

Later, I received private messages through Facebook. Several of my son's friends asked me how they could get in contact with his mother. I had no information, no phone numbers, only the Facebook connection, which he did not respond to. To have a child suffering from a traumatic injury, with no means of contacting him, is one of the worst feelings in the world. Prayer was my only hope.

<u>5 2</u>

THE NEWS OF MY SON LOSING A LIMB CAME WITH AN INITIAL
sense of shock, but an unusual peace replaced it. I sensed we
would rebuild our father/son relationship through this crucible of
tragedy.

Since I had no way of communicating with my son other than
Facebook, I posted a message asking him to tell me where he was.
He didn't respond to anyone's questions. I put the new social media
platform to the test. I posted a message asking if any of my
connections in Arizona could help me locate the hospital where my
son was.

A friend from high school was a trauma nurse, and she found
him. Due to privacy laws, she could not give me any information.
She called my son's room and spoke with him, telling him his father
was trying to reach him. Before she relayed my phone number, an
unidentified man grabbed the phone and in a hostile tone,
demanded I call his cell phone.

I thanked my friend for being the miracle in helping me find my
boy so quick. She wished me luck. Without hesitation I called the
cell number given, not knowing who I was calling. I got a voicemail
response, so I left a message with my name and phone number and
asked for an immediate return call. None came.

The day was Thursday when I called. I will never forget because
I had made plans for the following evening to go out with several
guys from church to see the movie "Courageous" on opening
night. Based on my doctor's suggestion, I had fostered relationships

with other males and thought it would be a good idea to ask them to join me to see that movie.

It was no coincidence everything came together the way it did. Thursday night I could not sleep. I may have slept an hour all night before going to work Friday morning.

I was zombie-like all day, as I tried to process everything. Since there was nothing I could do, I kept the movie night with the fellas, hoping for a nice distraction.

As the men gathered in front of the theater, I did something for the first time. I shared with the guys what was going on with my son and asked if they would pray with me. Fiercely independent, asking for help was never something I did well. Without hesitation they agreed, and we all locked arms right there on the sidewalk, while people filed past us into the theaters.

The movie is about intentional fatherhood as seen through the eyes of four police officers and their friend. As the story unfolded, I understood where I had failed as a man in both of my prior marriages, and maybe even my third.

I excelled in virtues such as loyalty, faithfulness, provision, and protection. My failures stemmed from apathy and passivity. I had not done well in leadership, specifically spiritual leadership. I realized one of my responsibilities, as a husband and a father, was to lead my family with a vision for the future.

Recalling all the years I looked forward to pushing up daisies from six feet under made me realize I had left my former wives in a state of uncertainty. I decided my failure in those areas was as destructive to the marriage as their respective infidelities had been.

About halfway through the movie, the main character's nine-year-old daughter is killed in a car crash. The crash occurred when the child was away from her parents, traveling in a friend's car. I thought of my own son, lying in a hospital bed somewhere, and I could not be there for him.

I lost all composure and sobbed. I didn't care what the surrounding people thought. That was a crushing moment. Looking around, I noticed I was not the only one in tears. The theater was full of men weeping over their own shortcomings.

After the film ended, the guys gathered again to pray for me and my son. That was a tender moment my doctor had referred to in his office. Somebody had my back. Distance may separate some of us, but those guys are still a big part of my life. All of them willing to provide help where needed, and I would do the same for them.

Within days of the discovery of my son's crash, his mother deleted all of his social media accounts, emails, and phone number for reasons I did not understand. She then transported him back to her home somewhere in Texas for rehabilitation. She changed her phone number too.

Once again, I lost communication with my son.

It made me angry that his mother would keep me out of his life, again. I released that anger and asked God to keep me from hardening my heart again. Never did I want to return to my dark place. I also prayed He would hold my son close and provide everything he needed to heal. I trusted God had a plan which He would show me someday, but until that day, He would have to give me what I needed to persevere.

It would be another six years before I found my son again. In those years, I often wondered what it was like for someone whose child had died. I couldn't help but feel they were better off than me. Forgive me if this sounds crass, but when a parent loses a child to death, closure comes, in most cases. In my situation, I lost my child when he was two, and again at twenty-four, though I knew he was still alive. The pain of loss remained in my heart. There was no closure.

53

SEVERAL MONTHS PASSED WITHOUT A WORD FROM MY SON. I wondered how he was doing in his recovery. Did he have complications with sepsis, or some other infection? The not knowing was difficult to handle.

Meanwhile, Amelia progressed with her reflux issue. While studying biology, I discovered she was likely born with a weak lower esophageal sphincter which allowed stomach acids to travel up her throat, causing burning and irritation.

I found a drug being prescribed for adults but not children. It took some convincing but our pediatrician finally agreed to prescribe it for Amelia, and it made a night and day difference. The drug was a proton pump inhibitor which reduced the production of stomach acid. Acid reduction allowed the esophagus and the L.E.S. to heal.

Our baby girl no longer screamed for hours every day. Her first year of life was intense, but we rejoiced in her ability to lie down and sleep without the acid burning her throat. In reflection, I thought I was executing a plan for my life but it was God who directed my steps. The switch from construction to bioscience made little sense, but in hindsight the purpose is clear.

For the third time since our wedding, our landlord informed us they intended to sell. With the rental market still boiling, we looked at houses on the Washington side of the river. My commute to work would be shorter and we would go back to our first church home.

We made the drive to Vancouver on a Sunday to attend church and look at houses while we were there. We enjoyed catching up with old friends and sharing our kids with them. After service, one pastor offered Shelly a position on staff at the church.

Asher was to start kindergarten that year, and we thought it would be great to have our kids attend the private Christian school affiliated with our church. We found a house to rent and signed a three year lease. The landlord guaranteed us he had no intentions of selling the property as it provided a second revenue stream for his family.

The things God did after we moved back to Vancouver were unreal. To recap, my salvation experience happened after a failed suicide attempt when I was twenty-two. That was my point of rock bottom. My twenties was a time when God took my hand and led me out of the pit. In my thirties He revealed Himself through signs and wonders. The first half of the forties the Lord did the transformational work of healing a broken and wounded heart. The latter half of that decade He revealed His purpose for me.

Through the following chapters you will see how my life comes full circle as the Lord redeems my struggles and pain. I give all glory to God; only He could make these things come to fruition.

Over the years, I have shared little segments of my story and when people hear of the tragedy and pain, they often ask what I did to overcome. They want to know what therapy worked, or what kind of counseling programs I went through.

I had next to nothing to do with my healing. About the only thing I can claim for myself, is I learned to trust in the God who made me, by placing my faith in Jesus alone. It was He who did all the work, which is why I share my story.

Right after we moved back to Vancouver, I received a tiny inheritance after my grandmother died. We decided it would be great to go to Disneyland that Christmas, and we invited many family members to join us. Our plans included taking my parents, my bride's parents, my sister, my sister-in-law, her husband and his family. All together there were fifteen of us. We made the reservations in May and had to keep it a secret from the kids until Christmas Day.

Just before Christmas a public shooting happened close to us, at a shopping mall in a Portland suburb. A few days later another mass shooting occurred in Newtown, Connecticut at an elementary school. I noticed the two shooters had something in common; they were both kids of absent fathers.

The school shooting hit me hard because of all the children murdered. At the same time; however, I experienced a deep empathy toward the shooter. I wondered how different his life might have been if his family hadn't splintered. Saddened by the senseless deaths in the mall shooting spree; the shooter in that case also garnered my empathy. Both young men had deep father wounds, as did I, and they both made poor choices in a cry for help. The emotional pain they suffered I found easy to relate to.

I could not despise the gunmen with the rest of the nation. I wanted to hate them, but I couldn't. It's easy to mourn for the innocent victims, but what about those who inflict the damage? I pondered that question a great deal after the December 11, 2012 mall shooting.

December 21, 2012 began much like every other day. I helped get the kids ready for school and once they were on their way, I jumped in the shower. Excitement increased for Shelly and I as we were just days away from surprising the kids with a most amazing Christmas gift—their first trip to Disneyland, on Christmas day!

In the shower that morning, the two shootings held my mind captive as I washed my hair. I felt God's presence, as if He was physically in the room speaking with me about a mission He wanted me to carry out. "I want you to bring hope to the hurting," was how it started.

As I rinsed the soap from my scalp, I got clear instructions on how to bring that hope. Those instructions were to coordinate a *flash choir* at the mall, the very mall where the tragic shooting had taken place. What?!? I knew nothing about flash choirs, how was I supposed organize such a thing?

A dialogue with God ensued in the shower, of all places. He gave me the exact location of where to set up, the date, the time, and the five songs we were to sing. The song arrangement had a specific order. If there was significance to the order, I was unaware of it.

1. Hark the Herald Angels Sing
2. Joy to the World
3. Silent Night
4. O Come, O Come Emmanuel
5. O Holy Night

I continued to refuse the assignment, asking God to find someone else as I was not qualified to do such a task. Just like Jonah, I tried to turn and run the other direction.

A lover of music, I appreciate those who make it, but I have no talent or musical ability. The Lord and I discussed the mission for several minutes, with me doing everything possible to refuse. A flash choir was not in my skill set.

In my resistance, I drew my bride into the mix. We already had tight plans for Christmas Eve and could not fit the event into our schedule, let alone pull it together. How grateful I am the Lord is so long-suffering with me.

That's it! This little encounter with the divine was just a result of holiday stress, coupled with my deep feelings of empathy regarding the tragic loss of life. I would require a test to confirm this mission was truly from God. If, by a miracle Shelly agrees to do it, that would serve as confirmation. On the flip side, if she responded by shutting it down I would be free to believe the interaction was a fluke.

Shelly came home and I shared the news as if it were no big deal. In joyous anticipation, I waited for the reply that would get me off the hook and set my mind free. She might think I hit my head in the shower or something.

My chin must have hit the floor when she responded, "Well, if God told you to do that, then I guess we need to get it done." That was not the answer I had expected from her, it was quite the opposite.

Dazed by her reaction, I sat before the computer to draft song sheets, create a flyer, and post the event on Facebook. Anyone else might have thought I did this kind of thing in my sleep, but it was not my strength getting it done.

Since I was already going crazy, I thought it best to call the mall management to inform them of our intention. Out of respect for their heightened tension, I wanted to forewarn them there may be a couple people singing songs on Christmas Eve.

As I left the voicemail, complete with my name and phone number, I wondered what the mall staff would think when they retrieved the message. If it sounded crazy to me, they would think I was off my rocker.

The plan came together so quickly. I asked for volunteers to act as captains to start each song. Five people responded with their song choice. Others responded to the post they would love to join in the festivity.

On Christmas Eve we went to the mall to meet any others who showed up, in the food court area. Some folks who said they wanted to come backed out due to fear that an alleged copycat had threatened to kill again. Surprising even myself, I had no fear of taking my bride and kids on the mission that day.

People gathered at the staging area, I gave the details of the mission God had given me, and then sent the song captains to their positions. They were placed in strategic locations so that each time a song started; it would come from a different place in the mall.

After the final song began, we were all to gather at one spot on the second floor so the collective voices could make the greatest impact with volume. When we finished the last song, shoppers and passersby clapped and whistled and someone suggested we get a group photo. Altogether, thirty-seven people showed up to take part, not including the people who joined in as they passed by. Carolers traveled from as far away as fifty miles to be a part of that event.

After taking photos, I noticed one of our family members walking toward me with a puzzled look on her face. As she approached, she said a woman insisted on meeting the person responsible for organizing the event. She introduced me to the elderly lady and then stepped away.

As the woman spoke, it sounded like complaining. Every time she got close to the singers, the next song would start somewhere else, and she had to work her way through the crowd, trying to join in. She seemed quite frustrated.

Then she asked me the source of my inspiration for doing the flash choir. I figured I had nothing to lose, so I gave her the truth. I shared with her how God had given me the mission in the shower just three days prior.

She continued ranting, or so it seemed. When everyone gathered together for the last song, she and her friends had turned around to backtrack when she noticed a woman leaning on the glass railing of the mezzanine. The woman held her face in her hands as she wept.

She stopped to console the lady and asked if she was okay. She then asked if the lady worked in the mall. The lady responded yes. Her third question was, "Were you here the day of the shooting?" Through tears the woman said she worked at Macy's, behind the counter at the mall entrance. She watched as the gunman passed her counter and raised his weapon, killing his first victim before her eyes.

The woman died in the very spot we had gathered to sing the last song, O Holy Night. The two ladies embraced and the one from the Macy's counter mentioned to the elderly woman she had given up hope in humanity after the shooting. When she heard our group sing those songs, O Holy Night being her favorite one, hope returned.

As the elderly woman shared this story, she reached up and placed her hands on my cheeks. "Son, if your mission was to reach just one person by what you did here today, then you have succeeded. But you have reached at least two, because you got me, thank you!"

We wished each other a Merry Christmas before she turned to walk away. I never met the lady who had witnessed the shooting, but that was okay. Satisfied knowing we touched her heart, I prayed she would find the healing she needed. My words cannot express the gratitude for what God allowed me to see that day. The results of a simple act of obedience can be profound.

5 4

OUR FAMILY TRIP TO DISNEYLAND WAS AWESOME! IT WAS so much fun to wake unsuspecting kids at 4 am to get ready for our flight. We had kept the Christmas surprise a surprise. After three days at Disney, we ventured south to San Diego to visit SeaWorld. It rained that day and being from the Pacific Northwest, liquid sunshine was normal so we watched the outdoor shows while others escaped the drizzle. Rain made for much shorter lines.

A fun trip it was, but also a blessing to have celebrated Christmas with our family in such a memorable way. The cherry on top was coming home to find snow on the ground. My bride saw the snow as another gift from God as she and the kids longed for a white Christmas.

After several months, I wanted to organize a small group of men to go through a Bible study together. I had heard no audible voice this time, but the matter weighed heavily on my heart.

The residual impact of the Courageous movie led me to think there might be other men in our church who could benefit from the content the movie delivered. I set out to find others who may be interested, and to my surprise several signed up.

The plan came together as we met to watch the movie together, some for the first time. The movie had more impact on me than the first time I watched it. I had led a couple other studies by then, but those groups were small and co-ed. After we watched the film together, I spoke, for the first time, to a group of a dozen men, several of whom I had never met.

My voice quivered with passion as I shared the reason for starting the group and how important it was for men to regain lost ground in the culture war. The following week, eight men gathered to spend a couple hours together on Thursday nights for the next sixteen weeks, learning and growing together.

It was within this group that God showed me what a real leader was. Seven of the most amazing men I have ever met, graciously encouraged me as I submitted to the Lord's will in learning to lead such a group.

One of the weekly sessions involved sharing our testimonies. Shared testimony, of God's work in our lives, strengthens the faith of others. The man to my left to shared first, and as we progressed clockwise around the table, one by one, I listened as each man talked about his own salvation experience.

Raised in Christian homes, most of the guys accepted Jesus as their Lord and Savior at a young age. Because of that faith, they avoided many of the traps and snares set by sin.

It was refreshing to hear testimonies of men who had done well in their spiritual walk, but I was not looking forward to sharing my own. As each man finished speaking, the pressure mounted. When it was my turn, I apologized to the group up front, letting them know my story was littered with wreckage and telling it would bring down the mood.

Nervous, I spoke about the darkness described earlier in this book. I gave a brief 30,000 foot overview, which lasted only a few minutes but seemed like a lifetime. When I finished sharing, I told the guys I was unworthy to lead a group of such honorable men. The man to my left responded by saying he sensed I was uniquely qualified to lead the group. Others lamented their testimonies lacked sensation, which made them feel useless as believers. I received their comments in humility, but I wished my "sensational" testimony, as they called it, was more like theirs.

One man from the group remarked how important the study was for men, and how more men needed access to the information we learned. Because our church had abandoned the corporate men's ministry model, guys were left to float like asteroids in their spiritual journeys.

"If men's ministry is that important, why don't you guys set it up and lead it?" I suggested. "I would support you."

While everyone supported reinstating the ministry, none would take the bull by the horns to get it done. I left that night with heaviness on my heart. They were right, more men needed to know what we learned in that study, for the sake of marriages and families all over our community.

Another rumbling in my spirit motivated me into action. For many years, my heart was like a solid stone, until the Lord's hand reached into my chest to crush that stone and refashion it into a heart of flesh. For a majority of my life men represented intense pain, but that was changing.

Many guys are stuck in a cycle of destructive patterns, passed down through the generations. Wounded and broken men, left to their own devices, wound and break others until someone with enough courage steps in to help break the chains.

Chain breaker...

God wanted me to break the chains in my family, so I followed the Lord's lead to see where it would go. Share my story... what does that look like God? I attended a Celebrate Recovery meeting which met at our church though its attendees included people from several other churches.

The gathering started with a potluck meal followed by a time of corporate worship and a keynote speaker. The guest speaker that night was a pastor from one of the larger churches in the area and as he spoke, he captured my full attention.

In candid detail, the man shared his story. He led a double life, with one foot in ministry as a pastor, and the other foot in the world as a sex addict. I hung on to every word as he admitted having a porn addiction. When the porn no longer satisfied, he solicited prostitutes. He did all these things while pastoring a church and raising his family, all of whom were unaware of his double life.

As he spoke, more scales fell from my eyes. Instead of dismissing the man as garbage scum, repulsed by his sin choices, I saw the heart of the man as opposed to the sin in his heart. That shift in paradigm was not of my own will, it was an act of divine providence.

The meeting continued as the large group broke into smaller focus groups for more discussion. There were groups for alcoholics, substance abusers, food addicts, anger issues, and more. I must have appeared lost standing there in the middle of the room as everyone filed past me to find their respective focus groups. Unsure where to go, I considered going home until someone came back in the room and invited me to join his group.

The focus of the group unannounced before we walked into a familiar classroom. It was the classroom where I taught third grade Sunday school; a room which held special meaning for me.

As we sat in a circle, the leader gave instructions, for my benefit as a guest, on what the protocols were for the discussion. Each man had command of the floor during his turn to speak. No one else could speak until the person finished. No questions, no comments, no suggestions.

After the first man shared, I realized I had joined the group focused on sexual issues. One by one, each man shared either success or failures they had experienced over the past week, as it related to their particular struggle. One had strong urges to give in to his same sex attraction, another talked about his failure abstaining from pornography. Most intriguing that evening was the confession of a guy who looked like a straight-laced dairy farmer.

He and his wife had adopted two young girls, sisters as I recall, and he struggled against the temptation to de-flower the middle school-aged girls. A constant battle for him, he admitted to finding release through viewing pornography. His testimony upended my issue with judgementalism as he was not someone I would suspect of any wrongdoing.

I found myself in a den surrounded by hungry spiritual lions. Like the biblical Daniel, the Lord was there with me, whispering in my ear to fear not. A tremendous sense of peace washed over me as I listened to each one give an account. I had no anger or feelings of disgust for those men, a different reaction for me.

God orchestrated the entire experience, to include the room where the meeting took place. If given the choice up front, I never would have selected this group. These men were engaging in activities which led many to act out their selfish lusts and desires on innocent children.

To my wonderment, I listened to every testimony and looked past their sins, straight into their hearts, much like the Lord Jesus does with all those who seek His forgiveness. Not condoning their actions and choices to sin, I could see the brokenness of each one.

At my turn to speak, I shared that I was a survivor of childhood molestation, sent by God to encourage them to repent of the sin which ensnared them. I told them that submission to the Lordship of Christ afforded them all a means of escape whenever temptations came their way.

Though none of these men had hurt me personally, I wanted to extend grace to them. Their sins I could not pardon, but by grace I could lead them back to the Savior who alone could wash them clean, and set them free from their bondage.

Many valuable lessons I learned that night. God showed me it was the hearts of sinners He was after, to heal and restore, not control by means of behavioral modification. In my anger towards people who had violated me, I had become a judge towards others, seeing the person as their sin rather than a person, like me, who commits sins. He taught me that the wrath of man never produces the righteousness of God. I learned that in the eyes of God, all sin is equal.

My sins of harboring anger, being judgmental, withholding forgiveness, and countless others, were just as heinous in His eyes as sins of rape, murder, and incest. Sure, degrees of consequence vary, but to a Holy God, one sin is as all sin.

Understanding that concept was freeing because it leveled the playing field. It means I am no better than you, or anyone else, and vice versa. The Bible says we are created in the likeness and image of God, each one deserving of love and respect.

That meeting opened the door to the abundant life Jesus said He came to give all who placed their faith and trust in Him. God had saved me at twenty-two but I was reluctant to leave the familiar surroundings of the prison of my hard heart. That night I became a free man.

Back to the Courageous study group the next week, I was excited to share my experiences from the recovery group meeting with the guys. Refreshed by a new mindset, we continued our study to learn what authentic fatherhood looked like.

Similar to the movie, our study concluded with a resolution ceremony, complete with brides and families. Officiated by a pastor at the church, we each signed the resolution, symbolizing our commitment to take our roles as men, husbands, and fathers seriously.

As anyone who has walked an authentic journey of faith can attest, trials and tribulations continue to test us. Jesus warned His followers about those, but He also told us to fear not because He has overcome the world.

Knowing this principle to be true, I still questioned God of His whereabouts when some new test came my way. Such was the case when my bride received notice that the church eliminated her position on staff. It was her pay we used to send our kids to school there and without her income; we saw no possibility of keeping them enrolled.

It had been a real blessing for her to work on campus beside the kids. If she had to find a job elsewhere, we would have to remove them from the private school and find other means of daycare to cover before and after school hours. The extra costs meant it would be prohibitive for my bride to even hold a job.

At a loss for what to do next, we waited. As we waited, the day drew closer to Shelly's last day on staff. A couple weeks before her last day, I sat alone in the sanctuary while my bride worked. My mind was in a funk and I was angry about the job loss.

Rather than ask the Lord for direction, I let Him know just how frustrated I was with the whole thing. An old nemesis slipped back into my mind, victimhood. Rather than look to the Lord for direction, I complained about the decisions others made which had a perceived negative impact on my family.

The pastor delivered his sermon as I continued in my complaints to God. White noise drowned out every other sound, and a familiar voice spoke the following words. "I have allowed all these things to happen in your life, for such a time as this, that through your story, my glory would be revealed. Now is the time to tell your story."

The white noise faded and the sound of the pastor's voice filled my ears. One day I hope to overcome my stubbornness in responding to the Almighty. To this incredible word from the Lord, I replied with a resounding, "NO!" What did He mean tell my story, to whom? No one in my history ever had time for it and reliving it was not my plan. I left church that day defiant, unwilling to do what God asked of me.

A few weeks later, I was talking with some guys from my study group about men's ministry. Before I joined the conversation, they had decided it should be me who went to pastoral staff to petition a return of the men's group.

I resisted. No way would I lead that ministry because, in my mind, I was unqualified to preach or teach anything to a large group of men.

5 5

WORD SPREAD OF A MAN IN THE CHURCH WHO DIED FROM a self-inflicted gunshot wound to the head. A man invested in the church, he volunteered in multiple ministries, and his kids attended the school there. Known for his generosity, he would give the shirt off his back to anyone in need.

Though I did not know him, I felt compelled to attend his memorial service. I sat in the back corner like a fly on the wall. Memorial services often focus on the person's good side. My soul connected with this man's sorrow and pain which emanated from the photos of him flashing across giant screens. An all too familiar pain, almost three decades after my attempted suicide, it felt like only days had passed.

The Lord took another opportunity to teach me something through this experience. He gave me questions to ponder such as, where does a man turn when sin has him weighed down? Who can help him heal from prior wounds? Where should he turn to relieve pressure?

Reflecting on the questions, a particular verse came to mind. James 5:16 states, "Confess *your* trespasses (sins) to one another, and pray for one another, that you may be healed. The effective, fervent prayer of a righteous man avails much." This verse does not say we should confess our sins to other men to be forgiven; only God has the power to forgive sin. It does suggest a great benefit to linking arms with a brother (s) for the purpose of sharing our burdens. The power of prayer multiplies when men pray for one another.

"OK Lord, so what does that mean for me?" I asked. The Spirit reminded me our church had no men's ministry, and that He wanted me to do something about that. Still, I resisted.

A few days passed and the busyness of life reclaimed its grip on me, allowing the experience at the memorial service to settle into the archives of memory. One evening, our regular family routine proceeded as expected and we tucked the children into bed. A perpetual night owl, I read as my bride drifted off to sleep. I read, and re-read, the same passages multiple times, distracted by a persistent thought.

As I recalled the events which had taken place over the last several months, "Give the men a voice" remained the forefront of my thought. I continued reading until my eyes grew tired. After turning off the lights, the thought lingered, "Give the men a voice", until I fell asleep.

The dream began with me standing in line at the Gates of Heaven. The line was long but everyone waited their turn. As I approached the gate, I could just make out a man who checked each person's name against a list in a massive book.

With the name checked off, the person entered with exuberance. With a dozen people in front of me, a figure tapped my shoulder, and asked me to step out of line and take a seat a few paces away. It was disconcerting when pulled out of line so close to the end. Trying to stay calm, I waited and watched, as each of the people ahead of walked through the gate. Things changed when the person behind me stepped up to have his name verified.

The guy was denied entry at the gate. As he walked past me, headed to places unknown, he looked at me. Our eyes met and at that moment I felt despair emanating from this stranger, greater than any I had ever known. The same scenario unfolded as each person who stood behind me in line met with the same fate.

The figure who pulled me out of the line stood next to me. I rose from the chair, to inquire of the faceless being, why all the people who stood behind me in line were being denied access. "They are going to their chosen destination," the being replied. "Where might that be?" I asked. "They are all going to hell."

It concerned me because I was the divider in the line. Fearful that my destiny would be the same, I asked my host; "Why them? What difference separated those in front of me from those behind me?"

In a monotone voice the host replied, "Those behind you never accepted the gift of salvation found in Jesus." But why wouldn't they, I wondered to myself. The host responded to my thought by saying, "They never heard the Gospel because you never shared your story."

I awoke, sitting bolt upright in my bed, terrified and sweating profusely. My bride tried to comfort me but the vision had shaken me to the core. My willful rebellion, against the instruction God had given me, contributed to all those souls spending eternity in hell. Why, because the opinions others intimidated me? That dream was a wake-up call which instigated a call to one of our pastors, asking for an immediate meeting with him.

Grateful he could fit me in later that morning; I arrived at his office still shaken. I shared my experiences with the trusted pastor, hoping he could offer clarity and direction. He listened close, and when I finished he said, "David, it sounds like God has a very distinct purpose for your life. Should you continue to resist that calling, you will continue to suffer spiritual unrest."

I had been trying to do the Lord's will, but in my own strength and understanding. I had attempted to keep the almighty God in a safe little box I could control, and whose steps I could direct. My pastor friend helped me understand I should respond like Samuel did in the Old Testament. Eli told Samuel to respond to the next call from the Lord in this manner, "Speak, for your servant hears."

We wrapped up our visit with the pastor offering a prayer for me before I walked out to my car. I sat in the parking lot for a few minutes, in complete silence and reverence. "Lord," I prayed, "I'm done fighting you. Forgive me and help me do what you are calling me to because I can't do it on my own."

I started the car and pulled away just as the next song played on the radio. It was a song I had not yet heard, entitled *Help Me Find It* by the Sidewalk Prophets. The first couple of stanzas *hooked* me as it seemed to mirror my prayer.

> I don't know where to go from here
> It all used to seem so clear
> I'm finding I can't do this on my own
>
> I don't know where to go from here
> As long as I know that You are near
> I'm done fighting
> I'm finally letting go

By the end of the second stanza, tears flowed from my eyes and all I could do was rejoice in knowing God was very much with me. As the song continued, it seemed ordained for me to hear at that moment of surrender.

I'm done fighting, I'm finally letting go. That was exactly right. I scheduled an appointment to meet with church leadership for the purpose of relaunching the men's ministry. The road to healing is sometimes long to make our courage strong. It took every ounce of courage I had to stand up for what I believed in, even if it meant standing up to the church.

No longer could I stand by and idly watch other guys self-destruct in ways I knew all too well. Negotiations with pastoral staff lasted six months, and I met with a pastor every week to discuss the ministry. One week he understood the need, the following week he thought it was a waste of the church's resources. In retrospect, it's clear that God orchestrated every detail. The resistance I faced from the church was less about them and more for me. The road blocks were the means God used to ignite the fire of passion within me for the souls of men.

About halfway through the negotiation period, I asked the Lord to send like-minded men would make up our core leadership team. I remembered that still, small voice saying, "Give the men a voice." The Lord brought together a structure of responsibility with roles given to men wired in specific ways. There were teachers, trainers, worship leaders, exhorters, administrators, and tech operators; men who bought into the vision.

Once they approved everything, we launched the ministry with a Saturday morning breakfast. We had a budget to feed 30 people, but I knew we would have over one hundred men show up. The pastor I worked with increased the budget to cover 60. I promised it would still not be enough to cover everyone.

The day of the breakfast 130 men walked through the doors and we had to send runners to the grocery store twice to pick up more food. Many men waited in line for over an hour while the crew scrambled to cook more.

The following week, we launched the Tuesday night gatherings where we came together to spend time in worship, study, and small group discussion.

For the next two years, the Lord led me as I did my best to lead the men He placed in my charge. We watched the group grow, both in numbers, and in terms of their awareness of their identity in Christ.

I watched men find their voice, and it was a joy for me to see them use it. The teaching style I used differed from past iterations. Rather than standing up and preaching to the men for an hour, I engaged them through dialogue rather than a monologue. There was so much growth which resulted from giving any man the opportunity to speak his thoughts. The Spirit of God achieved many amazing things in that group.

A different style men's group, we introduced gatherings designed to complement our Bible study. We met for bowling once a month as a way of building relationships and comradery. Once a month we served our community through various projects designed to give the men opportunities to live out their faith in tangible ways outside the church walls. We acted as the hands and feet of Jesus and blessed our community in a myriad of ways.

We continued to offer the Saturday morning breakfast to expose new guys to the fellowship, with the hope of them joining us on a regular weekly basis. By the second year, at one breakfast event we had 355 men in attendance. I remain in awe of that gathering. Never had I dreamed of standing before a large group, men in particular, to pray and share a message from the Bible. As I got myself out of the way, forsaking my own fears for the benefit of others, God could use even this broken vessel through which to shine His light.

During one of the teaching series, we studied the life of Joshua. In the study, I spoke about a man's legacy. Prepared to give the message that night, I went to check my mailbox before going to church. A book entitled, "Know That He Is", by W. Jasper Woody was in the box.

The author is my maternal grandfather, whom I mentioned briefly in chapter 10. My brother had attended his funeral and forwarded a copy of the hard cover book. For me, it was the Lord himself who sent the book as a special gift. I never knew my grandfather, but with his autobiography in hand, I read all about his life. He pastored churches for over fifty years. He owned and operated a local newspaper, a radio station, and served as the Mayor of Benton, Tennessee.

I read the entire book in two days. The book included photos of this man of great importance to me. What a treat it was to read a story of his legacy. The book was a fantastic visual representation to use for the legacy discussion at the men's group.

Perhaps the **pièce de résistance** of my tenure as a ministry leader came when our church hosted a men's event called *The Main Event*, sponsored by Life Way Men. It was a large event with many well-known Christian speakers. One of them was Stephen Kendrick, Co-producer of the movie Courageous, the movie which had a huge impact in my life. I had the privilege of being Stephen's driver while he was in town.

Not one to get star-struck by celebrities, I felt I owed this man a debt of gratitude. He was the faithful conduit who God used to move me out of the ruts of passivity and complacency. After I picked him up at the airport, we stopped for lunch on the way to his hotel. What a pleasure it was to have conversations about God with Stephen.

As we made our way toward the hotel, a song came on in my truck. The song was "Because He Lives" by David Crowder. Stephen reached over and turned the volume up loud. Like old friends, the two of us sang together as we traveled down the highway, a moment I will never forget.

5 6

THE NEW YEAR STARTED WITH MOM FALLING IN HER HOME, shattering her elbow. She lay there on the floor, unable to get up for five plus hours, until someone came to check on her. They got her to the hospital where she remained for several weeks. Many complications arose after the elbow break, to include blood clots in the lungs and pneumonia. It looked like my mom's days were numbered.

I wrote a note to her on social media to encourage her to stay strong in the medical struggles she faced. I hoped my words blessed and encouraged her, but mom never responded to the post. She had forgotten her password and couldn't get back into her account.

Considering the circumstances, my bride and I took our family on a road trip to visit mom (Nana). I printed the note I had written and took it along for her to read.

In the piece, I started by imploring her to recount the events she endured as a twenty-five-year-old. A young mother of three children, all under the age of five, having never traveled far, was in Thailand, a country far removed from her home state of Alabama.

My goal was to help mom regain strength by reminiscing over earlier tribulations she had experienced, and how she had found victory over them. She had survived a car crash. She helped save the life of her injured child, and no one died on the jungle hillside that day.

When one of my own children skins a knee or breaks a bone, I hurt with them, but I can only imagine the stress mom felt. I wanted her to remember how she got through such a traumatic experience and find that strength within herself to persevere through her current medical situation. I encouraged her to fight and not give up.

A friend from church read the piece and asked if she could write mom a letter too, from one mother to another, to offer more encouragement. I gave her both documents and two days later, after everyone else went to bed, she told me she had read them. She asked how I learned about the crash in Thailand. I thought I upset her based on the look she gave. Most details came from my father, and an attorney.

I hired an attorney, just before my twenty-fifth birthday, to sue the US government before the twenty year statute of limitations expired. I gave the attorney all the information I had and asked him to communicate with my father for further details. A few weeks later, the lawyer informed me my father deployed to Thailand on a solo tour of duty. He assumed all risk by taking his family. Since we were not "command sponsored" we had to find civilian quarters off post. He also pointed out my father took restitution money from the two soldiers who crashed into us. Between the two men, he received $165 USD. Acceptance of that money amounted to an out-of-court settlement.

She said I didn't need to change what I wrote on social media but not all the details were correct. I don't want to put out misinformation, so I asked which details were inaccurate. The story of my limb loss, as mentioned in earlier chapters, I have shared countless times across the years. After forty-three years, I learned the truth. There was a slight tone of anger in my voice after I discovered the story I shared all my life wasn't true.

My next question was, "Mom, why have you said nothing about the crash?" As I sat there, reviewing my mental files, I had no recollection of a single time when mom disclosed any information about it. Again I asked, "Why didn't you ever tell me anything, Mom?"

In a sheepish tone she replied, "I didn't want you to hate me I guess." Interesting response, I thought. "Why would I hate you?" I watched her countenance shift from anger to something akin to embarrassment as she shared. "The truth is nowhere near as spectacular as the story your father concocted."

Two US soldiers, who preferred prison over returning to the battlefield, as I understood all those years, did not exist. The driver was a Thai native. I couldn't understand why this little detail change would cause me to hate her. She continued sharing.

The young man was a first year college student who attended the University of Bangkok. He had never been far from home, and missed his family. What was there to hate about a homesick kid?

Both drivers disappeared after the crash. A day or two later, the Thai police and the US military police escorted a young man, and his parents, to the hospital where we were. The group requested to see our family. The parents of the young man were there to ask for mercy on behalf of their son.

With a list of serious charges, the young man's fate rested with my parents. He took a vehicle from the university (vehicle theft), had no driver's license, caused a collision involving bodily harm, and he fled the scene of the accident (hit & run). There was also potential for an added charge of vehicular homicide if I succumbed to the injuries.

Even without the vehicular homicide charge, the punishment was capital. My parents were to decide whether to go ahead with execution in the public square, or grant mercy.

My father blurted out, "Execute him!" Mom lay in the hospital bed receiving care for a concussion. As she listened to the conversation, her mind drifted to thoughts of me, a few doors down the hall in critical condition. Not knowing whether I would survive, mom stared into the other woman's tear filled eyes. To take another life, as payment for mine, was not the best choice. Mom granted mercy. He did not receive the death penalty but we don't know if he received any other form of punishment under Thai law.

That decision resulted in an argument between my parents. When everyone left the room, my father expressed his frustration with my mom and then chased the family outside, demanding restitution in the form of cash. The family agreed to pay and delivered a sum of $850 in US dollars. A large sum of money in those days, it may have been funds they saved for their son's college tuition.

The figure mentioned above of $165 was all that remained when my father reunited with us back in the States. Mom surmised that my father spent most of the money in the "red light" district after she and I were air lifted back to Ft Gordon, Georgia.

Not seeking vengeance on my behalf, and embarrassed by my father's recklessness with the restitution money, she never talked about the accident for fear I would hate her. She assumed it would be harmless to let me believe my father's version of the story.

My father's version did have a negative impact on me, as I held a strong grudge against our own military all those years. I suppose one might say there was a silver lining to believing his lies; they kept me from using drugs and alcohol. I never wanted to alter my mind and put myself at risk of injuring others.

My father had a tendency to be melodramatic and enhanced details for his own benefit. I presume that every time he shared the story after we came home to the States he added more detail. Each time, like the effects of a narcotic, he added more detail to garner the sympathy he so craved. With every telling the story grew.

Mom's silence on the matter has taken a toll on her own health. Up to that point, she had carried that secret with her for forty-three years. It's the reason she always encouraged me to believe I had no handicap, which she hoped would dull her guilt.

As a result of trying to bury the guilt, for many years she suffered from depression, which contributed to ongoing battles with sickness, mental fatigue, and multiple surgeries. The events surrounding the crash were her darkest days, she admits, and she could never get past them. That night I told her I couldn't hate her for granting mercy.

My response to this new revelation must have stunned her. A few weeks passed before we talked about the discussion we had that night. What I always assumed was a malicious act, committed by our own soldiers, was in reality an unintended accident.

I told her I had forgiven the "mystery soldiers". God had moved her to reveal the truth so I could forgive the actual person who caused the crash. I don't know how I will find the guy, but I will spend the rest of my days searching for him to grant mercy through genuine forgiveness.

This guy has lived his life with the guilt and shame of what he did. My mission is to release him from that bondage. He doesn't know whether I lived or died. I can only imagine his struggle, knowing his choices resulted in the severing of a child's hand. I pray God allows me to live to see the day when I can set the man free, in person.

<u>5 7</u>

AFTER LEARNING THE TRUTH SURROUNDING MY CRASH, I
researched to see if I could find the person responsible. The
task may appear impossible at surface level, but I have learned if
this truly is the will of God, then He will lead me.

I retrieved the medical records from storage and read every page;
transcripts mostly, written in code only medical professionals would
understand. The pages are copies of carbon triplicates so they
are difficult to discern.

On a page containing surgery notes I found the name of the
Chief Surgeon who saved my life. I searched his name on the
internet and found a doctor bearing the same name, a renowned
specialist in trauma surgery. I called the phone number associated
with the group of doctors on the website. The following day I
received a call back from a lady in human resources; she was not
familiar with the doctor but gave me a phone number to an office in
Florida.

After hanging up, I placed a call to the Florida office and left a
voicemail. I called mom to share my discovery, and as we chatted, I
found a picture of the doctor in question on the internet. Switching
from voice to a video call, I asked if she recognized the man in the
photo.

Mom studied the photo and said, "Well, he was younger the last
time I saw him, but that could be the right guy." Excited by the
discovery, I continued sleuthing.

The next day brought surprise as a doctor from Florida called in
response the voicemail I left. After sharing the purpose behind my

search, he said I found the right guy. They served in the Air Force together and he knew Dr. Alexander had been in Thailand in 1972.

Bingo, I found him!

Then the air let out of my sails when his colleague informed me Dr. Alexander died in 1992, from cancer. I was so close to being able to extend gratitude to the awesome man who had saved my life. His colleague said their wives still communicated, and if I would write an email stating the purpose of my search, he would ask his wife to pass it forward. It was worth a try, so I emailed that afternoon and included my contact information.

Three weeks later, I was in church when my phone rang. I didn't recognize the number, so I forwarded the call to voicemail assuming it was a telemarketing agency.

After church, my family and I grabbed lunch before going to serve a hot meal to a homeless community. My regular job at the outreach was to serve a Bible message but on that day I served tables. Someone mentioned the word voicemail which triggered me to step out and check mine. Telemarketers rarely leave messages so maybe this call was one I should have taken.

The message was from the wife of the doctor I was searching for. I called her back, and we enjoyed the most incredible conversation.

I gave her the reasons why I was searching for her husband. Apprehensive to say much at first, perhaps she thought I was looking to sue or make threats. Feeling more comfortable as the conversation continued, she shared her recollection of Thailand with me.

She followed her husband to U-tapao Air Base for the same reasons my mom had. Dodie arrived in Thailand just six days after us. She talked about how wonderful the fruit was, and how snakes often surprised her inside the hut she and the doctor called home.

The conversation was fun, and the more she spoke, the more she recalled until she exclaimed, "I remember you! You were the only pediatric patient the doctor had during his time in Thailand." She recalled conversations she had with her husband when he came home after long shifts at the hospital.

"You have a rare blood type, B-negative as I recall." A career nurse, at age 79, she was as sharp as any 25-year-old. I looked into how rare B- is and only an estimated 1.67% of the world population carries it.

"I can't believe I am talking to you!" she cried. With excitement I replied, "I can't believe I'm talking to you also!" Amazed as we both were, it was for very different reasons. For me, I felt I had struck gold finding her. That I was still alive fascinated her more.

Due to the rare blood type, the hospital put out an emergency search. They found six donors, scattered all across the Southeast Asia Peninsula. Soldiers came in from Laos, Cambodia, Vietnam, and as far away as the Philippines and Guam, to share the precious liquid of life we call blood.

Dodie continued, not only were the doctors concerned about rejection of the hand by my body, and the potential for infection, but the blood transfusions increased potential risks.

Many soldiers in those locations were illicit drug users and visited the red light districts where sexually transmitted disease ran rampant. Screening technologies were not what they are today and the good doctor was skeptical due to the increased risks posed by tainted blood. With no other choice, he moved forward with the transfusion.

Dodie asked if I had lived a hard life. "I have, but how do you mean?" I inquired. She asked if I had been back and forth to the hospital for recurring infection. "I have not returned to the hospital for any medical issues related to the amputation. That's why I wanted to express my deepest gratitude for the incredible work your husband did."

In disbelief, she asked again, "So you have never dealt with sepsis?"

"No sepsis. No infection of any kind." I replied. Dodie marveled, as did I upon further study of my medical records. After re-amputating the hand, the stump was debrided, cleaned, and a flap of skin lapped over the end before wrapping it in gauze and cast.

Loaded onto a B-52 bomber, I left Thailand with what was essentially an open wound. We landed at various bases along the way before arriving at Fort Gordon, Georgia twelve days later. When the plane departed, the doctor had no way of knowing when we would arrive in Georgia, or the number of stops it would make. Regardless of the duration, he did not believe I would survive the flight.

This new information blew me away. I told Dodie my mom knew just a few of these details. She said the doctor was a terrible husband, but an amazing physician. He would have only offered hope to his patients.

After sharing my recent discovery about the truth of who caused the accident, I told her I needed to find the man and extend grace and forgiveness to him.

"Why are you doing this?"

Forgiven of much myself, God wanted me forgive others in like manner. To find the man is a mission I will pursue until I draw my last breath. "All I can say is I hope you find success in your mission, it's an amazing thing you're doing!" she replied.

As we closed out our forty-five minute phone call, she asked if she could share the story with her grandsons. I thought it would be a wonderful thing for the two teenaged boys to hear a story which contributes to the legacy of their grandfather. The boys never met their grandfather, as he died before their birth, and they also lost both parents to cancer. It would be incredible if one or both of the boys followed in the footsteps of this outstanding surgeon, continuing the legacy of the doctor they know as grandpa.

5 8

I CAN'T BELIEVE IT, I FOUND HIM AGAIN! I FOUND MY SON! IT had been over five years since our last communication. After losing his leg in a motorcycle crash in 2011, he vanished. He suffered memory loss because of the crash which took a long time to recover.

The date was October 22, 2016 when I received the text confirming I had found my son. At Asher's basketball game that day, I was torn between rooting for one son, and connecting with another, the one I had not seen in three decades.

We lost the game that day, but we were all super excited to have heard from Gerrod again. All his life, Asher had grown up knowing he had an older brother somewhere in the world. We had the few pictures of Gerrod as a baby, and the two pictures I received due to a court order, to remember him by. Gerrod was nine years old in the pictures sent from court, and he had just turned twenty-nine the month prior to this text.

It was a miracle to be communicating with my firstborn again. I tried to contain myself during a lunch outing we had with friends after the game. During the meal, Asher grabbed my phone and began a text conversation with his "big" brother.

I was reluctant because I didn't want to put extra pressure on Gerrod. It was a "walking on eggshells" kind of moment, but wonderful to see two brothers engaged in an electronic dialogue with pictures of cars and pets going back and forth.

Between Asher and me, I don't know who wanted Gerrod back more. As a parent, I wanted my kids to share a tight bond with each other. Watching my younger kids staring at the phone as they awaited the next text response from Gerrod was like a gift from Heaven. It looked like Christmas in their eyes.

Text conversations continued both ways over the next several weeks. Gerrod was gracious when his siblings wanted to chat and was always kind to them. On one occasion, I believe it was in January 2017; Gerrod texted with a question about the divorce of his mom and me. He said he wanted the straight truth and had no time for games. I appreciated the opportunity, not because I wanted to lambast his mother, but because it gave us the opportunity to get to the next level in healing our relationship.

What I had to say would likely differ from what his mom told him. If it was straight truth he wanted, then straight truth was what he would get. I also let him know I had forgiven his mother. As she would always be his mother, I wanted him to know I respected that and had no desire to persuade him otherwise.

I told him his mother did what felt right in her eyes and if she was wrong, then she would have to answer for it, not him. It would be great to be on friendly terms with my former wife. We have a son together and I try to live out what Romans 12:18 says, "If it is possible, as much as depends on you, live peaceably with all men."

Doing my best to give just the straight facts, with no emotional response, I gave him my side of the story. Texting is a great form of communication, but it comes with a risk of being misunderstood.

Gerrod asked if he could call me direct to talk. It was the second time in twenty seven years I would speak to him; no doubt I would take the call. We connected on the phone and with actual conversation taking place, he was better able to understand my responses.

After the conversation ended, which lasted only a few minutes, I was as happy as a kid in a toy store. Reconciliation can sometimes be a painful process, and this one would not be easy, but it would be so worth it.

Some may find this statement strange, or perhaps even crude, but this thought ran through my head after he asked to call me, "*Son, I would drag my crippled body across a sea of broken glass just to hear your voice over a shortwave radio with a weak battery, even if all you said was that you hate me*". That's just how much I wanted to talk to my son.

In later text conversations I let him know I hoped one day he would see things from another perspective. One text I sent read, "Perhaps you could try to put yourself in my shoes son. I am just a dad who loves his son fiercely and has done everything he could to reconnect." He said he had contemplated that thought, which led him to respond. That was an answer to many prayers.

As conversations continued, I asked if he would consider meeting in person. Since the cost was more to fly the four of us to see him, it made more sense to have him come see us. An added benefit to visiting us, I thought, would be for him to get a rest from the stress he had gone through. My original goal was to have him fly in as a surprise for Asher's birthday, a fantastic gift for a boy who just wanted to know his older brother. The timing didn't work out with Gerrod's schedule, but it was exciting to know he was even open to the idea.

A few weeks later I asked again if he would consider a visit. He agreed to come and gave me dates of availability. I booked a flight right away. I remember thinking, "Wow, in twelve days, a meeting I had dreamed of and prayed about, for almost three decades, was finally coming to fruition. Could this be real?"

My emotions stirred. What would my reaction be when I saw my boy, now a grown man, in person? He was no longer the two-year-old little boy, whose vision of departure has never escaped my mind. Would I be able to speak? Would I be able to hold my composure?

The days dragged on. Excitement overshadowed all other feelings, save for one; doubt. *"Would he get on that plane?"*

Pressing onward, excitement and doubt battled it out until the morning he was to fly. He sent a text letting me know he was on the plane. I only slept two hours that night.

My son shared that after every deployment, as he watched his men reunite with their families for a hero's welcome, no one was there for him. I knew he had deployed to Afghanistan and Iraq at least three times. The thought of no one being there for him hurt my heart. I get choked up every time I see reunion videos on social media of service members returning home. My favorites are the ones where their families are unsuspecting and the return is a big surprise.

Even though he was no longer in the military, we planned to receive him as though he was, with flags waving as he entered the passenger pick up area.

At the airport, Asher and Amelia kept asking when the plane would land. The flight delayed over an hour, and the four of us waited on pins and needles.

The arrival screen showed his plane landed, and more people gathered in the area, waiting to receive their loved ones. Shelly and I held a flag between us that was six feet long. The flag was from the World War II era and once belonged to her grandfather. Asher on my left and Amelia to the right of Shelly, both kids waved hand held flags.

Time stood still, as the moment I had waited twenty-seven years and seventy-four days for, finally came to pass. My firstborn son walked through the doors into the pickup area and I asked Asher to hold my corner of the flag so I could meet my son. Stepping away from the family, I walked over to my boy and enveloped him in a big hug, his arms weighed down by his luggage.

His body shook, in part because of all the walking he did on his prosthetic leg that day. He was also nervous meeting a side of his family he had grown up not knowing. I held him tight and whispered, "It's OK son, I've got you." With that, I felt his body slump in my embrace. I held him there for about a minute, with no additional words exchanged.

There are no words available to describe how I felt.

It will take time to rebuild our relationship, and he may never feel call me dad again. Considering all we have been through apart, if all he ever calls me is a friend, it will be enough.

<u>5 9</u>

BEFORE YOU CAN GROW A FRUIT TREE IN YOUR BACK YARD, be it an apple, peach, pear, or plum, you must first plant a seed. In the process of growth, the seed you plant has to die before new life comes forth. The seed dies and new life begins as a sprout. With water and cultivation, the sprout becomes a tree. In time, along with careful pruning, the tree produces fruit.

And so it has been for me. When I began my journey of faith, I was at a place of wanting to die. In fact, I had tried to take my life only two days before surrendering it to Jesus. Just like the seed, death was a prerequisite to my growth, but not in the physical sense. From a spiritual standpoint, I had to die to myself.

By the time I pulled that trigger, I was already dead on the inside, in my mind anyway. I was at the lowest point I'd ever been in my entire life, before or since, but grace found me there. I let go of my broken heart, gave it to the Lord, and transformed just like the seed. As I died to my flesh, new life sprouted in my heart.

The sprout grows out of the dead seed pod but it has to climb up out of the darkness of the soil. The time spent coming up out of the soil depends upon the depth of the seed's burial. With all I had endured in my first twenty-two years of life, my seed was planted at a great depth, in soil comprised of clay and rock. The sprout knows to survive; it must break from the old to pursue new life.

The sprout puts forth great effort as it seeks to break through the soil. Sometimes it runs into rocks or other impediments which cause it to change course, resulting in delays getting to the top, yet it continues in response to the beckoning call of the light above.

Once the sprout reaches the top of the soil, there is breakthrough, into the glorious light of the sun. It draws energy from the light, and by the washing of water the sprout grows into a sapling. If sunshine and water cannot reach the sapling, it will wither and fade away. One must avoid blocking the supply of light and water.

In contrast, when the sapling basks in the light and takes in the water, steady growth continues. As the sapling grows, the good gardener will cultivate the soil, removing debris from around the tiny tree that could choke out the roots. With the soil cultivated, the sapling grows into a mature tree, but not without careful pruning.

The good gardener knows there are branches which will drain the tree of energy, reducing the tree's potential to bear good fruit, so he cuts them off. Pruning, a painful process the tree does not comprehend the need for, is an act of love. The good gardener wants the best for the tree, for it to yield much good fruit. This is the story of my life.

They say hindsight is 20/20 and I believe it is true. Looking back, I see God's handiwork. Keeping my focus and priority on Jesus helps me to have better vision in the present.

People often ask, if I could, would I go back and alter the past to avoid losing my hand. The answer is no. God had a purpose when He allowed the crash to happen. He displayed His sovereignty through the loss of blood, by sustaining my life until donor blood arrived.

What was God doing in that situation? Because of the rarity of my blood type, it would be plain to see He was weaving what would become an amazing tapestry, beginning by integrating my life with the lives of those who donated blood. Six donors, from different racial and ethnic backgrounds, came together in unity to preserve life. It's a beautiful picture.

The surgeon who worked on me was a world class physician, placed in Thailand at a specific time in history so his God-given gifts could bring healing to a little boy, a miraculous healing at that.

The Lord also showed himself faithful to His purpose when he sent a triple amputee veteran to teach me how to tie my own shoes, an excellent picture of mentorship.

In fact, God was there every moment. His word tells us He will never leave us, nor forsake us. I love the poem "Footprints", where at the end, the Lord responds to the author's question of why there were two sets of footprints in the sand, except during times of trouble and sadness when only one set of footprints was visible. His answer, "*When you saw only one set of footprints, it was then that I carried you.*" On numerous occasions in my walk with the Lord, there was only a single set of footprints.

I never dreamed I would write this book. Even after hearing the Spirit direct me to do so, I resisted for two years before I started. He has been gracious there too.

Grace is an amazing concept, yet most of us go through life never grasping the full meaning of it. We often use the word in ways that cheapen its meaning, such as, *"When do you think she will grace us with her presence?"* For me, grace has a much deeper meaning.

I've heard it used as an acrostic:

G – God's
R – Riches
A – At
C – Christ's
E - Expense

Another explanation is to compare grace with mercy. Grace is receiving that which we do not deserve while Mercy is not receiving that which we do deserve. While both attempts to describe the word grace may have merit, I think they still fall short of describing grace in depth.

I like this description; Grace, is God giving the greatest treasure to the least deserving. Perhaps you are asking yourself why I would title the book "Hooked by Grace". My choice of words for the title implies becoming an amputee as a five-year-old child was an act of God's grace toward me. By extension, that would also include surviving molestation, being mocked and ridiculed by others, enduring betrayal, and suffering great loss.

I love the way A. W. Tozer, the esteemed Christian theologian put it, *"It is doubtful whether God can bless a man greatly until He has hurt him deeply."*•

If that sounds crazy to you, until five years ago I would have agreed. I have since come to realize that in my years of walking with God, much of that time I spent trying to control Him. I wanted to keep Him contained in a nice little box, and many times I have viewed Him as a cosmic vending machine, there to dispense blessings of my choosing, and in my timing.

After the fortieth anniversary, or ampuversary, if you will, of becoming an amputee, I heard the voice of God tell me to share my story. My story is really His story. I am His, to do with as He pleases, to bring about His purposes.

Though I did not grow up as a practicing Christian, God was with me. When speaking to others about me, Mom would often use the cliché, *"He has the patience of Job."* In fact, she said it so often it became a mantra for me. Only recently have I given much thought to what she meant.

I used to think being compared to a different character in the Bible would be nicer, maybe someone like Joshua, or Daniel. But what if, by divine providence, mom was speaking prophetically over my life when she compared me to Job?

People think Job suffered affliction at the hand of God. He was a faithful follower yet lost everything he had. As I looked deeper at Job's story, what impressed me most was through it all, with the loss of his wealth, his property, and even his children, Job waited for the Lord to reveal His purpose in the suffering.

God did not inflict the tragedies Job suffered, but he allowed Satan to have his way with Job. Satan's goal was to destroy Job's faith, and thus, destroy the man. God allowed Satan to inflict great pain and misery on His faithful servant, but Job persevered, and remained steadfast in his belief that God was for him and not against him.

From my study of the book I found a verse which summarizes my faith. It has become my life verse, taking up prominent residence on my dining room wall in three inch tall letters. "Naked I came from my mother's womb, and naked shall I return there. The LORD gave, and the LORD has taken away; Blessed be the name of the LORD." Job 1:21.

I came into this world with nothing, and I will leave the same way. Everything I have is a gift that comes from God, and He holds the sovereign right to give, or take away anything He pleases. I believe there is freedom in this verse. Applying it to my own life, it removes so much of the pressure imposed by the world in which we live. All we need is the Lord.

To understand God is in complete control has helped guide me toward my purpose in life. On a macro level, one purpose is to know God, to love Him, and to make Him known to others, always pointing people to the cross of salvation. On a micro level, with the wide array of experiences I have had, I now have the privilege of relating to vast numbers of people across a broad spectrum of pain. Like He said, "I want you to bring hope to the hurting." That purpose is what drives me to share my story.

Perhaps there are places in my story you might say coincidence brought something about, but there are far too many times where God alone could have orchestrated the situation and the outcome.

Because Job was faithful, God restored that which he had lost. The Lord, by His grace, is doing the same for me. He has returned my oldest son; He has extended my family to include more children, and, He is adding to my legacy the gift of grandchildren. He is also using me to bring about restoration with extended family members.

While writing this book, I gave a Bible message at a local outreach to the homeless, and I felt the Spirit leading me to talk about forgiveness. Not so for every homeless person, but many find themselves on the streets because they made bad choices resulting in bridges burned.

The passage I shared was Matthew 18:21-35, the Parable of the Unmerciful Servant. Jesus said the Kingdom of Heaven was like a king who wanted to settle his accounts with his servants. Brought before the king, was a servant who owed millions of dollars. The servant pleaded for mercy as the king ordered everything he had sold, family and all, to repay the debt. Again, the servant pleaded with the king for mercy.

The king took pity on the servant and cleared his entire debt, allowing him to go free. Right away, the freed servant went after a fellow servant who owed him a hundred dollars, choking the man as he demanded repayment.

The man who owed the smaller amount pleaded for mercy from the freed man, but mercy he did not receive. The freed man had his fellow servant sent to prison. Upon hearing this, the other servants reported the freed one to the king.

The freed servant appeared before the king again. Because the man, forgiven of much, did not forgive his fellow man in like manner, the king ordered the man return to the jailers who would torture him until he repaid the original debt in full.

It has been my experience, more often than not, that when I share a Bible message, hoping to teach others something about God, that the Lord teaches me something about myself. Such was the case here.

The Lord revealed how I had been the unmerciful servant. At twenty-two, Jesus gave me the gift of salvation and forgave of all my sin, a debt I could never repay. The King canceled the debt of millions of I owed and set me free.

In that freedom; however, I still demanded restitution from others. I held grudges, bitterness, and a lack of forgiveness in my heart toward a multitude of other people. The debts owed me by others were large and small, but even the largest ones fell short of the millions forgiven of me.

The King, by His grace, allowed me to return to jail for years of torture. I remained a prisoner in my heart, holding onto the debts owed by others, awaiting restitution. A prisoner I continued to be for twenty-three more years until I finally realized the key which would set me free was in my possession the whole time. I was the jailer and the prisoner, therefore the torture was self-inflicted. The key, which would allow me to escape the prison of my heart, was forgiveness. Over these last five years I have settled every account, cancelled the debt of each one regardless of the amount.

That included forgiving my father for everything he had done, or not done. It meant releasing Robert from the molestation debt. I forgave my first wife for all the pain and loss caused, to include robbing me of a relationship with my son. One by one, I forgave each person who had ever wronged me. Lastly, I forgave myself.

After half a century of life, I am free.

Again, would I change specific things in my past? The answer is still no. I would not want to repeat much of it, but change it I would not, because all of it together has made me who I am, a man of God, imperfect but forgiven, and loved beyond description by a Savior who willingly left His rightful place in Heaven to die on a cross to redeem me unto himself.

Through it all, I have learned to forgive others as God has forgiven me. I have learned to love people the way Jesus loves me. I have also learned it is the Holy Spirit who directs my path and provides opportunities for me to share His forgiveness and love with others.

I am...Hooked by Grace!

ABOUT THE AUTHOR

DL Boothe enjoys time with his family engaged in many outdoor activities such as camping, biking, walking, kayaking, and exploring the magnificent beauty of the Washington and Oregon coastlines. He and his family serve in several ministries around the Greater Portland Metroplex, bringing hope to the hurting. They make their home in SW Washington.

Follow him on Facebook at:
https://www.facebook.com/David-Boothe-1207832792651039/

Made in the USA
San Bernardino, CA
16 May 2018